THE

OF
WALL STREET

Sandra S. Hildreth

D1111810

Longman Financial Services Publishing,
a division of Longman Financial Services Institute, Inc.

While a great deal of care has been taken to provide accurate and current information, the ideas, suggestions, general principles and conclusions presented in this book are subject to local, state and federal laws and regulations, court cases and any revisions of same. The reader is thus urged to consult legal counsel regarding any points of law—this publication should not be used as a substitute for competent legal advice.

Executive Editor: Kathleen A. Welton
Project Editor: Roseann P. Costello
Copy Editor: Rita Tatum
Interior Design: Edwin Harris
Cover Design: Paul Klein

© 1988 by Longman Group USA Inc.

Published by Longman Financial Services Publishing
a division of Longman Financial Services Institute, Inc.

Printed in the United States of America.

88 89 90 10 9 8 7 6 5 4 3 2 1

Bar charts reprinted by permission of Standard & Poor's Corporation, 25 Broadway, New York, NY, 10004. Point & figure charts reprinted by permission of Chartcraft, Inc., 30 Church St., New Rochelle, NY 10801. Charts concerning "How to Read the Wall Street Journal Reports" are reprinted by permission of The Wall Street Journal, © Dow Jones & Company, Inc. 1987. All rights reserved.

Library of Congress Cataloging-in-Publication Data

Hildreth, Sandra S.
    The A to Z of Wall Street.

    1. Investments—Dictionaries.   I. Title.
HG4513.H56   1988   332.6'03'21   87-22615
ISBN 0-88462-711-X

PREFACE

WELCOME TO THE WORLD OF WALL STREET!

In this book, you will find concise explanations for more than 2,500 common investment terms and phrases such as bull and bear markets, correction, initial public offering, zero coupon bond and fixed-income securities. In addition, you will find that LYONs, TIGRs and COLTS are not animals. Ginnie Mae and Freddie Mac are not relatives. CARs and FASTBACs cannot be driven. The Paris Club is not a popular night spot. And a wedge is not a golf club.

The A to Z of Wall Street was written to provide an understanding of the language of investing for both the individual and professional. As a stock/commodity broker, radio commentator and newspaper columnist, I have received many phone calls and requests for information about investments from a wide variety of people. The same basic question was being asked—to explain investment terms in a way that could be easily understood. Those answers were the beginning of this book.

Two years were spent researching the terms and phrases used in the investment field. A special effort was made to include as many new words and phrases as possible.

Technical charts from Chartcraft and Trendline are included to graphically explain such trading patterns as correction, head and shoulders, breakout, pennant, etc. At the end of this book is a section that provides a detailed explanation of various headings and abbreviations used in financial pages of newspapers. Actual reports from *The Wall Street Journal* have been included to further assist you in monitoring your own investments.

The A to Z of Wall Street could not have been written were it not for the help of many. My thanks go out to Kathy Welton and Longman Financial Services Institute for their inspiration, dedication, professionalism and confidence in the development of this book. I would also like to thank my employer, coworkers, friends and family for their continuous cooperation and support.

Ability to pay: The expected ability of the issuer to pay principal and interest payments on notes, bonds and other investments when the payments are due.

Above par: The current price of a debt security above the face (par) value, expressed as a percentage. (Example: A $5,000 bond quoted at 110 percent is priced at $5,500.)

Absolute priority rule: The order of priority in which a bankrupt company pays its debts.

Absorbed: Shares of a new issue that have been completely sold and, therefore, absorbed into the market.

Abusive tax shelter: A limited or private partnership that the Internal Revenue Service has disallowed for tax deductions.

Accelerated cost recovery system (ACRS):   Also known as the 3-5-10 Rule, referring to the depreciation schedules for vehicles (three years), equipment and machinery (five years) and leased buildings (ten years). A system of depreciation for assets put into service after 1980, granted by the Economic Recovery and Tax Act of 1981 (ERTA).

Accountant's opinion: The statement of an accounting firm's work and its opinion in the corporation's financial statement.

Account executive: A person licensed and registered for the solicitation of and the representation for clients in the buying and selling of securities. Synonymous with "stock broker," "investment broker" and "registered representative."

Accounting year: The twelve-month period (not necessarily a calendar year) adopted by some corporations for IRS reporting purposes.

Accounts payable: Amounts owing to creditors for goods and services.

1

Accounts receivable: The money owed to a company by customers for goods and services charged on an open account.

Account statement: The record of any transactions during the accounting period and their resulting effect on any debt or equity position.

Accredited investor: An investor who, under the guidelines of the Securities and Exchange Commission (SEC) Regulation D, must meet certain financial and investment experience qualifications to be allowed to invest in a private limited offering.

Accretion: The prorated return of a deep discount bond reflecting the effect of compounded interest-rate return. Also known as "original issue discount," or OID.

Accrual basis: An accounting method that recognizes income and expense items as they are incurred. *(See also: BASIS)*

Accrue: To accumulate, as the interest on money.

Accrued interest: Interest on a fixed-income security that has accumulated since the latest payment. The previous owner of a debt security is entitled to any interest that has been earned but not paid. The new owner pays the accrued interest to the previous owner. The next interest payment is paid in full to the new owner thus "paying back" the accrued interest the buyer had paid to the seller.

Accumulated dividend: The dividend due but not paid to holders of cumulative preferred stock. Accumulated dividends must be paid before any common stock dividends may be declared by the board of directors.

Accumulation: The purchase of a large number of a company's shares without driving up the price per share.

Accumulation area: A very narrow price range a stock trades for over a period of time. Bids to buy shares at a price above the accumulation range tends to push the price up. Figure 1. *(See also: DISTRIBUTION AREA.)*

Accumulation unit: An accounting measure that represents a contract (usually an annuity) owner's proportion of interest in a separate account (the portfolio) during the accumulation (deposit) period.

Acid test ratio: A stringent test of a company's liquidity calculated by adding the sum of cash, cash equivalents and accounts, and notes receivable then dividing that sum by the total current liabilities, a one-to-one ratio or better indicates a firm can meet its debt obligations without using its inventory.

Acquisition: When one company takes over controlling interest of another. *(See also: MERGER, POOL, TAKEOVER)*

FIGURE 1: Accumulation Area

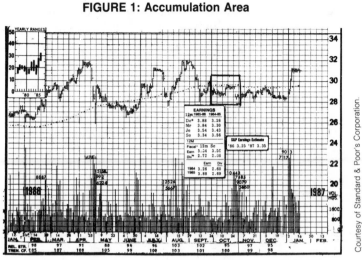

Courtesy of Standard & Poor's Corporation.

Across the board: Movement in the stock market that generally affects all stocks in the same way, either up or down. The "Board" or "Big Board" are terms synonymous with the New York Stock Exchange.

ACRS: Accelerated cost recovery system.

Active bond crowd: The New York Stock Exchange bond members who trade the most active bonds. *(See also: CABINET CROWD)*

Active box: The stocks held by a brokerage firm or hypothecated (pledged or assigned) by margin accounts. Used for collateral for securing broker loans or client margin loans.

Active market: Heavy volume in stocks, bonds or commodities as a whole or in individual issues. The spread (difference in bid and ask price) is usually narrower in an active market.

Active trading: A market condition in which there are many orders for the buying and selling of a security.

Actuals: Speculating in commodities, such as gold, pork bellies or soy beans that could result in delivery of the commodity if the contract is not closed out before the contract expires.

Adjusted basis: The base price of an asset after commissions and, in the case of stocks, any splits.

Adjusted debit balance (ADB): The formula for determining the position of a margin account calculated by netting the balance owing the broker-dealer firm with the balance in the special miscellaneous account (SMA) and any paper profits or losses on short accounts. Used to determine whether any withdrawals of cash or securities are available.

Adjusted gross income (AGI):   The taxable income of an individual after federally allowable deductions have been taken into consideration.

Adjustment bond: A bond issued after authorization from current bondholders of a corporation facing bankruptcy. The adjustment bond only pays interest when earned and replaces the outstanding bonds of the corporation.

Adjustments: The automatic price change of stocks and options on ex-dividend date due to a stock split or dividend (either stock or cash dividend).

ADR: American depository receipt.

Advance: A rise in value.

Advance-decline (A-D):   A ratio of those stocks that are declining versus those that are advancing, illustrating the general trend on the market.

Advance-decline line: A technical analysis of advancing or declining issues that forecasts the strength of the market. (*Synonym: BREADTH OF MARKET THEORY*)

Advance refunding: The exchange of maturing debt securities for issue of later dates.

Advisement: A recommendation, usually made after considering an investment's merits as matched to the investor's needs.

Affiliated person: Any person in a position to exert influence on the actions of a corporation, including but not limited to officers, directors and their families.

Afloats: Commodities loaded on shipping vessels but not at their destination.

Aftermarket: The markets and exchanges upon which all securities are traded that are not part of a new or secondary issue. (*Synonym: SECONDARY MARKET*)

Aftertax basis: The comparison of returns of corporate bond yields versus municipal bond yields after taxes have been taken into consideration.

Aftertax real rate of return: The rate of return on a security after tax liability has been taken into consideration.

Against the box: Selling shares of stock short that are actually owned by the seller who does not want to relinquish control of the stock.

Agency: The relationship between a principal and an agent who represents the principal in transactions with a third party.

Agency basis: Securities sold through normal broker transactions, executed through a national dealer market.

Agency issues: Debt securities (bonds) issued by authorized agencies of the federal government. These issues are backed by the issuing agency itself, not the full faith and credit of the U.S. Government.

Agent: An individual authorized by one person (the principal) to act on behalf of that person in transactions involving a third party.

Aggregate exercise price: The value of an option upon exercise figured by taking the underlying quantity and multiplying that figure by the exercise price. (Example: An option on 100 shares of stock with an option exercise price of 50 would have an aggregate exercise price of $5,000.)

Aggregate supply: The total amount of goods and services available for purchase at a given period of time. Also known as "total output."

Aggressive policy: Investing to get the maximum return on a portfolio by timing purchases and sales to coincide with expected market movements.

AGI: Adjusted gross income.

Air pocket stocks: Stocks that have plunged in price dramatically due to adverse news such as poor earnings.

Alien corporation: A corporation formed in: 1) a state other than that in which it does business, or 2) outside the U.S. Also known as a "foreign corporation."

Allied member: A general partner or voting stockholder of a member firm of the New York Stock Exchange who is not personally a member and, therefore, cannot do business on the trading floor.

Alligator spread: A combination of put and call options where the broker's commission "eats the investor alive" and is higher than the client's profits would be even if the market moved as expected.

All-or-none offering: An offering in which a brokerage firm agrees to devote its best efforts but, if a portion of the issue cannot be sold, then the entire offering is cancelled.

All-or-none order (AON):   An order in which the floor broker is instructed to execute the order in its entirety or not at all.

Allotment: The number of shares assigned to various underwriters of new issues for distribution.

Alternative depreciation system: A straight-line depreciation of 12 years on personal and 40 years on real property that may be elected by any taxpayer but is mandatory for property that: a) is used predominantly ouside the U.S., b) is leased to a tax-exempt entity or a foreign person, c) is financed by tax-exempt bonds or d) is imported from a country that maintains a trade restriction.

Alternative minimum tax (AMT):   Federal tax structure designed to ensure that all wealthy taxpayers pay at least some income tax.

Alternative order: Two simultaneous orders given to a registered representative by a client for the purchase or sale (not both) of a security with instructions to cancel one order should the other execute. (Example: A sell stop and a sell limit order is placed by one client. If the sell stop order executes, the sell limit is cancelled.)

American depository receipt (ADR):   A negotiable receipt in the form of a certificate for a number of shares of stock in a foreign corporation, bought and sold in the American securities markets just as any other U.S. stock is traded.

American Stock Exchange (AMEX):   The organization handles many firms that do not meet the criteria for membership in the New York Stock Exchange. Many small to medium companies as well as oil and gas stocks and most of the foreign stocks are traded on the AMEX. Also known as "Curb" because the AMEX started doing business on the curb of a downtown Manhattan street.

AMEX: American Stock Exchange.

Amortization: The reduction of the cost values of a limited life asset through an accounting procedure by periodic charges to income. *(See also: DEPRECIATION, DEPLETION, ACCOUNTING)*

AMPS: An acronym for Auction Market Preferred Stock.

AMT: Alternative minimum tax.

Analyst: A person who conducts research on securities, trends, corporations or other fields relative to the needs of the financial and economic community.

And interest: A phrase used in the purchase of bonds that means the buyer must pay the accrued interest to the seller.

Annual high: The highest price at which a security has traded in the preceding 12 months.

Annual low: The lowest price at which a security has traded in the preceding 12 months.

Annual meeting: The once-a-year meeting held by a corporation where all stockholders are invited to attend to vote, either in person or by proxy, on the company's directors and resolutions as well as be advised of past accomplishments and future plans.

Annual percentage rate (APR):   The cost of a debt expressed as a simple annual percentage.

Annual report: The yearly report sent to all shareholders of a company that gives the balance sheet, financial condition, events of the current year and forecasts of the upcoming year. *(See also: 10-K REPORT)*

Annuitant: The receiver of the distribution of an annuity contract.

Annuitize: The periodic distribution of an annuity, based on accumulation units.

Annuity: A contract between an insurance company and an individual that ordinarily guarantees a lifetime income to the person on whose life the contract is based in return for a lump sum or periodic payment to the insurance company.

Annuity beneficiary: The person who receives the benefits of an annuity policy upon the death of the annuitant.

Annuity owner: The owner of an annuity, thus entitled to make such policy decisions as the annuitant and beneficiary.

Annuity unit: The accounting measure used to determine the amount of each payment to an annuitant during the payout period.

Anticipated holding period: The time a limited partnership expects to hold any assets prior to selling.

Anticipation: Payment made before the actual due date.

AON: All-or-none order.

Appreciation: The increase in value of an asset.

Approved list: The list of possible investments approved by vote of the board of directors or trustees, usually in reference to mutual funds or fiduciary accounts.

Arbitrage: The purchase and sale of a security or commodity at the same time in separate stock or commodity exchanges to take advantage of any price difference.

Arbitration: A group of three to five individuals selected to settle disputes between brokerage firms or between a brokerage firm and a client.

Arrearage: The amount of dividends due but not paid on cumulative preferred stock.

Articles of incorporation: A document filed with a U.S. state by a company for the purpose of becoming a legal corporation. It includes the names of the directors, number of authorized shares and other pertinent information. Also known as a "charter."

Ascending tops: A chart pattern of the price of a stock that shows the peaks of the moving line are consistently higher than the previous peaks, considered bullish. Figure 2.

Asked price: The current price for which a security may be bought. For mutual funds, the price includes any sales charge that is added to the net asset value. Also known as "offering price." *(See also: BID PRICE)*

As of: A transaction completed on an earlier date then reported, with the settlement date figured from the original (as of) transaction date.

Asset: Anything that is owned.

Asset coverage: The amount of debt a company has that is covered by assets.

Asset-liability management: A financial strategy designed to maintain a specific asset to debt ratio.

Asset management account: A combination of banking and brokerage services in one account to provide checking, margin accounts, debit and credit cards.

Asset play: The purchase of a stock when the current price is below the book value.

Assigned: The transfer of an asset from one entity to another. (Example: When a client sells shares of stock, the shares delivered are assigned to the new owner.)

Assignment: A separate document accompanying a stock or bond certificate that is signed by the person named on the certificate or by the authorized company officer when owned by a company. Used for the purpose of transferring ownership. *(See also: STOCK POWER, BOND POWER)*

Assimilation: A new issue offering that has been completely sold to the public by the underwriter.

Associate member: A person who has purchased a right from the American Stock Exchange to execute orders through a regular exchange member.

At par: The situation when the current price of a debt security is exactly equal to its face value, expressed as a percentage. (Exam-

FIGURE 2: Ascending Tops

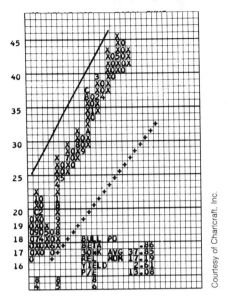

Courtesy of Chartcraft, Inc.

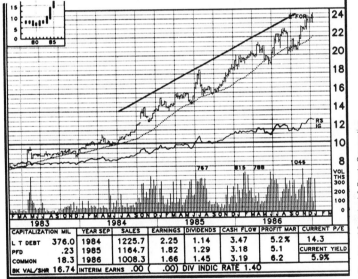

Courtesy of Standard & Poor's Corporation.

ple: a $5,000 bond quoted at 100 percent is priced at $5,000) *(See also: ABOVE PAR, BELOW PAR)*

At risk: The amount of the investment dollar that is subject to potential loss.

At risk rules: Tax rules that state losses may be taken only against sums of cash invested.

At the close: An order placed for stocks, commodities or options that are to be executed at the end of the trading session if possible. There is no guarantee that the order will be filled.

At the market: An order placed to be executed at the best possible price at the time of entering.

At the money: An option in which the underlying security is trading precisely at the exercise price of that option. *(See also: IN THE MONEY, OUT OF THE MONEY)*

At the opening: An order placed for stocks, commodities or options that is to be executed at the opening of the trading session or automatically cancelled if unable to be filled.

Attractive model: A financially attractive investment or portfolio.

Auction market: A market in which buyers enter competitive bids and sellers enter competitive offers simultaneously. The New York Stock Exchange is an auction market.

Auditor's report: The report of an accounting firm's work and its opinion of the corporation's financial statements.

Authority bond: A revenue bond issued by a government agency or a corporation formed to oversee a revenue-producing public enterprise.

Authority to transfer: A signed document that authorizes a transfer agent to transfer ownership from one party to another. Also known as a "third party release."

Authorize: To empower, commission or give authority.

Authorized stock: The number of shares of stock that a corporation is permitted to issue as stipulated in the corporation's state-approved charter.

Automatic reinvestment: The purchase of additional shares of stock using the dividends, capital gains or return of principal generated by that stock, usually in reference to mutual funds, or dividend utility stocks.

Automatic withdrawal: A fixed periodic payment from mutual funds set up on a monthly, quarterly, semi-annual or annual basis.

Average: A mathematical calculation of the price movements of a specific group of securities.

Average down: The lowering of the average price paid for stock by buying that stock as the price goes down. (Example: Paying $50 per share then buying more shares when the price drops to $45 and then $40. If the same number of shares were bought each time, the average price per share would be $45.)

Average up: The purchase of shares in a rising market to lower the overall average. (Example: Paying $50 per share, then paying $55 to $60. If the same number of shares were bought each time, the average price per share would be $55.)

Averaging: An investment strategy of investing a constant dollar amount or purchasing additional shares of a fund or security in order to average the overall investment.

Baby bond: A bond with a face value of less than $1,000.

Back-end load: A mutual fund or annuity investment that has the commission charges against redemptions of principal rather than purchase. Usually, the amount decreases by a certain percentage each year until there is no commission charge; used to discourage withdrawals by the investor.

Backing away: Failure by an over-the-counter market maker to honor bid and asked prices. The action is illegal under NASD's rules of fair practice.

Back office: All brokerage house and banking department personnel who are not directly involved in the buying or selling of securities.

Back up: A reversal of a stock market trend.

Backwardation: Future commodity prices that go progressively lower, inverse of contango.

Bad delivery: A certificate that has been received but is nontransferable to the new owner because proper paperwork or signatures are lacking.

Balanced drilling program: A limited partnership formed for the purpose of exploratory drilling for oil and gas and the drilling in proven fields.

Balanced mutual fund: A mutual fund that has its portfolio comprised of stocks and debt instruments.

Balance of trade: The difference between the imports brought into a country and the exports shipped out to other countries.

Balance sheet: A shortened version of a financial sheet that shows the total dollar values of all assets and liabilities of a company on a fixed date.

Balloon maturity: A bond issue that has very few bonds maturing in the earlier years and the majority maturing in the later years. Also known as "serial maturity."

Banker's acceptance: A time draft drawn on a bank by an importer or exporter that represents the bank's unconditional promise to pay the face amount at maturity, which is normally less than three months. Also known as "time draft letter of credit."

Banker's loan rate: The interest amount banks charge to other banks for short term loans, usually one to three days.

Banking holding company: A corporation that owns or controls one or more banks.

Bank quality: A bond rated by a rating service such as Standard & Poor's in the top four categories. AAA, AA, A and BBB are considered to be "bank quality." Bonds rated BB and below are considerd "junk bonds." (Caution: Bond ratings are subject to adjustment should the financial status of the issuer change.)

Bankruptcy: A legal action, whether voluntary or involuntary, taken by a business or individual as the result of the inability to pay debts.

Bank trust department: A service department of a bank that performs agent services such as estate settlement, trust and guardianship administration, retirement plan administration and estate planning.

Bar chart: A type of technical chart in which the closing or high, low and closing prices of a security are recorded each specified time, every 15 minutes, hourly, daily or other time period. Figure 3.

Barometer: Technical analysis of economic and/or market indicators to project future trends.

Barron's Confidence Index: A ratio of high quality bonds to low quality bonds that indicates investor confidence in the economy. Buyers of low-grade bonds tend to have confidence in the economy, while buyers of high-grade bonds tend to have doubts about the economy.

Base market value: The average price per share of a specific group of stocks at a given time, used as a basis of comparison for market indexes.

Basic grade: A specific grade as named in the exchange's futures contract. Any grade other than that specified is tenderable subject to price differentials from the basis.

Basis: 1) To find the cost basis of a share of stock, take the total purchase price or value when acquired, add the cost of purchase (i.e. commission, fee, etc.) and divide the result by the number of

FIGURE 3:   Bar Chart

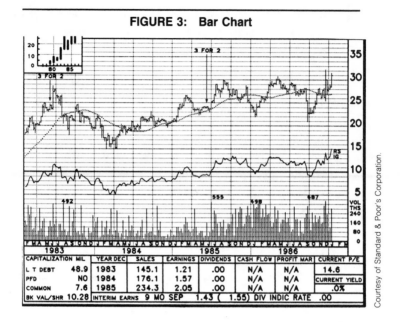

Courtesy of Standard & Poor's Corporation.

CAPITALIZATION MIL		YEAR DEC	SALES	EARNINGS	DIVIDENDS	CASH FLOW	PROFIT MAR	CURRENT P/E	
L T DEBT	48.9	1983	145.1	1.21	.00	N/A	N/A	14.6	
PFD	NO	1984	176.1	1.57	.00	N/A	N/A	CURRENT YIELD	
COMMON	7.6	1985	234.3	2.05	.00	N/A	N/A	.0%	
BK VAL/SHR	10.28	INTERIM EARNS	9 MO SEP	1.43 (	1.55) DIV INDIC RATE	.00			

shares held. 2) The price difference of a commodity over or under a designated future at which a commodity is sold or quoted. Also known as "cost basis."

Basis point: One one-hundredth (1/100) of a point, used to quote yields and prices, of various securities. (Example: the difference between 11.73 percent and 11.69 percent is four basis points.)

Baskets: The list of qualified or required entities as defined for federal tax purposes. (Example: The 1986 Tax Reform Act specifies five new baskets are added to foreign tax credits already in the Code which are: 1) passive income, 2) Subpart F shipping income, 3) financial services income, 4) high withholding tax interest of any person and 5) dividends from each noncontrolled foreign corporation that is 10 to 50 percent owned by the taxpayer.)

Bear: A person who believes the market is in a down trend.

Bearer bond: A nonregistered bond with interest coupons physically attached to the certificate. These must be removed and sent to the transfer agent for the interest payment. Ownership changes by simply handing the certificate to the new owner.

Bear market: A down trend in the stock market. (From the expression "bear down.")

Bear raid: An illegal attempt by investors of stock selling short to bring the price of that stock down so that their profits will be larger.

Bear spread: Buying and/or selling a combination of stocks, options or commodities designed to take advantage of an anticipated drop in the market.

Bed-bug letter: A letter sent by the Securities and Exchange Commission (SEC) to the issuer of a public offering (new issue) that lists corrections to the registration which must be made prior to the SEC release. *(Synonym: DEFICIENCY LETTER)*

Bell: The signal that announces the opening and closing of the exchanges. No trading can occur before the opening bell or after the closing bell.

Bellwether: A stock that trades in such large volumes as to tend to influence the whole market, thus indicating a general trend. Due to the extremely large number of outstanding shares, IBM has long been the stock market bellwether.

Below par: The current price of a debt security below the face (par) value, expressed as a percentage. (Example: A $5,000 bond quoted at 95 percent is priced at $4,750.)

Beneficial owner: The actual owner of an asset, even though the asset may be held in another name, such as a brokerage firm's street name.

Beneficiary: The receiver of the proceeds of a will, insurance policy, annuity or other similar contract.

Best efforts offering: A new issue offering in which an investment banker agrees to distribute as many units as possible and to return any unsold units to the issuer.

Best's rating: An unbiased rating by A.M. Best Co. of insurance companies' financial soundness. A+ being the highest rating.

BETA coefficient: The measure of a stock's volatility relative to the rest of the market. A rating of 1.0 implies the stock historically moves with the market, while 0.0 is reserved for cash and ratings approaching 2.0 are historically highly volatile. Also known as BETA.

Bid and asked: The current quote of a security. The "bid" is the price for which a security may be sold and the "asked" is the price for which a security may be bought.

Bidding up: The moving up of the bid price of a stock, usually the result of a large block trying to be bought. In order for the block trade to execute, as the offering price moves up because of the large buy order, the bid also must be moved up to facilitate the purchase of the entire block.

Bid price: The current price for which a security may be sold. *(See also: ASKED PRICE)*

Bid wanted (BW):   An indication a holder of a security wants to sell and will entertain bids on a negotiated basis. Usually announced in the "Pink Sheets," a national daily listing of over-the-counter securities and their market makers.

Big bang: The "shot heard round the world" on October 27, 1986 when the London Stock Exchange eliminated fixed brokerage commissions.

Big board: The nickname for the New York Stock Exchange (NYSE).

Big boys, the: Managers of multi-million dollar portfolios, generally those of mutual funds, insurance funds, retirement funds and brokerage firms.

Big eight: The eight largest U.S. accounting firms measured by total audited sales.

Big rubber ball: A big "bounce" in a security or the market as a whole, either up or down that will return just as far as the original bounce.

Bill, U.S. Treasury: A U.S. Government-issued debt security sold at a discount to face value in maturities of one year or less. Also known as "T-bill."

Black Friday: The original stock market disaster occurred on Friday, September 24, 1869, when a group of financiers tried to corner the gold market and started a business panic and depression.

Black ink: Profits made from an investment.

Black Monday: Two large stock market crashes that both occurred on a Monday. The DJIA dropped 12.8 percent on October 28, 1929 and dropped 22.6 percent on October 19, 1987 for a 508 point loss.

Blanket fidelity bond: A fidelity bond brokerage firm must carry to protect against employee dishonesty, includes securities forgery and fraudulent trading.

Blanket mortgage: A mortgage on the entire assets of an individual or company.

Blanket recommendation: A recommendation made to a large group of investors to buy or sell a particular security, or securities in a particular industry regardless of the individual's investment objectives or portfolio size.

Blind pool: A limited partnership that does not specifically state the assets to be bought with the proceeds raised.

Block: A large number of shares of stock or option contracts that are to be bought or sold.

Blowout: A new issue generating such investor interest that all shares are quickly sold. As a result, the issue is "oversubscribed," meaning that there are more orders than stock available. Also known as a "hot issue."

Blue chip company: A highly respected company. From the gambling use of blue chips as the most valuable, this phrase indicates a company with consistently good products, earnings and steady growth patterns.

Blue List, The: A daily trade publication that lists the current municipal bond offering of banks and brokerage firms across the nation.

Blue sky laws: The expression used to indicate whether a security is registered by the state in which the securities are to be sold. Believed to have originated when a judge, ruling on the merits of a particular stock, stated the stock had about the same value as a "patch of blue sky."

Board maker: A member of the Chicago Board Options Exchange who accepts orders for options that are not capable of immediate execution. When and if the order can be executed, the "board maker" does so on an agency basis then notifies the member firm that had entered the order.

Board of arbitration: A group of three to five individuals selected to settle disputes between brokerage firms or between a brokerage firm and a client.

Board of directors (BOD):   Individuals elected by shareholders to establish corporate management policies.

Board of Governors of the Federal Reserve System: The seven-member board of the Federal Reserve System who set banking regulation policies. Said to be the most economically influential policymakers in the U.S.

Boiler room: A place where high pressure salespeople call "sucker" lists of investments in often illegal, fraudulent, highly-speculative securities and oftentimes nonexistent products. Also known as "bucket shops."

Bond: A debt instrument in which the issuing authority, whether a corporation or a municipality, promises to repay a loan on the expiration date and the interest at specified intervals, usually semi-annually.

Bond fund: A mutual fund with a portfolio consisting of bonds to provide fairly stable income with a minimum of capital risk.

Bond power: A form of assigning ownership by appointing an attorney-in-fact with the power to make a transfer of ownership. Also known as "assignment."

Bond rating: A rating assigned to bonds by independent rating service such as Standard and Poor's or Moody's after an unbiased evaluation of the ability by the issuer to pay principal and interest. (Caution: Bond ratings are subject to adjustment should the financial status of the issuer change.)

Bond ratio: A ratio used to determine a company's bond capitalization. Measured by dividing the total amount of bonds due after one year by the same number plus the total equity figure.

Bond swap: The sale of municipal bonds with lower than current interest rates with the proceeds used to purchase bonds with higher interest rates.

Book: 1) The total amount of a security available from a specialist that may be purchased. 2) The record kept by a specialist of open buy and sell orders. 3) As relates to a syndicated offering: a) The number of indications of interest, b) The total number of units offered. 4) The act of recording information. 5) Any business account records such as journals or ledgers.

Book entry: Securities that are in registration form only and do not have certificates issued.

Book loss: Loss that is on paper only, as the assets have not been sold. Also known as "paper loss" and "unrealized loss."

Book profit: Profit that is on paper only as the assets have not been sold. Also known as "paper profit" and "unrealized profit."

Book value per share: An accounting method used to determine a company's net worth on a per share basis. Figured by taking all assets, subtracting all liabilities and dividing the results by the shares outstanding.

Borrowing power of securities: The amount of money that may be borrowed using securities as collateral.

Boston Stock Exchange (BSE): A regional stock exchange.

BOT: Securities market terminology for bought.

Bottom: The lowest point or price a security has reached in a given period of time. Figure 4.

Bottom fisher: An investor who purchases stocks of companies that are at lows, usually bankrupt or near-bankrupt companies.

Bought deal: A firm commitment of completion by an underwriting team regarding a new issue.

FIGURE 4:   Bottom

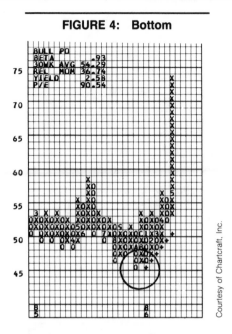

Courtesy of Chartcraft, Inc.

Bourse: French for "purse," used in France, Switzerland and Belgium as their name for the stock exchange.

Boutique: A specialty-type of small brokerage firm that specializes in few clients and few product lines.

Box: The physical location of security certificates. The name evolved because the brokerage firms and banks originally held certificates in a large metal box or tray.

Branch office manager: The manager of a branch office of a bank or brokerage firm.

Breadth of market theory: A technical analysis of advancing or declining issues that forecasts the strength of the market. Also referred to as "advance-decline."

Breadth of the market: An analysis of how many available issues were actually traded and therefore are participating in a current movement.

Break: The sudden upward or downward price movement of a security.

Break-even point: The selling price of an investment that, when liquidated, produces neither a loss nor a gain.

Breaking the syndicate: The termination by a syndicate of the underwriting agreement.

FIGURE 5:   Breakout

Through Support

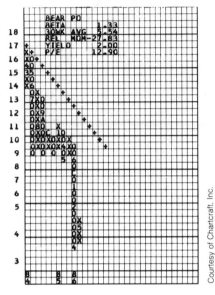

Courtesy of Chartcraft, Inc.

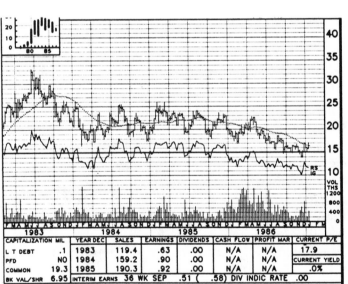

Courtesy of Standard & Poor's Corporation.

Through Resistance

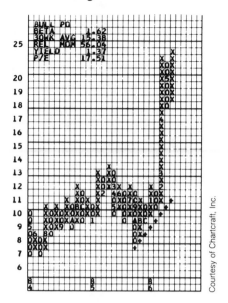

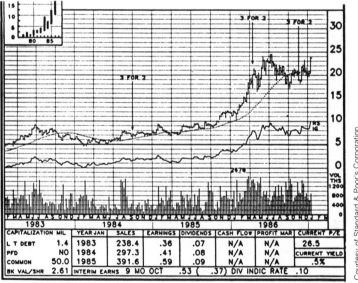

Breakout: In technical analysis, a decline through a support level or an advance through a resistance level (*See Also: SUPPORT LEVEL, RESISTANCE LEVEL*) Figure 5.

Breakpoint: The dollar amount of an investment in a mutual fund that qualifies for a lower sales charge.

Breakpoint sales: Sales of mutual funds at or just below a breakpoint.

Broad tape: A continually running tape (report) of major news developments and financial information provided by Dow Jones News Service.

Broker: An agent who specializes in stocks, options and/or commodities acting as an intermediary between the buyer and seller.

Broker-dealer: A brokerage firm which operates as both brokers and principals.

Broker's loan rate: The interest rate charged for the loan of money between brokerage firms.

Broker's loans: Money loaned to brokerage firms from banks or other brokerage firms.

Bucket shop: A brokerage firm (now almost extinct) that illegally puts customers orders in a "bucket," confirms a price to the customer but does not actually execute the order until the price is more favorable, with the firm pocketing the difference. Also known as "boiler room."

Bulge: A quick, temporary rise in price.

Bull: A person who believes the market is in an uptrend.

Bull market: An uptrend in the stock market. (From the expression "a bull charges forward.")

Bull spread: Simultaneously buying and/or selling a combination of stocks, options or commodities designed to take advantage of an anticipated rise in the market.

Bunching: 1) The combining of several buy or sell orders for a security into one for execution on the floor of an exchange. 2) Patterns on the ticker tape reflecting a series of trades in one stock.

Burn: Slang, said of a broker who excessively trades a client's account in order to generate additional commissions, an illegal manipulation.

Burnout: The exhaustion of a tax shelter's benefits.

Business cycle: 1) The period of time, usually an average of 2½ years in which the Gross National Product moves from the base line to the top of a rise then to the bottom of a fall then rises back to the original base line. 2) The length of time needed to turn raw materials into a finished product.

Business day: A a day in which a stock, bond, option and/or commodity exchange is open for business during the hours set by each individual exchange.

Butterfly spread: The buying of two calls and the simultaneous selling of two calls, all with different strike prices and/or expiration months. The premiums on the buy side are lower than the premiums on the sell side. The spread is most profitable when the underlying stock price is stable.

Buy: To purchase or acquire goods or services in exchange for cash or cash equivalents.

Buy and write strategy: The purchase of a security and the simultaneous selling of a call option against that security.

Buyer's market: A market that is favorable to the buyer rather than the seller. The supply of sell orders are greater than the demand to buy creating an atmosphere of lower prices.

Buyer's option: A settlement contract that calls for delivery and payment according to the number of days specified by the buyer. *(See also: SELLER'S OPTION)*

Buy in: A procedure of buying a security in the open market that occurs when the seller of a security fails to deliver the security sold. Any resulting losses are charged against the seller's account.

Buying climax: A dramatic and rapid rise in the price of a stock, often followed by an equal lowering of the price.

Buying on margin: Buying securities in a margin (open loan) account at a brokerage firm using stocks, bonds, SMA and cash as collateral. Closely regulated by the Federal Reserve Board.

Buying power: In a margin account, the dollar amount of additional securities that may be purchased using only the Special Maintenance Account (SMA), a bookkeeping entry that works along the same lines as an open loan account.

Buy limit order: Instructions for a security to be bought no higher than the amount stated on the order.

Buy minus: An order to buy a stock at a lower than current price.

Buy on the bad news: The purchase of a stock that has declined following bad news on the premise that the stock will rise again.

Buy on the close: To buy at the close of a trading session at a price within the closing range.

Buy on the open: To buy at the open of a trading session at a price within the opening range.

Buy order: An order to purchase a security or commodity placed by a client to a broker-dealer.

Buyout: The purchase of controlling interest in another company.

Buy program: Buy orders of such volume and of many different securities that the market as a whole rises, sometimes dramatically, usually implemented by a "signal" when a computerized chart/plot program indicates a buy program is advisable. (Example: The institutional investor's computer generated a buy signal to purchase 10-million shares of stock of various companies causing the market to go up 17 points in 10 minutes.) Also called "computerized buy program."

Buy stop order: An order to buy a security at the best possible price after the stop price has been touched. The order could be filled at a price other than is indicated at the stop price because the order becomes a market order once the stop price is touched. (Example: A buy stop order to buy the XYZ Company at $45 was triggered. The buy stop order then became a market order and filled at $45 ⅛, the next best available price.)

Buy the book: An order to purchase as many shares of a company as are available at the current offer price.

Cabinet: The metal storage rack containing limit orders pending execution by the specialist or market maker.

Cabinet crowd: Members of the New York Stock Exchange (NYSE) who deal in infrequently traded bonds.

Cabinet security: An infrequently traded stock or bond listed on a major exchange.

Cage: The banking or brokerage firm's cashiering department that receives and delivers securities and payments.

Calendar: A list of securities soon to be offered for sale as a new or secondary offering.

Calendar spread: The purchase of two options on the same security with different expiration dates.

Calendar year: The accounting reporting method using January 1 through December 31 as the fiscal year.

Call: 1) A type of option contract giving the buyer the right to buy and the seller the obligation to sell a specific number of the underlying security at a specific price on or before a specific date. 2) The right by the issuer to redeem a debt security prior to the maturity date.

Callable: 1) A bond issue that may be redeemed by the issuing authority at a stated date(s) in the future prior to the maturity date. 2) A preferred stock that may be redeemed by the issuing corporation.

Call date: The date an issuing authority may redeem a debt security as stated in the original indenture (agreement).

Call feature: The part of a bond's indenture (agreement) that outlines the schedule and price of redemptions prior to the stated maturity.

Call loan rate: The interest rate charged for the loan of money between brokerage firms.

Call option: A contract giving the right to buy (to the buyer) and the obligation to sell (to the writer) a specific number of the underlying security at the stated (strike) price on or before a specific (expiration) date.

Call premium: The per-unit price of a call option times the number of units in the contract. (Example: An option with a premium of two on 100 shares of stock has a total cost, not including commissions or fees, of $200.)

Call price: The price at which a debt instrument with a call feature may be redeemed.

Call protection: The length of time during which a debt instrument may not be redeemed or called.

Call provision: The part of a bond's indenture (agreement) that outlines the schedule and price of redemptions prior to the stated maturity.

Call spread: The simultaneous purchase and sale of call options with different expiration dates and/or exercise prices.

Called away: The term used when a debt security with a call date has, in fact, been called (redeemed) by the issuing authority.

Canadian stock: Stocks incorporated in the country of Canada listed on U.S., Canadian and foreign exchanges or sold as ADRs.

Cancel: Rescind (void) an order to buy or sell a security. *(See also: GOOD TIL CANCELLED ORDER)*

C & F: Cash and freight.

Cap: The top or maximum increase allowed by the terms of a contract. Usually refers to the highest amount of interest which may be charged on a floating rate debt.

Capital: Accumulated cash and property.

Capital appreciation: The increase in value of an asset.

Capital asset: An asset such as buildings or equipment with a life expectancy in excess of one year.

Capital Asset Pricing Model (CAPM):   A sophisticated model showing the relationship between expected risk and expected return based on the theory that investors demand higher returns for higher risks.

Capital budget: A company's long-time financing program.

Capital expenditure: The amount of money used to purchase or improve capital assets.

Capital flight: The movement of money from one country to another.

Capital formation: The creation or expansion of capital assets that produce goods and services resulting in economic expansion.

Capital gain: Profit realized from the sale of an asset. Deemed to be long term if held longer than the time stipulated by federal income tax laws and short term if held for less. Caution: Tax laws change on a periodic basis as to the length of time and other provisions for capital gains. It is advisable to check with a tax attorney, accountant or other qualified advisor regarding capital gains.

Capital gains distribution: The distribution of capital gains by a mutual fund to the fund's shareholders.

Capital gains tax: Federal income tax assessed on the profit or loss generated by the sale of an asset. *(See also: SHORT TERM CAPITAL GAIN OR (LOSS), LONG TERM CAPITAL GAIN OR (LOSS)*

Capital goods: Goods used in the production of other goods.

Capital intensive: 1) The requirement of a large investment in capital assets. 2) A high proportion of fixed assets to labor.

Capital investment: The amount of money used to purchase or improve capital assets.

Capitalization: The total of all securities issued by a company including common stock, preferred stock, bonds, debentures and surplus.

Capital loss: Loss realized from the sale of an asset. *(See also: CAPITAL GAIN)*

Capital market: The segment of the securities market that deals in long-term debt and equity securities.

Capital preservation: An investment which is designed with the least amount of principal loss risk as possible.

Capital requirements: The long-term and working capital (cash) needed for the normal operation of a business.

Capital stock: The total of all outstanding common and preferred shares of stock representing ownership of a company.

Capital structure: The sum of a company's long-term debt, capital stock and all surplus. *(See also: INVESTED CAPITAL, CAPITALIZATION)*

Capital surplus: Equity not otherwise classified as capital stock or retained earnings.

Capital turnover: The annual sales of a company divided by the average equity. Used to determine the extent to which the company is able to grow without additional capital.

CARDs: A debt security backed by credit-card receivables. An acronym for Certificates for Amortizing Revolving Debts.

Carry forward: A term used in the calculations of federal income that indicates amounts of gains or losses that may be taken in subsequent tax years.

Carrying charge: 1) The charges needed to carry commodities, including interest, storage and insurance. 2) The fee (interest) a brokerage firm charges in a margin account for any debit balances. *(See also: MARGIN)*

Carrying market: Refers to commodities, where a futures contract is higher in price to the cash or spot price reflecting the costs such as interest, storage, feed or insurance associated with owning a commodity.

CARs: A debt security backed by auto loans. An acronym for Certificates of Automobile Receivables.

Cartel: A group of individuals or businesses who agree to influence prices by regulation of production and the marketing of a product, illegal in a number of countries including the U.S.

Cash: 1) Capital. 2) Paper currency, coins, balances in checking and savings account and negotiable money orders.

Cash account: The account at a brokerage firm in which the client pays for all transactions in full. *(See also: MARGIN ACCOUNT, SPECIAL CASH ACCOUNT)*

Cash and freight (C & F): The cash and freight charges added for delivering an actual commodity to the port of destination.

Cash assets ratio: A test of a company's liquidity, figured by adding the sum of cash and marketable securities then dividing the result by the total current liabilities.

Cash basis: The accounting method that defines revenues as cash received and expenses as cash paid out.

Cash commodity: A commodity that is owned and delivered as the result of a completed contract.

Cash cow: A business that generates a continuous flow of cash, usually due to the repeated purchasing of a company's products.

Cash dividend: The cash payment to a company's stockholders generated from the current earnings or accumulated profits. Must be declared by the board of directors.

Cash equivalents: Securities of such high liquidity and safety that they are considered virtually as good as cash. Usually money market funds or Treasury bills.

Cash flow: The money derived from a company's operations. Could be a negative or a positive figure.

Cashiering department: The brokerage firm department that receives and delivers securities and payments. Also known as the cage.

Cash market: The completion of a transaction that transfers ownership of a commodity from the seller to the buyer for immediate delivery and payment. *(See also: FUTURES MARKET)*

Cash on delivery (C.O.D.):   A delivery transaction requiring payment in full before the delivery can be completed.

Cash order: A transaction calling for the seller to deliver and the buyer to pay for the securities being traded on the same day as the transaction. Also known as cash sale, cash trade.

Cash position: The total amount of money in an account that is not being used to secure a position in any way, such as collateral for a margin account.

Cash sale: A transaction calling for the seller to deliver and the buyer to pay for the securities being traded on the same day as the transaction. Also known as cash order, cash trade.

Cash surrender value: The amount of money that would be returned to the owner of an insurance policy should the policy be cancelled (surrendered).

Cash to futures: The price relationship of a commodity's cash price to the future contract price.

Cash trade: A transaction calling for the seller to deliver and the buyer to pay for the securities being traded on the same day as the transaction. Also known as cash order, cash sale.

Cash value: The amount of money which may be taken from an accrual contract such as a whole life insurance policy.

Casualty insurance: Insurance that protects the owner against property loss, damage or resultant liability, with the exclusion of policy limitations.

Casualty loss: Financial loss as the result of damage to property by a sudden, unexpected or unusual event.

CATS: An acronym for Certificate of Accrual on Treasury Securities.

Cats and dogs: Highly speculative and therefore very risky stocks.

CBOE: Chicago Board Options Exchange.

CBOT: Chicago Board of Trade.

CD: Certificate of deposit.

CEO: Chief executive officer.

Central bank: The Federal Reserve System section responsible for the issuance of money, administration of monetary policy, holding the reserve deposits of other banks and engaging in transactions to facilitate the conducting of business and protect the public interest.

Certificate: A piece of paper, usually ornate, signifying ownership, indebtedness or a factual event.

Certificate of Accrual on Treasury Securities (CATS): A U.S. Treasury issue sold at deep discount to maturity value. A zero coupon security as no interest payments are made. (Caution: When held in a taxable account, taxes are paid on the "phantom income" on an accrual basis just as if the interest had been received.)

Certificate of deposit (CD): A debt security issued by a financial institution, usually a bank or savings and loan, with a stated date of maturity and interest rate.

Certificateless municipals: Municipal bonds that are in registration form only and do not have certificates issued.

Certified check: A bank guaranteed and issued check.

Certified financial planner (CFP): A designation granted by the Institute of Financial Planners (Denver, Colorado) to individuals who have passed certain requirements and exams involving the coordination of a client's banking, investment and insurance needs. A CFP may charge a fee and/or commission to his or her clients.

Certified public accountant (CPA): An accountant who has passed certain exams and professional requirements and has become licensed in the state in which the individual resides.

Certified stock: A physical commodity that has been approved as a deliverable grade. Also usually certified as to quality.

CFP: Certified financial planner.

CFTC: Commodity Futures Trading Commission.

Chairman of the board: The presiding officer of the board of directors of a corporation, may or may not be the actual head authority of the company. *(See also: CHIEF EXECUTIVE OFFICER)*

Chapter 7:   The chapter of the Bankruptcy Act of 1978 that deals with liquidation of an insolvent (bankrupt) company and the distribution of any assets.

Chapter 11:   The chapter of the Bankruptcy Act of 1978 that deals with the reorganization of an insolvent (bankrupt) company in an attempt to avoid total liquidation of the company and its assets.

Chapter 13:   The chapter of the Bankruptcy Act of 1978 that deals with the liquidation of assets for an insolvent individual.

Chart: The past price movements of a security placed on graph paper that will, hopefully, give indications of possible future price moves, used for stocks, options, bonds and commodities. Figures 6 and 7.

Charter: The document filed with a U.S. state by the founders of a corporation in order to become a legal corporation, includes such information as the corporate name, director's names and the number of authorized shares. Also known as "articles of incorporation."

Chartist: A technical analyst who uses chart patterns to help forecast future price movements.

Check: 1) A demand instrument drawn against deposited funds for a specific amount of money payable to a specific person or entity. 2) To stop or curb an event (Example: To check the rise in interest rates, a change in monetary policy was implemented.)

FIGURE 6:   Bar Chart

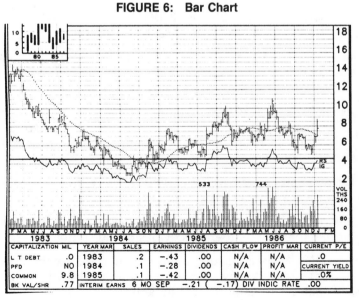

Courtesy of Standard & Poor's Corporation.

FIGURE 7:   Point and Figure Chart

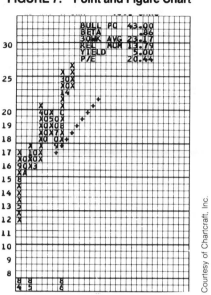

Courtesy of Chartcraft, Inc.

Checking the market: Canvassing securities market makers for a bid or asked price.

Chicago Board of Trade (CBOT):   A futures exchange located in Chicago, Illinois, where certain commodity futures and options on those futures (if available) are traded.

Chicago Board Options Exchange (CBOE):   The first national securities exchange for the trading of listed options.

Chicago Mercantile Exchange (CME):   A futures exchange located in Chicago, Illinois, where certain commodity futures and certain options on those futures (if available) are traded.

Chief executive officer (CEO):   The principal officer of a firm responsible for the activities of the company, usually the chairman of the board but could be another officer such as president or executive vice president.

Chief financial officer (CFO):   The principal officer in charge of a firm's financial affairs, in some firms called a controller or comptroller.

Chief operating officer (COO):   The principal officer of a firm responsible for the day-to-day activities of the company.

Chinese wall: The wall through which insider information must not pass from corporate adviser to investment traders who could make use of that information to reap huge profits.

Churn and burn: An illegal manipulation. Slang for a broker who excessively trades a client's account in order to generate additional commissions.

Churning: The excessive buying and selling of securities in a client's account, usually a ploy by the broker to generate commissions.

Cincinnati Stock Exchange (CSE): Established in 1887, it is the first completely automated stock exchange, known as the "Cincinnati Experiment." Uses no floor traders, but a sophisticated computerized trading system.

Circle: A term used as an indication of interest in the purchase of a security. The security in question appears on a list, is physically circled and has the name of the potential buyer noted.

Class: 1. A group of securities with similar features (Example: Preferred stocks are a class of securities). 2. Options of the same type, either puts or calls. (Example: The XYZ Company calls are one class.)

Class A/Class B stock: Classified stock.

Classified stock: A corporation's stock that has been separated and given separate features, such as voting privileges as set forth in the company's charter, and given specific designations, such as Class A or Class B.

Clean: 1) Free of debt. 2) Without document requirements. 3) A match of corresponding buy and sell orders for securities. Also known as a "natural."

Clear: 1) The collection of funds on which a check was drawn. 2) Assets not being used as collateral. 3) Profit after expenses. 4) Securities legally acceptable for transfer. Also known as "negotiable."

Clearances: The total amount of marine shipments of a specific commodity as of a given date from domestic and foreign ports.

Clearing house funds: Funds drawn by check or draft that are transferred through the Federal Reserve System and usually require three days to clear. *(See also: FEDERAL FUNDS)*

Client: A person who has engaged the services of an agent in order to transact business.

Close: 1) The last price of a security on a business day. 2) The last half hour of trading on exchanges. 3) The consumation of a sale or transaction.

Close a position: The transaction that liquidates a position. (Example: Selling a call option previously bought or buying a stock that was previously sold short.)

Closed corporation: The shares of a corporation in which there is no trading market because the majority of shares are owned by only a few stockholders.

Closed-end fund: A mutual fund company with a fixed capitalization. May only issue the number of shares authorized in the company charter.

Closed-end investment company: A mutual fund company with a fixed capitalization. May only issue the numbers of shares as authorized in the company charter. *(See also: OPEN-END INVEST-MENT COMPANY)*

Closed-end management company: A mutual fund company with a fixed capitalization. May only issue the number of shares authorized in the company charter.

Closed out: The forced liquidation of a client's position in order to satisfy a margin call, if the client is unable to meet the debt by an additional deposit of cash or securities.

Closely held: A situation when a large percentage of shares of a publicly-traded corporation are owned by only a few stockholders.

Closing price: The last price at which a security traded on a business day.

Closing purchase: The transaction that liquidates a position. (Examples: Selling a call option previously bought; buying a stock that was previously sold short.)

Closing quote: The final bid and asked of a security on a business day.

Closing sale: The last price at which a security traded on a business day. (Example: Selling a call option previously bought, buying a stock that was previously sold short.)

Closing transaction: The transaction that liquidates a position. (Example: Selling a call option previously bought; buying a stock that was previously sold short.)

Code of procedure: The National Association of Securities Dealers (NASD) code that addresses the procedure of dealing with violations of NASD rules and regulations and customer complaints.

Collateral: Assets pledged by a borrower to secure a debt obligation.

Collateralize: The pledge, assignment or hypothecation of assets to secure a loan.

Collateral trust bond: A corporate debt security backed by other securities.

Collectibles: A individual's collection of any rare object such as jewelry, coins, stamps, antiques, etc.

Collection: The presentation of a negotiable item, such as a check or interest coupon, to the place at which it is payable.

Collection ratio: The ratio of a company's accounts receivable to the average daily sales.

COLTS: An acronym for Continuously Offered Long-Term Securities.

Combination: The simultaneous buy (or sell) of a put and a call option with different exercise prices and/or expiration months.

Combination bond: A bond backed by the full faith and credit of the governmental issuing authority, as well as the revenue from the project financed by the bond.

Combined account: A margin account having both long and short positions in different securities.

Combined distribution: An offering of a combination of new (primary) and previously-issued (secondary) securities.

COMEX: Commodity Exchange of New York.

Comfort letter: An independent auditor's letter stating that the information in the registration statement and prospectus of a new issue are correctly prepared and that no material changes have come to the auditor's attention since its preparation. Required by the Securities and Exchange Commission to be attached to all offerings.

Commercial paper: A short term debt instrument issued by a company.

Commingling: The mixing of a client's securities with those in another account, legal only with prior written consent of the client.

Commission: The fee paid to a broker (agent) for the purchase or sale of a security.

Commission broker: A broker who charges a commission when acting as agent in the purchases and sales of securities.

Commission house: A broker-dealer firm that buys and sells actuals or future commodities contracts for client's accounts.

Committee on Uniform Securities Identification Procedures (CUSIP): The committee that assigns identification numbers for securities.

Commodity Futures Trading Commission (CFTC): Established in 1974 by the U.S. Congress to police matters of information and disclosure, fair trading practices, registration of firms and individuals, protection of customer funds, record keeping, and the maintenance of orderly futures and options on futures markets.

Commodity: An actual physical product as distinguished from the "future," such as gold, live cattle, wheat, Japanese yen, lumber and pork bellies.

Commodity contract: The agreement to deliver a specific amount of a commodity in exchange for cash.

Commodity Exchange of New York (COMEX):   A regional futures exchange where certain commodity futures and options on those futures, if available, are traded.

Common market: Headquartered in Brussels, Belgium, an economic alliance formed in 1957 comprised of many foreign countries to foster trade and cooperation among its members.

Common stock: Units of ownership in a corporation.

Common stock equivalent: Preferred stock, convertible bond, warrant or right to purchase stock at a specified price or discount from market price.

Common stock fund: A mutual fund with a portfolio comprised of common stock, usually has objectives of capital growth.

Community property: Assets owned jointly by a married couple with equal rights as to dividends, interest, earnings and appreciation.

Company: An organization engaged in providing goods or services.

Competitive bidding: The submission of sealed bids by underwriters who want to be awarded the privilege of underwriting an issue of securities, usually of general obligation municipal bonds.

Complaint: A formal or informal expression of pain, grief or dissatisfaction.

Compliance: The adherence of any and all rules and regulations imposed upon individuals and businesses by various laws and governing bodies.

Compliance department: A department within each exchange and brokerage firm to oversee activities and ensure adherence of the Securities and Exchange Commission rules and regulations.

Compounded interest rate return: An investment in which the return or yield is reinvested in the account with interest being paid on the entire amount, including the credited interest.

Compound growth rate: The rate of growth compounded over a number of years, used to project the future growth rate of a company.

Compound interest: Interest paid on principal and on accumulated interest. *(See also: SIMPLE INTEREST)*

Comptroller: The chief financial officer of a company. Also known as Controller.

Computerized buy program: Buy orders of such volume and of many different securities that the market as a whole rises, sometimes dramatically, usually implemented by a "signal" when a computerized chart/plot program indicates a sell program is advisable.

Computerized marketing system: The use of a computer to analyze trends in individual issues as well as the market in general. Used to generate buy and sell signals.

Computerized sell program: Sell orders of such volume and of many different securities that the market as a whole loses value, sometimes dramatically, usually implemented by a "signal" when a computerized chart/plot program indicates a sell program is advisable.

Concession: Compensation paid by an issuing authority to the underwriter on a per-share or per-bond basis.

Conduit theory: The passing of tax liability on interest, dividends or capital gains from one entity to another. (Example: A regulated investment company passes all dividends, interest and capital gains to the individual investor who then assumes all tax liability.

Confidence theory: A ratio of high quality bonds to low quality bonds that indicates investor confidence in the economy. Purchasers of low quality bonds have confidence in the economy while buyers of high grade bonds tend to have doubts about the economy.

Confirmation: A written notice to the buyer or seller of a security detailing the name, price, commission or fee and trade date of the transaction.

Conflict of interest: The illegal act of representing two opposing sides of a transaction.

Conglomerate: A corporation with highly diversified operations.

Consent to loan agreement: An agreement signed by margin account clients that authorizes the brokerage firm to lend the clients' securities to itself or other firms. *(See also: LOAN CONSENT AGREEMENT)*

Consideration: An item of value given in exchange for a promise or act.

Consolidated balance sheet: A shortened version of a financial sheet that shows the total dollar values of all assets and liabilities of a company on a fixed date.

Consolidated financial statement: The complete financial statement of a parent company that lists all assets, liabilities and operating accounts of itself and all subsidiaries.

Consolidated Tape System (CTS):   The telegraphic system which prints or displays the stock symbol, volume and last sale price usually within one minute of the transaction.

Consolidating: The narrowing of a security's price range usually as a result of increased trading volume in the security.

Consortium: A group formed to promote a common objective. (Example: An insurance company may form with other insurance companies to underwrite a multi-million dollar policy of such a high dollar amount which would be financially impossible for one company to accomplish.)

Constant dollar plan: An investment strategy designed to maintain a portfolio at a constant dollar amount.

Constant ratio plan: An investment strategy designed to maintain a constant predetermined ratio of debt to equity positions in a portfolio.

Constructive receipt: The date established by IRS rules in which interest or dividends would have been paid to a taxpayer whether or not that taxpayer actually received the payment.

Consumer debenture: A financial institution investment note marketed directly to the public.

Consumer goods: Goods and services for personal and household use.

Consumer Price Index (CPI):   The U.S. Bureau of Labor Statistics measure of changes in consumer prices, includes cost of housing, food, transportation, utilities, entertainment and other services.

Contango: Futures prices that go progressively higher reflecting carrying costs, such as storage, financing and insurance. (The inverse of backwardation.)

Contingent order: An order placed for a security that is only to be executed as the result of another order's execution. (Example: If an order to buy 100 shares of XYZ stock executes, a contingent order is activated to sell an option on the newly-acquired stock.)

Contra broker: The broker on the opposite side of a transaction. (i.e., The broker acting as the buying agent is contra broker to the broker acting as the selling agent.)

Contract: An agreement between two or more parties by which rights or acts are exchanged for lawful consideration.

Contract grade: A grade of a commodity which has been officially approved by an exchange as deliverable in settlement of a futures contract.

Contractual plan: A type of accumulation plan of some mutual funds in which the investor makes a firm commitment to invest a specific amount of money in the fund during a specific time. *(See also: PENALTY PLAN, PREPAID CHARGE PLAN)*

Contrarian: An investor who makes decisions based on doing the opposite of what the majority of other investors are doing, (i.e., buying when the market is going down or selling when the market is going up.)

Controlled commodities: Commodities regulated by the rules and regulations of the Commodities and Exchange Act of 1936.

Controller: The chief financial officer of an organization. Also known as Comptroller.

Controlling interest: Ownership of more than 50 percent of a corporation's voting shares or a higher percentage of ownership than any other shareholder.

Control person: A director, officer or other affiliate of a company or a stockholder who owns at least ten percent of any class of a company's outstanding securities.

Control securities: Securities of an issue owned by a control person or by a holder of the controlling interest of a company.

Conventional mortgage: A residential mortgage loan granted by a bank or savings and loan that carries no insurance by the Federal Housing Administration or guarantee by the Veterans Administration.

Convergence: When the prices of a future's contract and the underlying cash commodity meet as the contract nears the maturity date. Figure 8.

Conversion: The exchange of a convertible security into the converted security. (Example: A convertible bond exchanged for common shares as per the terms of the bond.)

Conversion parity: The state of having a security that can be converted into another, both having equal dollar value.

Conversion price: The dollar amount of the bond's par (face) value that is exchangeable for one share of stock. *(See also: CONVERSION PRICE OF THE BOND)*

Conversion ratio: The number of shares per $1,000 bond or debenture that a holder would receive if the debt security were converted into shares of stock. *(See also: CONVERSION RATE)*

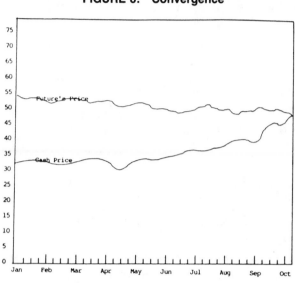

FIGURE 8:   Convergence

Conversion value: The total market value of common or preferred stock that the holder would receive if the debt security were to be converted into shares of stock.

Convert: To exchange one security for another. May or may not require additional money to accomplish the conversion.

Convertible security (CV):   A bond, debenture or preferred stock that may be exchanged for common stock or other security as stated by the terms of issuance.

Cooling-off period: The minimum 20 days between the filing date and the effective date of a registration statement for a new issue.

Copartnership account: A partnership account in which the individual members are empowered to act on behalf of the partnership as a whole.

Cornering the market: An illegal purchasing strategy to achieve price control of a security or commodity by the buyer.

Corporate Alternative Minimum Tax (AMT):   The minimum federal tax rate which corporations must pay, enacted with the 1986 Tax Reform Act.

Corporate bond: A bond issued by a corporation with a stated interest rate and maturity backed by equipment, buildings, assets or by signature only (debenture). Under current tax laws corporate bond income is federally taxed by individuals at their tax rate. *(See* *also: DEBENTURE, EQUIPMENT TRUST CERTIFICATE, MUNICI-PAL BOND)*

Corporate bond calendar: A list of corporate bonds soon to be offered for sale as a new or secondary offering.

Corporation: A form of business organization in which the total worth of the company is divided into shares of stock, each share representing a proportionate unit of ownership that carries certain rights and responsibilities as well as limited liability. Chartered by a U.S. state or the federal government.

Correction: The opposite movement of the price trend of a security, commodity, option, bond or index. Figure 9.

Correlation coefficient: The statistical measure of the degree of relation of the movements of two variables.

Correspondent: A financial institution that regularly performs services for another in an otherwise inaccessible market. (Example: A brokerage firm may use a correspondent in a foreign exchange where the brokerage firm is not a member.)

Cost basis: The total purchase price or value when acquired, includes the cost of purchase (i.e., commission, fees, etc.)

Cost of carrying: 1. The charges needed to carry commodities, including interest, storage and insurance. 2. The right (interest) a brokerage firm charges in a margin account against any debit balances.

Cost-of-Living Index: The U.S. Bureau of Labor Statistics measure of changes in consumer prices, includes costs of housing, food, transportation, utilities, entertainment and other services. Also known as Consumer Price Index (CPI).

Cost of sale: The total purchase price or value when acquired, includes the cost of purchase (i.e., commission, fees, etc.)

Cost push: Inflation caused by higher production costs, especially wages.

Cost records: Records kept by an investor or business to substantiate costs and dates of purchases.

Council of Economic Advisers: Economics advisers appointed by the President of the U.S. to provide counsel on economic policy.

Coupon: The interest rate as stated on a debt security, because at one time very few bonds were owner registered. They were bearer bonds, or bonds that had small coupons attached to the actual certificate that had to be detached and sent to the transfer agent in order for the interest to be paid. Each coupon stated the interest rate, hence the use of "coupon" to mean interest rate on a bond.

FIGURE 9:   Correction

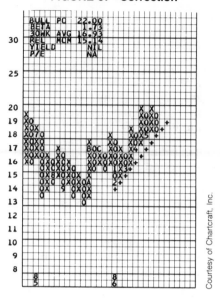

Courtesy of Chartcraft, Inc.

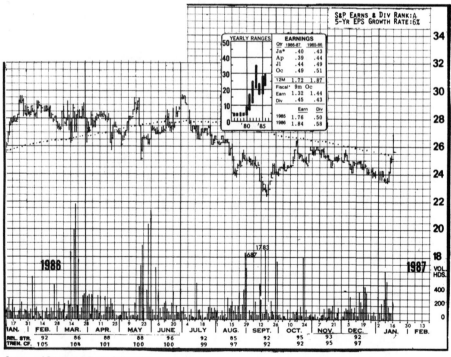

Courtesy of Standard & Poor's Corporation.

Coupon bond: A nonregistered bond in which the interest coupons are physically attached to the certificate to be taken off and sent to the transfer agent for the interest payment. Ownership changes by simply handing the certificate to the new owner. Also known as "bearer bond."

Coupon yield: The interest rate as stated on the face of the bond.

Covenant: The promise to perform all duties as required in a trust endenture of formal debt agreement.

Covenant of equal coverage: A promise in an indenture that states the issuer will not pledge any of its assets if doing so would result in less security to the debtholders covered by the indenture agreement. Also known as "negative pledge clause."

Cover: To buy back securities or commodities that had previously been sold short, thus closing a position. *(See also: CLOSING TRANSACTION)*

Covered call writer: The owner of a security who sells a call option against that security.

Covered option: An option position that is offset (covered) by an equal position in the underlying security. (Example: The seller of two calls on the XYZ company owns 200 shares of the XYZ company that would be used to deliver to the call buyer should the buyer decide to exercise the call.)

Covered put writer: The owner of a put option who sells a put of the same class with an equal or longer expiration date and an equal or higher exercise price.

CPI: Consumer Price Index.

Crash: The abrupt drop in stock prices as witnessed in the crash of 1929 that precipitated the Great Depression.

Credit (CR): 1) The accounting entry that increases liabilities and decreases assets. 2) Balances due to the owner of an account. 3) An increase in equity.

Credit agreement: A signed statement by a client agreeing to the rules of a margin account. (Securities pledged as collateral will be held by the brokerage firm, those securities may be repledged by the brokerage firm to finance the account and the brokerage firm may sell the securities if needed to protect its financial interest in the account.)

Credit analyst: A person who analyzes the creditworthiness and determines the credit rating of individuals, corporations and/or municipalities.

Credit balance (CR): The amount of money remaining in a client's account after all commitments have been paid in full.

Credit rating: The formal credit evaluation of an individual, corporation or municipality taking into consideration financial history and repayment capabilities.

Credit risk: Generally refers to the amount of risk that an issuer of bonds may default in the payment of either principal or interest. *(See also: AT RISK)*

Credit spread: A situation when one option is bought and another option of the same type is sold and the premium of the one sold is higher than the one bought.

Credit union: A not-for-profit financial institution empowered to provide banking services, usually formed by employees of a company or large organization.

Crop year: The period of time from the harvest of a crop of one year to the time of harvest in the next year.

Cross: A securities transaction with the same broker acting as buying and selling agent. A legal transaction if the security is first publicly offered at a price higher than the bid.

Crossed trade: A prohibited maneuver of offsetting buy and sell orders without reporting the transaction to the exchange.

Crowd: The trading population of an exchange grouped in the area of activity of interest. (Example: All bond traders congregate in the area of an exchange concerned with trading bonds. All live hog traders congregate in the exchange pit (area) where hogs are traded. Each group is a "crowd.")

Crown jewels: The most highly valued entities of a company.

Crush: A commodity phrase used when soybean contracts are bought, and soybean meal and soybean oil are sold. Usually a crush is put on by the producer of soybean meal and oil. Also known as Putting-on-the-Crush.

Cum dividend: Refers to a stock whose buyer is entitled to receive the declared dividend. Literally means "with dividend." *(See also: EX-DIVIDEND)*

Cum rights: Literally means with rights. Refers to a stock that is traded with rights which allow the owner to purchase an additional number of shares at a specified price.

Cumulative preferred stock: A preferred stock with a provision that states any dividends not declared by the board of directors must be paid before any dividends may be declared for the common stock.

Cumulative voting: A method of voting for corporate directors that allows the total amount of a shareholder's voting rights to be divided according to the shareholder's desire. (Example: A shareholder with 100 voting rights may choose to cast all 100 votes for one director or possibly 20 for one and 80 for another.)

Curb: American Stock Exchange.

Currency futures: Commodity contracts that are for U.S. dollars, British pounds, Japanese yen, Swiss francs, French francs or German marks.

Current assets: Assets of a company that are expected to be converted to cash, sold or used during one accounting year.

Current coupon bond: A bond with a coupon rate within ½ point of the current market rate.

Current liabilities: Money owed and payable during one accounting year.

Current market value (CMV):   The current value of securities in an account based on closing prices of the previous business day.

Current maturity: The interval of time between the date a bond is issued and the date it matures. Also known as "original maturity."

Current ratio: A measure of a company's liquidity calculated by dividing the total current assets by the total current liabilities.

Current return/yield: Figured by taking the stated interest rate and dividing that figure by the price. The current yield will be the same as the stated interest rate if the price is par (100 percent). The current yield will be higher when the stated interest rate is at a discount and will be lower if the stated interest rate is at a premium. (Example: A seven percent bond priced at 100 percent has a seven percent current yield, a price of 95 percent has a 7.36 percent current yield and a price of 105 percent has a 6.6 percent current yield.)

Cushion bond: A callable bond selling at a premium with a coupon rate higher than current market interest rates. Tends to be less volatile in an unstable interest rate market.

Cushion theory: Relates to stock that has a high percentage of short positions that technical analysts consider bullish, as a rise in price of the stock will trigger the short holders to start buying to cover thus making the price go even higher.

CUSIP: Committee on Uniform Securities Identification Procedures.

Custodian: An institution or individual responsible for the protection of the property of another.

Custodian account: An account created for the benefit of a minor or incompetent but controlled by an adult.

Customer: One who buys consistently at a given establishment.

Customer's loan consent: An agreement signed by margin account clients that authorizes the brokerage firm to lend the client's securities to itself or other firms. *Synonym: LOAN CONSENT AGREEMENT.*

Customer's man: An out-of-date term referring to a stock broker, used before women started working for brokerage firms.

Customer statement: The record of any transaction during the accounting period and their resulting effect on any debt or equity position.

CV: Convertible security.

Cyclical stock: A stock price that tends to go up in certain seasons and down in others because of the type of goods or services produced by the issuing company.

Daily trading limit: The maximum price movement a commodity may make, up or down, in any one trading day.

Daisy chain: Trading among a group of persons in a particular security at successively higher prices, creating a false image of trading activity in the hopes of generating buy orders in the general market to bring the price even higher. Once the price does become higher, the group of manipulators sell their positions, a fraudulent and illegal maneuver.

DARTS: An acronym for Dutch Auction-Rate Transferable Securities.

Dated date: The date a debt instrument, such as a bond, starts accruing interest.

Date of record: The date on which a shareholder must be registered on the books of the company to be eligible to receive a dividend.

Day order: An order to buy or sell which, if not executed, is automatically cancelled at the end of the trading day on which it was entered.

Day trade: The purchase and sale of a security transacted on the same day.

Day trader: An individual who speculates in securities, options and/or commodity futures markets by buying and selling positions on the same day or possibly overnight. Also known as a "scalper."

Dealer: An individual or firm in the securities business who buys and sells securities as a principal rather than as an agent.

Debenture: A promissory note (bond) backed by the full faith and credit of a company and usually not secured by any specific property.

Debenture stock: A common stock issued that provides a fixed payment on a periodic basis.

Debit (DR):   An item of debt recorded in an account.

Debit balance: The portion of a security's purchase price that is covered by credit extended by the broker-dealer firm to the margin customer.

Debit spread: The purchase and sale of two similar options, where the value of the option purchased is greater than the one sold.

Debt: An amount one party owes another.

Debt instrument: A security signifying a loan to the issuer and usually paying a stated interest rate at specified intervals for a stated length of time, such as a certificate of deposit or corporate, municipal or government bonds.

Debt position: 1) The total amount of debt owed by an individual or other entity. 2) The total value of debt securities in a portfolio.

Debt retirement: The repayment of a debt.

Debt security: The general name for bonds, notes, mortgages, preferred stock and other forms of paper evidencing amounts owed and payable.

Debt service: The number and amount of required payments of principal and interest on a debt.

Debt-to-equity ratio: The ratio of total debt to total stockholder's equity.

Debtor: The entity owing a debt.

Decay: A term to describe when the value of the securities in a portfolio is declining.

Declare: The authorization by a companies board of directors of a cash or stock dividend.

Decline: Reduce or go down in value.

Deduction: An expense allowed by the Internal Revenue Service against adjusted gross income.

Deed of trust: The written agreement between a corporation and its creditors that details the terms of the debt issue including rate of interest, maturity date(s), call features, collateral and means of payment.

Deep discount bond: A bond selling for a discount of 20 percent or more from its par (face) value.

Deep in-the-money call option: An option with an exercise price that is well below the current price of the underlying security.

Deep in-the-money put option: An option with an exercise price that is well above the current price of the underlying security.

Deep out-of-the money call option: An option with an exercise price that is well above the current price of the underlying security.

Deep out-of-the money put option: An option with an exercise price that is well below the current price of the underlying security.

Default: The inability by an issuer of a debt security to pay interest and principal as due.

Defensive industry stocks or issues: An industry that is relatively unaffected by business cycles, such as food and utilities. Also known as "defense stocks."

Defensive policy: A method investors use to minimize the risk of losing principal by using predetermined buy and sell parameters.

Deferral of taxes: Tax liability on an investment that has been deferred to a later time.

Deferred account: An account that postpones tax liabilities until funds are withdrawn, such as a retirement account.

Deferred annuity: An annuity contract in which payment of principal and earnings are to begin at some date in the future.

Deferred interest bond: A bond issued at a discount to face value which pays no current interest. The stated interest is a calculation of the difference in issued and maturity values on a compounded rather than simple interest basis. (Caution: Both taxable and non-taxable deferred interest bonds are available. When taxable, the income tax is due on the annual accured interest as if actually received.) (*See also: PHANTOM INCOME, ZERO COUPON BOND, ORIGINAL ISSUE DISCOUNT BOND.*)

Deficiency letter: A letter sent by the Securities and Exchange Commission (SEC) to the issuer of a public offering (new issue) that lists corrections to the registration that must be made prior to SEC release. (*See also: BED-BUG LETTER*)

Deficit financing: Borrowing by the government to make up for a revenue shortfall.

Defined benefit pension plan: A retirement plan designed to provide a specified amount to employees who retire after a set number of years. Tax liabilities are deferred until funds are withdrawn.

Defined contribution: The amount, as defined by current law, which an individual or corporation may invest in a retirement plan.

Deflation: The persistent and appreciable fall in the general level of prices.

Deflator: A statistical factor designed to adjust the difference between real value and value affected by inflation.

Deflection of tax liability: The shifting of tax liability from one taxpayer to another to take advantage of a lower tax bracket.

Delayed delivery: An out-of-the-ordinary transaction allowing the seller to deliver the certificate at any time within a period ranging from 6 to 60 days as specified by the seller.

Delayed opening: Postponement of trading a security beyond the normal opening of a day's trading session because market conditions have been judged by exchange officials to warrant such a delay, usually an imbalance of orders or pending corporate news.

Delinquency: Failure to pay a debt when due.

Delisting: The removal of a stock from an exchange's list of tradable securities.

Deliverable grade: A grade of commodity which has been officially approved by an exchange as deliverable in settlement against a futures contract.

Delivery: 1) The tender and receipt of the actual commodity (or warehouse receipts covering such commodity) in settlement of a futures contract. 2) The presentation of cash or certificate(s) as a result of the completion of a transaction.

Delivery against cost/sale: Delivery of securities made to a buyer's account simultaneously in exchange for cash. (*See also: DELIVERY VERSUS PAYMENT.*)

Delivery date: 1) The date on which a commodities future contract becomes deliverable. (Caution: Commodity futures contracts oftentimes become deliverable before the contract month.) 2) The fifth business day following a regular way trade for stock. 3) The day following a transaction for bonds and options.

Delivery month: The specified month within which delivery may be made under the terms of a futures contract.

Delivery notice: Notification from the seller to the buyer of a futures contract of intent to deliver that specifies date, destination and quality adjustments.

Delivery points: The actual place designated by futures exchanges at which the physical commodity covered by a futures contract may be delivered in fulfillment of such contract.

Delivery versus payment (DVP): Delivery of securities made to a buyer's account simultaneously in exchange for cash. Also known as "cash on delivery," "delivery against payment," "delivery against sale."

Delphi Forecast: A forecast of a panel of experts who have been given the same information and asked to make market forecasts based on the information, collectively review the results then make changes based on the group's decisions. Believed to be a more realistic forecast than any given by an individual. The panel is called the jury of executive opinion.

Delta: The rate of increase or decrease of an options value in relationship to the underlying security price. An "at the money" option will have a delta of 1:1.

Demand deposit: An account balance which, with proper notice, may be withdrawn by check, automatic teller or transfer.

Demand pull: A type of inflation that results from too much money and too few goods.

Denationalization: The transfer of a government-owned company to private ownership, usually by means of a public stock offering.

Denomination: The face value of a coin, currency and securities. *(See also: PAR)*

Depletion accounting: An accounting practice regarding natural resources consisting of charges against earnings based upon the amount of the asset taken out of the total reserves in the period for which accounting is made. It does not represent any cash outlay nor are any funds earmarked for the purpose.

Depletion allowance: A tax preferential treatment (if allowed by law) given to investors of producing oil or gas properties.

Deposit: 1) Items, including cash and securities, that are placed in trust with a financial institution for a customer's account. 2) Money given by a buyer as a sign of good faith in the expectation of fulfillment of a contract.

Depository receipt: A negotiable receipt in the form of a certificate for a number of shares of stock in a foreign corporation, bought and sold in the American securities markets just as any other U.S. stock is traded.

Depository Trust Company (DTC): A central securities certificate depository through which member firms use computerized bookkeeping entries to effect security deliveries.

Depreciation: A bookkeeping entry that charges off the cost against earnings, less salvage value, of an asset over its estimated useful life.

FIGURE 10: Descending Top

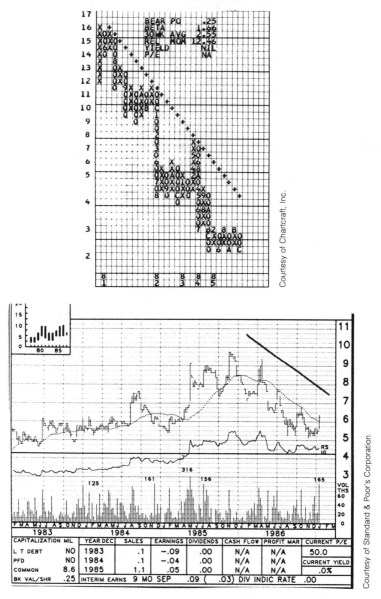

Courtesy of Chartcraft, Inc.

Courtesy of Standard & Poor's Corporation.

Deregulation: The reduction of governmental control designed to allow the concept of free enterprise and the economics law of supply and demand to create a more efficient marketplace.

Descending tops: A chart pattern where each new high price of a security is lower than the previous high. Figure 10.

Devaluation: An adjustment of a country's currency value relative to the price of gold or the currency of another country.

Developmental drilling program: A limited partnership that drills for oil and gas in proven areas and to previously successful depths.

DI: Disposable income.

Diagonal spread: The simultaneous purchase and sale of options of the same class but with different exercise prices and expiration dates. (Example: A diagonal spread position is taken consisting of the purchase of one XYZ January 45 call and the sale of one XYZ April 50 put.)

Diamond investment trust: A unit trust that invests in high quality diamonds.

Differential: 1) The extra per-share charge, usually one eighth of a point, imposed on odd lot orders (as opposed to round lot orders evenly divisible by 100). 2) The difference between the buy (bid) and sell (asked) price of a security. 3) The premium paid for a better grade or discount allowed for a lesser grade on the delivery of an actual commodity.

Digits deleted: The first digit of a price dropped from a ticker tape due to fast conditions (heavy trading). (Example: 1s49½ meaning one lot traded at 49½ would show on a fast tape as 1s9½.)

Dilution: The effect of earnings per share and book value should all stock convertible securities, warrants, rights and options be exercised. *(See also: FULLY DILUTED EARNINGS PER COMMON SHARE)*

Dip: A slight drop in the price of a security after a sustained upward trend.

Direct obligation: A debt obligation issued by an entity, such as the U.S. government, with the payment of interest and the repayment of principal paid directly by the issuing entity. *(See also: INDIRECT OBLIGATION)*

Director: A person elected by shareholders of a company to serve on the board of directors to make various decisions on the shareholders behalf, such as the appointment of operating officers and the declaration and payment of any dividends.

Direct participation program: A limited partnership in which all investors participate directly in the cash flow and tax benefits of the underlying investment.

Direct placement: A conditional offering of non-registered securities, the requirements of which must be strictly adhered to. (Caution:

The number of investors as well as the qualification rules are subject to change. It is advisable to consult with a tax attorney prior to the formation or investment in a direct placement.)

Disbursement: The paying out of monies due as a result of a loan or an expense.

Disclosure: The complete release of all pertinent information, whether negative or positive, that might influence an investment decision.

Disclosure statement: The statement required of all new issues that releases any and all pertinent information, whether negative or positive, that might influence an investment decision.

Discount: The amount by which a preferred stock or bond is priced below its par (face) value. *(See also: BELOW PAR)*

Discount bond: A bond which is priced below its par or face value.

Discount broker: A registered representative who takes unsolicited orders from clients for the purchase and/or sale of securities, gives no advice and charges commissions on a flat fee, per trading unit or other basis.

Discounting the news: The drop or rise of a stock in anticipation of bad or good news about the company.

Discount rate: The interest rate charged to member banks that borrow from the Federal Reserve.

Discount yield: The yield of a debt security sold at a discount to face value. The yield is based on the difference between the discount price and the par value, expressed on an annual basis. (Example: A $100,000 U.S. Treasury bill due in 90 days bought at a price of $98,000 has a discount yield of 8.1 percent arrived by dividing the discount amount by the face value, dividing the number of days in a year by the number of days until maturity then multiplying the resulting two figures.)

Discretionary account: An account where the client gives the registered representative authority to buy and sell securities, including selection, timing, amount and/or price to be paid or received.

Discretionary income: Personal income remaining after essentials such as housing, food and utilities are deducted from the disposable income.

Discretionary order: An order to buy or sell a security giving the broker the power to decide when to place the order and/or at what price.

Disinflation: The situation when retailers are not able to pass higher prices on to their customer resulting in lower profits, fewer pay raises and a slowing of the economy.

Disposable income (DI): Personal income remaining for spending or saving after all taxes have been deducted.

Distributing syndicate: A group of investment bankers formed to underwrite and distribute a new or secondary issue of securities.

Distribution: 1) The payout of funds, such as cash or stock dividends and capital gains. 2) The sale of a large block of stock in such a manner as to not adversely affect the price. Inverse of accumulation.

Distribution area: The narrow price range which a stock has traded for a period of time. Offers to sell at a price below the distribution area tends to push the price down. (*See also: ACCUMULATION AREA.*) Figure 11.

FIGURE 11.   Distribution Area

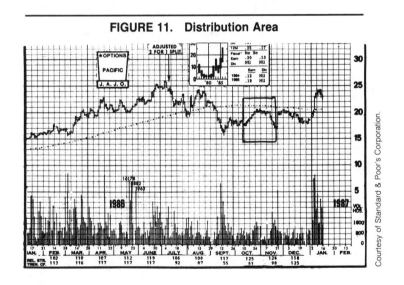

Courtesy of Standard & Poor's Corporation.

Diversification: The spread of investments among different types of securities and/or various companies in different fields.

Diversified management company: A management company that must have at least 75 percent of its assets in cash, receivables and/or securities, with no more than 5 percent in any one company and it cannot own more than 10 percent of a voting company's stock.

Divestiture: The disposition of an asset, investment or subsidiary by purchase, liquidation or distribution.

Dividend: A portion of a company's earnings that are paid to shareholders on a pro rata basis, amount and pay date as declared by the board of directors. May be paid from current or past earnings.

Dividend exclusion: The amount of dividends excluded from taxes by rules of the Internal Revenue Service.

Dividend payout ratio: A ratio calculated by dividing the dividends paid on common stock by the net income available for common stock.

Dividend reinvestment plan: The method of automatically reinvesting a shareholder's dividends into additional shares of stock.

Dividend requirement: The amount of earnings needed to pay dividends on issued preferred stock.

Dividend rollover plan: A short term investment method involving the purchase of a stock a few weeks before the exdividend date and selling a short time later. Stock prices are adjusted down by the amount of the dividend on exdividend date and tend to rise back to the predividend price within a short period of time.

Dividend yield: The annual percentage of return, figured by dividing the annual dividend amount by the per share cost basis of the securities.

DJIA: Dow Jones Industrial Average.

DK: Don't know. Indicates a lack of information about a company, transaction or record of transaction.

DNR: Do not reduce.

Dog and pony show: A lecture, seminar or other type of setting used by wholesalers, investment bankers and/or brokers to interest investors in a financial product of offering.

Dollar bonds: Municipal bonds quoted and traded on a dollar rather than yield to maturity basis.

Dollar cost averaging: A method of buying mutual fund shares with a fixed dollar amount at regular intervals, buying more shares when the price is down and less when the price is up.

Domestic corporation: A corporation doing business in the state in which it was incorporated. *(See also: ALIEN CORPORATION)*

Done deal: Slang for a contract or trade that is complete except for the final confirmation.

Donoghue's money fund average: A report of the seven- and 30-day average yields of all major money market funds. Also reflects the

FIGURE 12.   Double Bottom

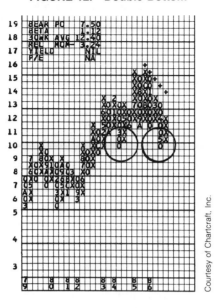

Courtesy of Chartcraft, Inc.

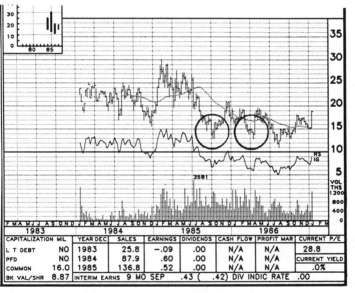

Courtesy of Standard & Poor's Corporation.

average maturity dates of the money market fund's investments, reported to be an indication of interest rate patterns (i.e., short term indicates rising interest rates while long term indicates lowering interest rates).

Do not reduce (DNR):   A good until cancelled order that stipulates the limit price shall not be reduced as a result of cash or stock dividends.

Don't fight the tape: Don't trade against the market trend as reported on the broad tape (i.e., don't buy in a down market or sell in an up market).

Don't know (DK):   A reply sent back to a requester of a quote or other information that means there is no information available to the best of that person's knowledge.

Double-barreled bond: A municipal bond whose principal and interest payments are backed by the issuing authority and a larger municipal entity, such as the city or state of issuance.

Double bottom: A technical chart pattern showing the price of a stock that has dipped to a low trading area, recovered, then dipped to the low trading area again. Figure 12.

Double declining balance depreciation method: An accounting method of doubling the annual depreciation rate over the straight line method.

Double taxation: 1) The taxation of dividends at the corporate level and then again at the personal income level. 2) Taxing at the state and at the federal level.

Double top: A technical chart pattern that shows a high, a correction, then another high. Figure 13.

Dow Jones averages: Price weighted average based on specific groups, including the 30 Industrial, 20 Transportation, 15 Utility, 65 Composite, 40 Bond and Municipal Bond Yields. The numbers preceding each group indicates the number of issues that make up the average.

Dow Jones Composite Average: A measurement of price movement of the total numbers of stocks in the Dow Jones Industrial Transportation and Utility Average.

Dow Jones Industrial Average (DJIA):   The most widely recognized market indicator made up of 30 large and actively traded industrial stocks. The stocks included in the DIJA composite list change from time-to-time due to mergers, trading activities or other factors.

Dow Jones Transportation Average: A measurement of price movement of 20 of the largest and most active transportation stocks.

Dow Jones Utility Average: A measurement of price movement of 15 of the largest and most active utility stocks.

Down-and-out option: A put or call option that is far enough out of the money as to be considered worthless.

FIGURE 13.   Double Top

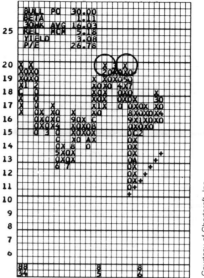

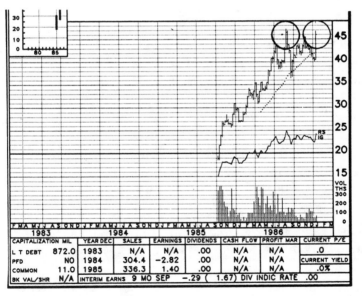

Courtesy of Chartcraft, Inc.

Courtesy of Standard & Poor's Corporation.

Downside protection: The lowest value which an asset is estimated to possibly fall.

Downside risk: The possible risk of an investment losing its value after taking market conditions into consideration.

Downtick: A term used to designate a transaction made at a price lower than the preceding transaction. Also known as a "minus tick."

Down trend: The situation in which a security or the market as a whole is going down more than it is going up.

Downturn: The shift of the market or economic conditions from an up trend to a down trend.

Dow Theory: A theory of market analysis based upon the performance of the Dow Jones Industrial and Transportation Averages. Says to confirm an upward or downward trend if both averages move above or below a previous important high or low.

Drilling program: A limited partnership invested in drilling for oil and/or gas. (*See also: DEVELOPMENTAL DRILLING PROGRAM, EXPLORATORY DRILLING PROGRAM, BALANCED DRILLING PROGRAM, OIL AND GAS LIMITED PARTNERSHIP*)

Dual listing: A stock that is listed on more than one exchange.

Dual-purpose fund: A closed-end investment company that offers income shares and capital (growth) shares.

Dual security: A bond or preferred stock that is guaranteed by an entity other than the issuer as to the timely payment of interest or dividends and principals.

Due bill: A statement showing the transfer of a security's title of rights, or showing the obligation of a seller to deliver the securities of rights to the purchaser.

Due diligence: The careful investigation necessary to ensure that all pertinent information of an issue has been disclosed.

Due diligence meeting: A meeting between an issuer and an underwriter to discuss details of a pending issue. Includes the preparation of the registration statement and the prospectus.

Dump: To close positions in securities very quickly.

Dumping: The selling of large amounts of shares with no consideration of the effect the selling will have on the market.

Duplicate confirmation: A copy of a confirmation that a client has requested in writing to be sent to an attorney or agent of the client.

DVP: Delivery versus payment.

Each way: One broker acting as agent on both the buy and the sell side of a security transaction.

Early exercise: The election by the buyer of an option to exercise the terms of the option contract prior to the expiration date.

Early withdrawal penalty: A penalty assessed only if funds are withdrawn early from a fixed term account, such as a certificate of deposit, retirement or annuity account.

Earned income: Income that is derived from personal income such as wages, tips, commissions, bonuses, etc. Does not include rental, dividend or interest income.

Earned surplus: The amount of net income remaining after all dividends have been paid to common and preferred shareholders.

Earning power: Money generated per dollar of invested capital of a company, calculated by adding net income and interest expense and dividing that total by the total amount of invested capital.

Earnings: Wages, salaries or profits.

Earnings per share (EPS):   The net income available for common stock divided by the number of shares of common stock outstanding.

Earnings per share after dilution: The earnings per share when all convertible securities, such as convertible preferred stock and convertible bonds, have been converted.

Earnings report: An income statement issued by a company showing its earnings or losses, income earned, expenses and net result over a given period of time.

Earnings-to-price ratio: The inverse of price to earnings ratio. Shows the relationship of earnings per share as compared to the current stock price.

Eastern account: A municipal bond underwriting agreement in which each participant is responsible for selling a percentage of the offering and must make up any overall deficit at the member's percentage rate. (Example: A member has agreed to sell 20 percent of an offering, sells 30 percent, total sold was 90 percent so member must make up 20 percent of deficit regardless of original amount sold by member. *(See also: WESTERN ACCOUNT)*

Easy money: Money that is easily obtained with fairly low interest rates because the money supply is high. Easy money tends to generate economic growth and inflation.

Econometrics: A mathematical computation showing relationships between key economic forces and the probable effect on both.

Economic and social risk: The impact that international and social events may have on national or world economics.

Economic expansion: At least two consecutive quarterly gains in the Gross National Product.

Economic growth rate: The rate of change in the Gross National Product, expressed as an annual percentage. Two consecutive quarterly drops mean recession while two quarterly growths mean expansion.

Economic indicators: Key economic factors that show the direction of the economy, including unemployment, inflation, factory utilization and balance of trade.

ECU: European Currency Unit.

Edge Act: A federal act, passed in 1919, that, if allowed by state law, permits banks to conduct business in other states. The act has been expanded several times since 1979 to further deregulate banking restrictions.

Effective date: The date the registration of a new issue becomes effective and the securities are available for purchase.

Effective rate: The actual return, if held to maturity, of a debt interest, calculated by taking the dollar amount of the annual return, dividing by 365, multiplying that figure by the number of days until maturity, adding the amount of discount or subtracting the amount of premium, (whichever is applicable), dividing the sum by the number of years held then dividing that figure by the total investment amount. (Example: For a 10 pecent coupon bond bought at $90,000 due in six and a half years. (2,370 days), the average annual return if held to maturity is 12.8 percent.)

Effective sale: The last price of a round lot that, when the odd lot differential is added, determines the price of an odd lot.

Effective yield: The actual yield of a debt security based on the interest rate being paid, price paid and length of time held.

Efficient market theory: The theory based on the assumption that new information is reflected immediately in the price of a stock, which becomes a "fair price" and is therefore perfectly efficient. *(See also: RANDOM WALK THEORY)*

Efficient portfolio: A portfolio that is receiving the maximum amount of return based on expected risk or the minimum amount of risk based on the return.

Either or order: Two simultaneous orders given to a registerd representative by a client for the purchase or sale (not both) of a security with instructions to cancel one order should the other execute.

Elasticity of demand and supply: A measure of personal spending habits as the result of price changes.

Eligible securities: Securities that are eligible to a) be traded by Federal Open Market Committee: b) be accepted by the Federal Reserve for loans at the discount window; c) have loan value in margin accounts; d) be deposited at the Options Clearing Corporation as collateral for short option positions; or e) be traded in the over the counter market even though listed on an exchange.

Employee Retirement Income Security Act (ERISA): Passed in 1974, the law gives the federal government power to oversee the establishment, operation and funding of most nongovernmental pension and benefit (retirement) plans.

Employee Stock Ownership Plan (ESOP): A qualified retirement plan in which the funds are invested in the company's stock or, in some cases, in other company's stocks. (Caution: An ESOP is regulated by federal law and is therefore subject to change.)

Endaka: Japanese for "yen shock," the result of the economic trauma due to the recent dramatic appreciation of the yen against the dollar.

End load: A mutual fund or annuity investment that has the commission charges against redemptions of principal rather than purchases. Ordinarily, the amount of commission decreases by a certain percentage each year until there is no sales charge.

Endorsement: The owner's signature on a security certificate or stock/ bond power making the certificate negotiable for transfer to a new owner or trustee.

Energy complex: Commodities used in the making of energy, (i.e., crude oil, gasoline and heating oil).

Energy mutual fund: A mutual fund with a portfolio comprised solely in energy stocks, such as oil, gas, solar and energy-saving device manufacturing companies.

Enterprise: A business of any kind.

Entrepreneur: An individual willing to assume the risks of business ownership. Usually refers to those engaged in new, innovative companies.

EPS: Earnings per share.

Equilibrium price: The highest profit of goods for the cost, manufactured at the best rate for demand.

Equipment bond/trust certificate: A bond, generally issued by a railroad, proceeds of which are used to purchase new equipment, the title to which is held in trust until the bond is paid off.

Equipment leasing partnership: A limited partnership engaged in the purchase of equipment for lease to end users, such as computers, piggy-back trucks, shipping barges and airplanes.

Equity: 1) Ownership of assets including common and preferred stock holders. 2) Excess of the value of securities over debt balance in a margin account.

Equity financing: Capital financing by the use or issuance of common or preferred stock.

Equity kickers: An added inducement to make an investment more attractive by using equity securities or enhancements, such as rights, warrants, convertible features or other equities.

Equity position: The total value or number of securities, usually stocks, representing ownership.

Equity reit: An organization with investments in real estate. The formation charter usually calls for as much as 90 percent of the earnings to be returned to the shareholders.

Equity security: A security, usually stock, representing ownership.

Equity turnover: The annual sales of a company divided by the average equity. Used to determine the extent to which the company is able to grow without additional capital.

Equivalent bond yield: The yield of a bond sold at discount as compared to a coupon bond. (Example: A Treasury Bill due in 90 days with a face value of $1,000 bought at $975 would be equivalent to a 10.4 percent coupon bond.)

Equivalent taxable yield: The yield of a corporate bond compared to a municipal bond after an individual's tax bracket has been taken into consideration.

ERISA: Employee Retirement Income Security Act.

Escheat: The power of a state to hold in trust or dispose of abandoned property, usually bank accounts and insurance policies, that can be claimed by the rightful owner should the owner be found.

Escrow: Funds, property or securities held in trust by a third party until conditions of a contract have been met.

Escrow receipt: The notification from an approved bank that guarantees securities are on deposit at the bank and will be delivered should an option written against the security be exercised.

ESOP: Employee Stock Ownership Plan.

Estate: Everything an individual owns and/or owes.

Estate planning: The preparation of an individual's investments, assets, insurance and all other properties through the use of a will, trust and/or transfer of property to minimize estate taxes and facilitate the administration of the estate when the individual dies.

Estate tax: The tax imposed by the state or federal government on an inheritance.

Eurobond: A bond issued by the government or a corporation in one country and denominated in its currency but sold outside that country.

Eurocurrency: European currency held in banks outside of the country issuing the currency.

Eurodollar: U.S. currency held in banks outside the U.S.

Eurodollar bond: A bond that pays the interest and principal payments in Eurodollars (U.S. dollars deposited in banks outside the United States.)

Eurodollar certificate of deposit: A certificate of deposit issued by a bank outside the U.S. with interest and principal paid in Eurodollars (U.S. dollars deposited in banks outside the United States).

European Currency Unit (ECU):   Developed by member nations of the European Common Market consisting of Western European currencies for the purpose of simplifying transactions among themselves. Some American and foreign corporations have issued bonds that are denominated in ECUs.

Evaluator: An independent, disinterested third party who assigns a value on assets with a limited market.

Evening up: Said of a trader who, for any reason, is completing transactions by the selling of long positions or the buying of short positions.

Ex-all: Without dividends, rights, warrants or any other items attached.

Excess equity/margin: The amount of money in a margin account that is over the federal requirement.

Excess profits tax: A special general federal tax on business earnings imposed during a time of national emergency.

Excess reserves: The amount of money a bank holds over and above the Federal Reserve Requirements.

Exchange: A place of business organized for the purpose of providing an orderly and efficient marketplace for the trading of securities such as stocks, bonds, options and commodities.

Exchange acquisition/distribution: A block of stock that is crossed on the floor of an exchange with no prior announcement on the broad tape.

Exchange offer: An offer to exchange one type of security for another, usually as a result of a possible friendly merger.

Exchange privilege: The right of an investor to switch from one fund to another within a family of mutual funds, usually with no sales charges to the investor. Could have a nominal transfer fee.

Exchange rate: The amount of currency of one country needed to convert to currency of another country.

Exchange trade: A block of stock crossed on the floor of an exchange with no prior announcement on the broad tape.

Excise tax: State or federal tax imposed on specific luxury manufactured goods, such as tobacco and alcohol.

Exclusion: The elimination of all or a portion of an item or items.

Ex-date: The last day that a stock trades with the latest declared dividend, usually four business days prior to record date. After exdate, the purchaser of the stock is not entitled to the dividend.

Ex-dividend: Literally means "without dividend." A buyer of stock on or after the exdividend date is not entitled to receive the latest dividend declared by the board of directors of a company.

Ex-dividend date: The last day that a stock trades with the latest declared dividend, usually four business days prior to record date.

A buyer of the stock after the ex dividend date is not entitled to receive the dividend.

Execute: Used to indicate a "fill" or completion of an order to buy or sell a security.

Execution: A completed transaction, either a buy or a sell of a security.

Executor: Someone authorized by the last will of a decedent to manage the financial business of an estate.

Exempt security: A security exempt from the registration requirements of the Securities Act of 1933.

Exercise: Action taken by a buyer of an option requiring the seller of the option to fulfill the option contract terms. In the case of a call, the buyer buys the underlying security from the seller and for a put, the buyer sells the underlying security to the option seller.

Exercise limit: The number of the same type of option contracts that can be exercised in a given period of time.

Exercise notice: Notice to the seller of an option that the buyer wishes to fulfill the terms of the option contract. In the case of a call, to purchase the security from the option seller; in the case of a put, to sell the security to the option seller.

Exercise price: The price at which the underlying security of an option may be exercised.

Eximbank: Shortened name for the independent federal agency established in 1934 to borrow from the U.S. Treasury to finance exports and imports.

Ex-legal: A municipal bond that does not have the required legal opinion attached or printed on it.

Exotic shelter: A tax favored investment in an unusual product.

Expense ratio: A comparison of a mutual fund's management fees and overhead expenses to the average net asset value, expressed in cents per $100 of investment.

Expiration: The date a contract expires and no longer has value.

Expiration cycle: 1) Stock: The cycle of option expiration dates available for specific securities, may be one of four cycles; a) January, April, July and October; b) February, May, August and November; c) March, June, September and December; or d) Closest consecutive three months plus one of the other three cycles. 2) Commodity: Options on futures expire on; a) Cycle c above in the case of index and financial futures, and b) The months the underlying commodity future is available for trading.

Expiration date: The date on which an option expires valueless and is no longer tradable or exercisable.

Expire: To terminate or die, as in the case of an option contract that has passed its expiration date.

Expire worthless: A long call or put option contract that has surpassed the expiration contract and is no longer tradable or exercisable. All premium paid for the expired option is a loss.

Ex-pit transaction: The trading of a commodity off the floor of the exhange at specified terms.

Exploratory drilling program: A limited partnership that invests in searches for undiscovered oil or gas reserves.

Ex-rights: A security trading without rights attached.

Ex-store: A selling term used for commodities in warehouse.

Extra dividend: A dividend declared by a company's board of directors that is in addition to the regularly declared dividends.

Extraordinary item: An unusual and nonrecurring event. Must be detailed and explained in a company's quarterly or annual report.

Ex-warrants: A security trading without warrants attached.

F: Used in uppercase in newspaper quotes to denote the security trades in a foreign market.

Face amount certificate: A security issued by a mutual fund company that guarantees the face amount after the buyer has invested a specific number of fixed payments. There is also a surrender value, based on the amount invested, should the certificate be presented for payment prior to maturity.

Face value: The dollar value of a bond upon maturity that appears on the face of a bond certificate. Not indicative of the market value, especially in the case of deep discount or original issue discount (zero coupon) bonds. *(See also: PAR, PRINCIPAL)*

Fail position: Securities not delivered by the seller or to the buyer.

Fail to deliver: Failure by the seller to deliver securities sold.

Fail to receive: Failure by the buyer to receive securities bought.

Fair average quality (FAQ): A standard deliverable quality of a commodity. Differentials will be assigned for deviations from the FAQ. A premium is paid for higher quality or a discount is allowed for lower quality commodities.

Fair market value (FMV): The current market value of a security determined by supply and demand.

Family of funds: The total number of mutual funds with different investment objectives accomplished by various investment methods managed by one mutual fund company. Usually, exchanges may be made between funds within the family of funds with no additional commissions but they may have a nominal transfer fee.

Fannie Mae (FNMA): Federal National Mortgage Association.

FAO: For the account of.

FAQ: Fair average quality.

Farm out: The passing out of responsibilities from one person or entity to another.

Farm prices: The prices paid to farmers for their products, published by the U.S. Department of Agriculture the 15th of each month.

Farther in: An option contract that expires earlier than another. (Example: A September option expires "farther in" than a December option).

Farther out: An option contract that expires later than another. (Example: An April option expires "farther out" than a January option.)

Fast market: High volume of orders in the option's market. New orders and reports on transactions may be delayed until an orderly market is re-established.

FASTBACs: A debt security backed by auto loans. An acronym for First Automotive Short-Term Bonds and Certificates.

Favorable trade balance: Situation when a nation's exports are in excess of imports.

Favorite fifty: The 50 companies which are the most highly favored investments by institutional investors. Also know as the "nifty fifty."

FBO: For the benefit of.

FDIC: Federal Deposit Insurance Corporation.

Fed, The: Federal Reserve System.

Federal agency security: A debt instrument issued by an agency of the federal government that is not a direct obligation of the government. (Examples: Federal National Mortgage Association, Federal Farm Credit Bank and the Tennessee Valley Authority)

Federal Deposit Insurance Corporation (FDIC): The federal agency established in 1933 that guarantees funds on deposit (up to federally-established limits) of member banks and performs other duties designed to facilitate mergers or prevent failures.

Federal Farm Credit Bank System: Established in 1971 to consolidate services to farmers and farm related enterprises through a network of 12 Farm Credit districts, with each district including a Federal Land Bank, Federal Intermediate Credit Bank and a Bank for Cooperatives.

Federal funds: Money on deposit at Federal Reserve Banks including funds in excess of bank reserve requirements. (Note: Proceeds from checks to be cleared are considered to be federal funds the day after the receiving bank has received the money from the sending bank.)

Federal funds rate: The interest rate member banks charge one another for short term, usually overnight, loans.

Federal Home Loan Bank System: Established in 1932 and made up of 12 regional Federal Home Loan Banks. The system supplies credit reserved for savings and loans, cooperative banks and other mortgage lenders. Provides services to noncommercial mortgage companies not covered under the Federal Reserve System.

Federal Home Loan Mortgage Corporation (FHLMC, Freddie Mac):   A publicly-chartered agency owned by savings institutions engaged in the business of buying mortgages from lenders, grouping the mortgages into "pools," then selling the pools in the open market.

Federal Housing Administration (FHA):   Federally-sponsored agency founded in 1934 that insures lenders against loss on residential mortgages.

Federal Intermediate Credit Bank (FICB):   One of the banking institutions included in the Federal Farm Credit System that makes funds available to institutions that extend credit to crop farmers and cattle raisers.

Federal Land Bank (FLB):   One of the banking institutions included in the Federal Farm Credit System that makes funds available for buying land, refinancing debts or other agricultural purposes to institutions who extend credit to crop farmers and cattle raisers.

Federal National Mortgage Association (FNMA, Fannie Mae):   A federally-sponsored publicly-owned corporation engaged in the business of purchasing conventional, FHA, VA and Farmers Home Administration mortgages.

Federal Open Market Committee (FOMC):   The key committee of the Federal Reserve System that meets secretly to set short-term monetary policy for the Federal Reserve System.

Federal Reserve Board: The governing board of the Federal Reserve System, comprised of seven presidentially appointed members (subject to Senate confirmation), for terms of 14 years. Sets policies such as reserve requirements, bank regulations, discount rate, margin requirements and carries out the instructions of the Federal Open Market Committee regarding the tightening and loosening of credit.

Federal Reserve Open Market Committee: The Federal Reserve System committee that meets secretly to set its short-term monetary policy. Also known as the "Federal Open Market Committee (FOMC)."

Federal Reserve System: The central bank of the United States with the primary responsibility being to control the flow of money and credit. To tighten money (raise interest rates), the Federal Reserve System sells government securities. To ease the money supply (lower interest rates), the fed buys government securities.

Federal Savings and Loan Insurance Corporation (FSLIC): The federal agency established in 1934 that insures deposits, within certain specific guidelines, in member savings institutions.

Federal Trade Commission (FTC): The federal agency established in 1914 to promote free and fair business competition and prevent monopolies and activities in restraint of trade, administers the antitrust and consumer protection legislation.

Fed funds: Federal funds.

Feds: The name given to decision makers of the Federal Reserve Board.

Fed wire: Considered "the central nervous system of money transfer in the United States." Enables all federal banks and federal monetary agencies to transfer funds and securities among themselves by a high-speed, computerized communications network.

FHA: Federal Housing Administration.

FHLMC: Federal Home Loan Mortgage Corporation.

Fictitious credit: A credit balance in a client's margin account that is not available to the client for withdrawal due to Regulation T requirements.

Fictitious quotation: Any bid or offer of which the quotation system network is unaware.

Fidelity bond: A bond required to be carried by brokerage firms to protect against employee dishonesty, includes securities forgery and fraudulent trading.

Fiduciary: Any person legally appointed and authorized to represent and act in another's behalf, governed by state laws.

Fiduciary responsibility: The responsibility of a fiduciary—trustee or other type of custodian—to act in another's behalf in a prudent and careful manner.

FIFO: First in, first out.

Fifteen-minute delay: The delay required by law in the transmission over public facilities of ticker tapes.

Filing date: The date a security's registration statement is filed with the Securities and Exchange Commission.

Fill: To complete or execute a transaction.

Fill-or-kill order (FOK): Instructions to the floor broker to buy or sell the entire amount of a security order immediately or kill (cancel) the entire order.

Fill price: The execution price of an order to buy or sell a security on a per item basis. (Example: An order to buy 100 shares of stock at market was executed at a fill price of $27 per share.

Final analysis: A term used to describe the end result of an action taken.

Final prospectus: The final prospectus of a new offering that includes the price, delivery date and the underwriting spread of the security.

Financial Accounting Standards Board (FASB): An independent board of certified public accountants who establish uniform accounting practices generally adhered to by corporations in the preparation of financial reports.

Financial analyst: A person who conducts research on securities, trends, corporations, or other fields relative to needs of the financial and economic community.

Financial condition: The overall picture of a company's assets, liabilities and equities as of a certain time, usually quarterly or annually, as shown on the financial statement.

Financial futures: Commodity contracts based on financial instruments such as T-Bills, Japanese yen, British pound and other currencies.

Financial institution: Any institution engaged in the collection of funds from the public to place in financial assets such as stocks, bonds, money market instruments, bank deposits or loans. Includes banks, brokerage firms, savings and loans, nondepository institutions such as insurance companies and retirement plan companies, credit unions and savings banks.

Financial market: Any market engaged in the exchange of capital and credit securities in the market, such as stock, bond, commodity, option and foreign exchange markets.

Financial planner: A person who advises clients on the investments available for the client's needs, such as insurance, growth and income securities.

Financial planning: A structured investment plan of an individual which encompasses all needs such as insurance, real estate, retirement, asset accumulation and debts.

Financial position: The overall picture of a company's assets, liabilities and equities as of a certain time, usually quarterly or annually, as shown on the financial statement.

Financial pyramid: A graphic illustration used in financial planning that shows the proportionate relationships of low, medium and high risk investments and approximate portions of funds which would ideally be invested in each. Low risk investments, shown as the base of the pyramid includes insurance, fixed income securities, CDs, savings and other safe items. The middle portion of the pyramid includes assets and investments in which there could be fluctuations in values such as real estate and stocks. The top (and least proportionate share) of the pyramid includes investments such as commodities and options of the highest risk in which all or more of the amount invested is at risk.

Financial risk: The possible risk of an investment losing its value after taking market conditions into consideration.

Financial statement: Includes a balance sheet and income statement and any other statements necessary to provide a written record of a business, organization or individual's total financial status.

Find a home: The search for a buyer of a security or other investment.

Finder's fee: A fee given to a person who has referred business to another.

Firm: A general term for any organization engaged in the business of providing goods and/or services.

Firm commitment underwriting: The underwriting of a security in which the brokerage firm commits to buy the entire issue and assumes the total financial responsibility for any unsold shares.

Firm market: 1) A market condition in which there are sufficient buyers of items for sale to effectively stabilize prices. 2) A bid or offering price stated by a market maker and is not identified as a nominal or subject quote.

Firm order: A written or verbal order that is subject to cancellation only by formal written or verbal notice by the client.

Firm quote: Term referring to any round lot bid or offer price stated by a market maker and not identified as a nominal or subject quote.

First board: A commodity future delivery date as established by the commodity exchange trading in the future.

First call date: The first date a debt security may be redeemed at a specific price as stated in the indenture.

First in, first out (FIFO):   1) An accounting method of assuming the first goods produced (and costs of same) are the first to be sold. 2) The accounting method whereby principal is returned to an investor before any interest earned.

First mortgage: The primary lien against a specific piece of property having precedence against all other liens.

First notice day: The first day on which notices of delivery may be issued in the specified delivery month.

First preferred stock: A preferred issue of stock that has preferential claim on dividends and assets over all the preferred and common stock of a company.

FIRSTS: An acronym for Floating-Interest Rate Short-Term Securities.

Fiscal policy: White House and U.S. Congressional tax and spending policies.

Fiscal year: A 12-month accounting period designated by a company. Can be any 12-month period, not necessarily a calendar year.

Fit: Term used to describe the perfect match of an investor's portfolio requirements to a particular investment.

Fitch sheets: The sheets from Fitch Service listing successive trading prices during the day for all listed securities on major exchanges.

Five day pay rule: The settlement rule that states delivery and payment shall be completed by the fifth business day following the buy or sell of a security.

Five-hundred dollar rule: The Regulation T rule that states margin requirements of less than $500 are exempt from mandatory remedial action. (Caution: Brokerage firms may elect to have a lower dollar amount exempt from mandatory remedial action, (i.e., While the Reg T amount is $500, a brokerage firm may have $300 as its in-house exempt amount.)

Five-percent markup policy: A general guideline of the National Association of Securities Dealers for the maximum markup on security transactions.

Fix: The daily or twice-daily price determination of a commodity, such as gold or silver after an assessment of the supply and demand. Used by both buyers and sellers in the trading of the actual commodity.

Fixed annuity: An insurance annuity policy in which the interest and length of term are fixed (guaranteed).

Fixed assets: Tangible physical properties used in the production of a company's product.

Fixed charge coverage: The comparison of a company's income to debt payments. Used as a measurement of safety of a bond and enters into the calculations to determine a bond's rating.

Fixed costs: A company's costs that remain constant regardless of income, such as rent, interest expense and salaries.

Fixed income fund: A mutual fund which has income as its stated objective through the use of interest and dividends.

Fixed income investment: A security that pays a stated rate of return until maturity. Includes corporate, government and municipal bonds as well as preferred stock and some annuities.

Fixed income security: An investment in a security, such as bond or annuity, that pays a constant dollar amount at periodic intervals until maturity or the length of the contract.

Fixed price: The price at which a new issue is offered to the buying public.

Fixed rate security: A type of debt instrument such as a loan, mortgage or bond in which the interest rate is constant and does not change for the life of the contract.

Fixed term: The length of a time a contract or investment stays in force.

Fixed term investment: A security, usually debt, in which the maturity date is fixed by terms of the indenture.

Fixed trust: An investment company security sold in units consisting of a portfolio of securities, usually bonds. A fixed trust returns the principal of retired issues to the investor on a pro rata basis and is a self liquidating trust.

Fixing: Trading in a new security for the purpose of stabilizing its price above the established offering price. (*See also: PEGGING*)

Flag: A technical chart pattern that shows a general up or down trend, a volatility of prices in a fairly narrow range, then a continuation of the trend. Figure 14.

Flash: The designation used when the broad tape is running more than five minutes behind due to heavy volume and tape is interrupted to display the "flash price" of a heavily traded security.

FIGURE 14.   Flag

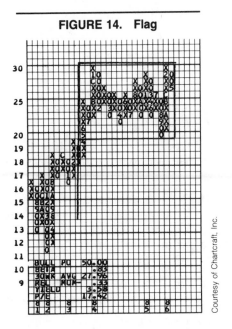

Courtesy of Chartcraft, Inc.

Flat: 1) Bonds trading with no accrued interest: 2) A market condition where there is very little volatility. 3) A company having no inventory.

Flat bonds: Trading without accrued interest being due to the seller, the buyer will receive interest if and when paid. Usually refers to bonds in default but can mean a bond is sold on the day the coupon is due.

Flat market: Very little volatility. Usually, a movement of five points or less on the Dow Industrial Average is considered flat.

Flat scale: A bond trader's term describing serial bonds with little or no difference in yields, regardless of the length of time until maturity.

Flat tax: Tax applied at the same rate to all levels of income.

Flexible exchange rate: A change in the value of a foreign currency rate in response to supply and demand.

Flight to quality: The switch of investments to the safest possible security.

Float: 1) The period of time between presentation and clearance of a check. 2) The number of outstanding shares available for trading.

Floater: Slang expression for floating rate note, a debt security with a variable interest rate.

Floating an issue: The initial public offering of a new or secondary security.

Floating debt: A debt that is constantly renewed, usually only a nominal amount of the principal and all of the interest is paid to the debt issuer.

Floating exchange rate: The change in value of a foreign currency rate in response to supply and demand.

Floating-Interest Rate Short-Term Securities (FIRSTS): A fund or trust that is comprised of floating-interest rate securities of three to five years or less.

Floating rate note (FRN): A debt instrument with a variable interest rate tied to another factor, such as the Consumer Price Index (CPI) or Treasury rate. Ideally, the debt interest rate will rise or fall according to the factor involved, protecting the income of the issuer as well as the payout of the holder.

Floating supply: The number of outstanding municipal bonds or a company's shares of stock available for purchase.

Floor: The trading area of a stock, option or bond exchange.

Floor broker: A person who buys and sells listed securities on the floor of the exchange where the person is a member.

Floor official: An exchange employee whose primary function is to settle disputes immediately about priority or precedence in the settlement of the auction procedures.

Floor ticket: Information received from a registered representative regarding the buy or sell of a security by a client given to a floor broker so the order can be executed.

Floor trader: A registered competitive trader who is a member of an exchange, trades for his or her own account and is governed by rules similar to those of a specialist.

Flotation costs: The actual costs to the issuer involved in bringing a new issue to the public.

Flower bond: A Treasury bond purchased at a discount to face value used to settle estate taxes.

Flow of funds: A statement in a municipal bond resolution outlining the application of revenue.

Flow-through of income and expenses: Income deductions and credits of a partnership are passed (flowed through) to each individual partner's tax return as though each partner had generated the income and expenses directly.

Fluctuation: The range in a) prices of securities b) interest rates or c) The economy.

Fluctuation limits: The maximum up or down price movement a commodity may make in any one trading day.

FMAN: An abbreviation of the option cycle consisting of options that expire in February, May, August and November. (*See also: JAJO, MSJD*).

FMV: Fair market value.

FNMA: Federal National Mortgage Association.

FOB: Free on board.

FOCUS Report: A monthly and quarterly report detailing capital, earnings, trade flow and any other pertinent information broker-dealers must make to a self-regulatory organization. Short for Financial and Operational Combined Uniform Single Report.

FOK: Fill-or-kill order.

FOMC: Federal Open Market Committee.

Forbes 500: The top 500 publicly owned corporations ranked by sales, assets, profits and market value as published annually by Forbes Magazine. (*See also: FORTUNE 500*)

Forced conversion: A method of forcing conversion of a bond, usually accomplished by the issuer calling a convertible bond when the market value of the stock is higher than the redemption price.

Forecasting: The projection of future trends based on past performance and current information.

Foreign corporation: A corporation formed in a) a state other than that in which it does business, or b) outside the U.S. Also known as an "alien corporation."

Foreign crowd: New York Stock Exchange floor brokers who trade in foreign bonds.

Foreign exchange: The type of payment involved in the settlement of debts between countries.

Foreign fund: A mutual fund with a portfolio consisting of foreign company stocks.

Foreign stocks: Stocks issued by companies registered in a) any state other than state of residence, b) a foreign country.

Formula investing: A technique of switching investments from one type to another according to a predetermined set of parameters. (Example: Switching from stocks to bonds when the market is on a downtrend and interest rates are on an uptrend.)

For the account of (FAO):   A designation of the account in which a deposit of cash or securities is to be made.

For the benefit of (FBO):   A designation of the person for whom a custodian account is opened. (Example: An Individual Retirement Account names the custodian and lists "for the benefit of" the individual who owns the account.)

Fortune 500:   Lists compiled by Fortune Magazine of the 500 largest a) U.S. and b) Non-U.S. industrial corporations in sales. *(See also: FORBES 500)*

For valuation only (FVO):   A quote from a market maker used to establish a security's value. Not a firm bid or offer. *(See also: FOR YOUR INFORMATION)*

Forward contract: The purchase or sale of an actual commodity at a specified price for exchange of payment and delivery at a specified future date, can be used as a hedge when used to offset a future contract.

Forward exchange contract: A forward contract involving foreign currency at a specific exchange rate.

Forward pricing: The pricing system used by open-end mutual funds whereby all buy and sell orders are filled at the net asset value as determined at the end of the trading session on the day the order is received.

Forward shipment: A contract that covers actual commodities to be shipped at some future date.

For your information (FYI):   A courtesy quote from a market maker, not a firm bid or offer, used when establishing a value on a security. *(See also: FOR VALUATION ONLY)*

401(k) plan: A salary reduction plan that allows an employee to make pre-tax contributions as allowed by law and by company policy on a tax-deferred basis to a company pool. May be withdrawn by the employee upon retirement, severance from the company or other reasons as outlined in the plan.

Fourth market: The trading of securities from one institution to another without the services of a brokerage firm.

Fraction: Securities trade in dollars and fractions of dollars based on the "two bit, four bit, six bits, a dollar" formula, meaning $.25, $.50, $.75 and $1.00 and fractions of same. (Examples: 1, ¾, ½, ¼, ⅛, 1/16, 1/32, 1/64)

Fractional discretion order: An order placed for the purchase or sale of a security giving the floor broker discretion within a fraction of a point. (Example: An order to buy 100 shares of XYZ Company at 49 with ¼ means the floor broker may execute the trade at the best price up to 49¼).

Fractional point move: The change in the price of a security reported as a fraction of a dollar, usually in increments of ⅛'s. U.S. Treasury Securities trade in 1/32's and some stocks move as little 1/128.

Fractional share: The receipt by a shareholder of a portion of a whole share generated by stock dividends, mergers or reinvestment election.

Fraud: The intentional deceit or concealment of facts for personal gain to the detriment of others.

Freddie Mac (FHLMC):   Federal Home Loan Mortgage Corporation.

Free and open market: A market in which price is determined by natural supply and demand.

Free box: The vault or storage area at a bank or security firm where fully paid for (free) securities are stored.

Free credit balance: Cash in a client's account that may be withdrawn at any time and is not being used as collateral against a margin balance.

Free crowd: Slang term used for the New York Stock Exchange active bond crowd.

Freed up: The underwriting syndicate's release from an obligation to sell a security.

Free on board (FOB):   Delivery charges of a commodity which are included in a seller's invoice only to a certain specified point. Delivery beyond that point is at the buyer's expense.

Freeriding: An illegal practice of buying a security then selling with no intention of depositing the purchase amount.

Freeriding and withholding: The failure to make a bona fide (real) public offering at the public offering price by one of the members of the participating distributors. Usually occurs with "hot issues," that are expected to go up in value substantially shortly after the offering. A violation of the National Association of Securities Dealers Rules of Fair Practice.

Free right of exchange: The transfer from one owner to another with none of the usual costs involved. (Example: Stocks held in a brokerage firm's "street name" exchanged into the name of actual owner or the switch from a bearer status to a registered status.)

Free security: A security in a margin account which is fully paid for.

Friendly merger: The combining of two companies for the mutual benefit of all shareholders accomplished on a friendly, rather than unfriendly basis.

Friendly overture: The initial contact by suiter to a targeted company in an attempt for a friendly takeover.

Friendly takeover: The purchase of one company by another for the mutual benefit of all shareholders accomplished on a friendly, rather than an unfriendly basis.

Front-end load: For insurance, annuities and mutual funds, the system of collecting sales charges on the purchase and not on the sell.

Front running: A trader with advance knowledge of a block transaction that should affect the price of the security who engages in option trading to take advantage of the knowledge.

Frozen account: A securities account in which any purchase must be paid for in full before any order may be entered. An account is usually frozen for failure to pay for purchases in a timely manner.

FTC: Federal Trade Commission.

Full coupon bond: A bond with a coupon rate at or very near to the current market interest rate.

Full disclosure act: The term used as a reference to the Securities Act of 1933 which requires the full and fair disclosure of all material information about the issuance of a new security.

Full faith and credit: A debt security issuer's pledge that the full reputation and possible taxing power will be used in the payments of interest and principal. Not backed by buildings or equipment.

Full-service broker: A broker who provides a full range of information and services to a client. (*See also: DISCOUNT BROKER.*)

Full trading authorization: A power of attorney granted to someone other than the account owner giving authority for full trading privileges in the account including the transfer of funds and securities.

Fully diluted earnings per (common) share: Earnings per share of a corporation assuming all convertible and exercisable securities have been converted to common shares.

Fully distributed: A new issue that has been completely sold to the public rather than to dealers or traders.

Fully valued: A term used to describe a stock whose price is fair and reasonable when compared to the earning power of the company. (*See also: UNDER VALUED, OVER VALUED*)

Fundamental research analysis: The analysis of industries or companies based on sales, assets, earnings, goods or services, markets and management. Does not consider the supply and demand factors such as price, volume, trends and chart patterns technical researchers use in their analysis of a company.

Funded debt: The long term debt obligation of a company not including common or preferred stock.

Funding: The deposit of money into an account for a specific purpose, such as a retirement plan, trust account or debt retirement.

Fund manager: The entity responsible for the investment decisions of a mutual fund.

Fund switch: The transfer of funds from one mutual fund to another. May or may not be within the same family of mutual funds.

Fund, the: The entity responsible for general administration and supervision of the investment portfolio of a mutual fund.

Fungibles: Something that is interchangeable with another, such as dollar bills, common shares of the same company and wheat to soy beans.

Future time value: The value of a security after such factors as the cost of living and interest rates have been taken into account.

Futures contracts: Contracts traded on a commodity exchange specifying a future date of receipt of delivery on a hedge or speculation basis. Includes financial instruments, grains, meat, indexes, precious metals and other commodities. Also known as futures.

Futures market: A commodity exchange where futures contracts are traded.

FVO: For valuation only.

FYI: For your information.

Gap: A term used if one day's price range does not overlap the price range of the previous day. (Example: A stock with a price range of 30⅛ to 31 on one day and a range of 29 to 29½ the next day is said to have a gap.)

Garage: The nickname for the annex floor north of the main trading floor of the New York Stock Exchange.

Gather in the stops: The selling or buying of a stock in sufficient quantities to drive the price up or down to a point where stop orders are known to exist. This triggers the stop orders driving the price to further stop areas creating "snowball" effect. Stop orders can be suspended in the security should the exchange deem it advisable.

Gemstones: An investment which is considered very stable but which also has a good chance of rising in value much higher than comparable items.

General account: The Federal Reserve term for a client's margin account.

General ledger: The formal ledger including all the financial statements of a company.

General loan and collateral agreement: The agreement between brokers and banks which allows the pledging (rehypothecation) of securities in margin accounts to be used as collateral for broker loans.

Generally accepted accounting principles (GAAP): The basic doctrine set forth originally by the Accounting Principals Board of the American Institute of Certified Public Accounts and endorsed by the Financial Accounting Standards Board which explains and defines the rules, conventions and broad as well as detailed procedures of standardized accounting procedures.

General mortgage bond: A bond secured by a blanket mortgage of a company's property. (Caution: May be subordinate to other mortgages.)

General obligation bond (GO):   A municipal bond backed by the full faith, credit and taxing authority of the issuer for the payment of interest and principal.

General partner: The managing partner in a limited partnership who makes all decisions and takes all the partnership's legal risks.

General revenue: Revenue of state and local governments not including revenue from utilities, sales of alcoholic beverages or insurance trusts.

General revenue sharing: Funds from the federal government to all states, Indian tribes, cities, towns, townships and Alaskan native villages that may be used for any purpose.

Get out: The selling out of a long position or buying back of a short position.

Gift tax: When the value of gifts given on an annual basis exceed the amount specified by law, the excess value is federally or state taxed, levied against the giver. (Caution: Gift tax liability is subject to change. It is advisable to contact a tax attorney, accountant or other qualified advisor for the current values.)

Gilt-edged: A term meaning a security has a proven record of dividend or interest payments and is considered very high quality and a highly desirable investment.

Gilts: British government bonds and money-market securities.

Ginnie Mae (GNMA):   Government National Mortgage Association.

Ginnie Mae pass-through: A collection of mortgages guaranteed by the Government National Mortgage Association and sold to investors in original face amounts. The interest and partial principal payments are made by the trustee on a monthly basis.

Gives up: A third party transacting business for a second party through a first party giving the name of and all commissions to the first party.

Glamor stock: A stock in great investment favor by individual and institutional buyers. Usually has gained favor by a consistently growing sales and earnings record.

Glass Steagall Act of 1933:   Legislation passed to protect the banking industry from failure as occurred in the Great Depression, included provisions for deposit insurance and the prohibiting of banks performing services reserved for brokerage firms. Several deregulation bills passed since 1933 give banks more freedom to make their own choices about areas of responsibility.

GNMA: Government National Mortgage Association.

Gnomes of Zurich: Term coined during the sterling crisis of 1964 by labor ministers of Great Britain to describe the financiers and bankers in Zurich, Switzerland, who were engaged in foreign exchange speculation.

GNP: Gross National Product.

GO: General obligation bond.

Go ahead: A violation of the Rules of Fair Practice of the National Securities Dealers whereby a broker's personal account is traded before the client's account.

Go around: The process used by the Federal Open Market Committee when canvassing primary bank and nonbank dealers for bids and offers of government securities.

Go-go fund: The nickname given mutual funds that specialize in highly speculative securities.

Going away: One or more serial maturities of a municipal bond purchased in large amounts by an institutional investor or by a brokerage firm to place in inventory for future sales.

Going down the tubes: An expression used when the price of a security is going opposite of the desired direction. (Example: The price of XYZ Company has dropped $5.00 in the last two days, so it's going down the tubes.)

Going long: The purchasing of a stock, option or commodity as an opening (or first) transaction.

Going private: The movement of a publicly-held corporation to a privately-owned corporation accomplished by the purchase of all outstanding shares of stock by an individual, a group of investors or the company itself.

Going public: The movement of a privately-held corporation to a publicly-owned corporation accomplished by a public offering of part or all of the company's shares of stocks.

Going short: The selling of a stock, option or commodity as an opening, or first, transaction. A security sold short must, at some point in time, be delivered or bought back.

Gold bond: A bond, usually issued by a mining company, backed by gold with the interest payments pegged to the price of gold.

Goldbug: An analyst who recommends gold as a safe haven for investors concerned about possible disasters in the world economy.

Golden handcuffs: The contract a broker signs with a brokerage firm that states should the broker move to another firm, a portion of earnings received shall be returned to the original firm. Used to discourage the frequent movements from one brokerage firm to another.

Golden parachute: A contract given to a top executive providing lucrative benefits should the company be taken over resulting in the executive's loss of position.

Gold fix: The daily or twice-daily price determination of the price of gold after an assessment of the supply and demand.

Gold mutual fund: A mutual fund that invests in gold mining stocks, either U.S., Canadian and/or foreign mines such as South Africa.

Gold standard: The monetary system in which a currency is convertible to a fixed amount of gold. Also known as "hard money."

Good delivery: A security certificate that has been made negotiable by the proper signatures and/or necessary paperwork.

Good faith deposit: A token amount of money showing a client's desire and intention to complete a contract.

Good money: Funds which have been on deposit at least one day at a Federal Reserve Bank. Also known as Federal Funds.

Good this month order (GTM): An order to buy or sell a security that is to stay in effect until executed or is automatically cancelled by the registered representative at the end of the last business day of the month in which it was entered.

Good this week order (GTW): An order to buy or sell a security that is to stay in effect until executed or is automatically cancelled by the broker-dealer at the end of the last business day of the week in which it was entered.

Good til cancelled order (GTC): An order to buy or sell a security that is to stay in effect until executed or cancelled by the client.

Government bond calendar: A list of government issued debt securities soon to be offered for sale.

Government bonds: Direct debt obligations of the U.S. Government. Carries the safest rating of all bonds. Includes Treasury bonds, notes, bills and savings bonds.

Government National Mortgage Association (GNMA, Ginnie Mae): A government owned corporation that purchases mortgages and, in certain cases, guarantees timely payment of principal and interest.

Governments: A term used to mean bonds, bills or notes issued by the U.S. government.

Government securities: Debt instruments issued by federal agencies. Not a direct obligation of the U.S. Government.

Grades: The various qualities of commodities according to accepted trade usage.

Grading certificate: Certificate that attests to the quality of a commodity graded by official inspectors, graders or testers.

Graduated rate structure: Tax rates that get "gradually" higher as income increases.

Graduated security: A security that has moved its listing from a small exchange to one that is larger and more prestigious.

Graham and Dodd method of investing: An investing technique outlined in "Security Analysis" by Benjamin Graham and David Dodd, published in 1930. Involves buying undervalued securities with good earnings possibilities for the potential rise to the "true" value of those securities.

Grain complex: Those commodities used in the processing for feed, meal and oil, such as wheat, soybeans, oats, rye, barley, rapeseed and flaxseed.

Grandfather clause: A provision usually written into new rules that allows previously granted qualifications to continue to qualify. (Example: 1) Bonds issued as municipal would continue having the municipal designation even though new laws might not allow a certain type of municipal bond to be issued after a certain date. 2) A person with a license to sell a certain product would not be required to take additional courses or tests required by persons not yet licensed.)

Grantor: The seller (writer) of a put or a call option. The grantor (seller) receives the premium paid by the buyer for the right to execute the terms of the option contract. *(See also: EXERCISE)*

Gratuity fund: A special fund set up by the exchanges to benefit families of deceased members.

Graveyard market: The type of market that is like a graveyard, in that those who are in can't get out and those who are out don't want in. Caused by a bear market in which losers can't afford to take the loss and those not in the market prefer to stay on the sidelines in a cash position.

Green shoe: An underwriting provision that allows the syndicate to purchase additional shares of an offering from the issuer at the original price. Used to allow the covering of any shares sold short by the syndicate.

Greenmail: Payment to a potential acquirer by a takeover target in return for an agreement that the potential acquirer will cease the takeover pursuit.

Gresham's law: The economic theory named for Sir Thomas Gresham, Master of The Mint in the reign of Queen Elizabeth II, that states; given currency with the same nominal value, the more desirable (usually of metallic content) will be horded while the less desirable (usually paper) will be circulated, giving rise to the saying "bad money drives out good."

Gross estate: The total value of a deceased person's estate before any liabilities are deducted. After liabilities, the remaining is called the net estate.

Gross lease: A property lease under which the lessor (landlord) pays all expenses normally incurred in ownership. *(See also: NET LEASE)*

Gross National Product (GNP): The dollar value of all final goods and services produced in the U.S. "Normal" GNP is the quarterly total and "real" GNP is the total after inflation has been taken into consideration.

Gross profit: Sales of goods after the cost of producing the goods have been deducted.

Gross sales: The total amount of invoiced sales before returns or other adjustments are made.

Gross spread: The dollar difference between the offering price of a new issue and the amount received by the issuer.

Group of ten: The ten countries organized to try to coordinate monetary and fiscal policies to promote a more stable world economics system, includes Belgium, Canada, France, Italy, Japan, The Netherlands, Sweden, the United Kingdom, the United States and West Germany. Also known as the "Paris Club."

Group net: A buy order given by a nonsyndicate member to a manager of a municipal securities syndicate agreeing to pay the public offering price leaving the spread in the account for the syndicate. (Example: Given a public price of 100 percent and a member price of 99 percent, a nonmember agrees to pay the 100 percent leaving the 1 percent as additional profit to the syndicate.)

Group sales: Sales of a new issue offering to an institutional investor, credited to the syndicate as a whole and not to an individual member.

Growth: Used as a generic term to indicate the rise in value of a security that represents ownership, such as stock, options or commodities.

Growth fund: A mutual fund that invests in securities expected to grow in value. *(See also: GROWTH STOCK)*

Growths: The description of a commodity according to an area of growth, such as country, district or place of processing.

Growth stock: Stock in a company that pays little or no dividends but is expected to grow in value at a fairly rapid pace.

GTC: Good til cancelled order.

GTM: Good this month order.

GTW: Good this week order.

Guarantee: The promise to pay a debt or asume an obligation of another by a guarantor should the primary entity fail to perform.

Guaranteed annuity: An insurance product that guarantees a specific rate of interest for a specific period of time.

Guaranteed bond or stock: A bond (or preferred stock) that is guaranteed by an entity other than the issuer as to the timely payment of interest or dividends and principal.

Guaranteed income contract: An insurance product that, upon payment of a specific amount and, after a specified number of years, guarantees a specific dollar amount of income.

Guaranteed payment: The payment of interest and/or principal which have been guaranteed by a specified entity or account.

Guaranteed stock: Preferred or common stock which have had the dividends guaranteed by the parent company.

Guarantee letter: A letter of credit issued by a commercial bank on behalf of a customer who has written a put option. Specifies both the dollars and the put contract involved and promises to pay a specified sum when, and if, the put option exercise notice is received.

Guarantee signature: A certificate issued by a bank or brokerage firm office vouching for the authenticity of a person's signature. (Caution: Not the same as a Notary Public statement in which a signature was witnessed.)

Guardian: One who manages securities or funds for a minor or an incompetent.

Gun jumping: Slang for: 1) Trading in a security based on information not yet made public (insider trading). 2) Soliciting buy orders for a new issue not yet registered by the Securities and Exchange Commission.

Haircut: A slang expression used for the formula a broker-dealer firm uses in the valuation of the firm's net worth. Securities are "given a haircut" (or adjustment) according to the risk involved. (Example: A government security will have a 10 percent adjustment, most equities will have a 30 percent adjustment and fail (yet to be delivered) securities with little-to-no chance of being received are given a 100 percent adjustment.)

Half-life: The period of time a Ginnie Mae pass through certificate is expected to have half of the principal remaining in the pool after mortgage prepayments and defaults had been paid to the holder of the certificate.

Half-stock: Preferred stock with a par value of $50 rather than the standard $100.

Hammering the market: Intense selling short in securities felt to be overvalued and ready for a dramatic drop in price.

Hard currency: 1. Metallic coins rather than paper currency. 2. Currency issued by an economically strong country. Also known as "hard money."

Hard dollars: The actual amount paid for research or other services regardless of what actual costs (soft dollars) had been incurred in providing the information. (Example: A research function may have been performed at a cost of $5,000 (soft dollars) but only $1,000 (hard dollars) was charged to the client.)

Hard money: 1) Metallic coins, such as gold or silver, rather than paper currency. 2) Currency issued by an economically strong country such as the U.S. or Great Britain.

Head and shoulders: A technical chart pattern that looks like the silhouette of the front view of a head and both shoulders. Indicates the price of a security has risen in value, stayed constant for a while, goes higher, stays constant for a short while, goes down to

FIGURE 15.   Head and Shoulders

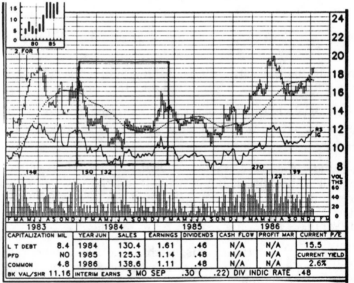

Reverse Head and Shoulders

the previous stable level, levels off again for a while, then drops in value to the approximate area at the beginning of the formation. A reverse pattern, called a "Head and Shoulders Bottom," is with the head and shoulders upside down. Figure 15.

Heavy market: A condition in which there are more sellers of a security than there are buyers, resulting in falling prices of that security.

Hedge clause: A clause contained in a research report or security evaluation disclaiming responsibility for the accuracy of the information taken from what was considered to be reliable information sources.

Hedged tender: The selling short of a security that is to be tendered under the anticipation that less than the full amount of securities held will be tendered.

Hedge fund: 1) Slang for a limited partnership speculating in securities with the limited partners taking the risk and the general partners sharing in the reward. 2) A fund that uses hedging techniques to increase the return.

Hedging: A protective procedure designed to minimize losses due to adverse price fluctuations. Used when actual securities or commodities are owned or are to be bought with offsetting positions of options or futures.

Hemline theory: A stock market theory in which the length of the hemlines of dresses directly corresponds to the prices of stocks. "The closer to the ground a hemline approaches, the more bearish the market; conversely, the shorter the hemline, the more bullish the market."

Highballing: A fraudulent swap technique by which a security is purchased above its current value (keeping the seller from having a loss), then swapped for a different security above its current value (creating a built-in gain for the original swapper).

High flyer: A highly speculative stock with sharp drops and rises of the price in a relatively short period of time.

High-grade bond: A bond with the highest Standard & Poor's ratings of AA or AAA.

High powered: An investment with better-than-average expectations of making high profits for the investor.

High-premium convertible debenture: A bond convertible at high premium to stock, usually with a coupon of relatively high interest rate.

Highs: The stocks that, during a business day, have reached new annual high prices.

High-tech stocks: Stocks involved in highly technical fields such as computers, biotechnology and electronics.

Historical trading range: The range in the price of a security since being offered for sale to the public.

Historical yield: The actual annual yield of a mutual fund.

Hit: A term used when a targeted price has been achieved or a desired trade has been accomplished.

Hit the bid: A term used when a seller is willing to accept the bid price of a security.

Holder of record: The owner of a security on a company's register at the close of the business day on the record date assigned by the company.

Holding company: The parent company who owns the securities of another, usually with voting control.

Holding mail: The keeping of confirmations, statements and other notices by a brokerage firm of no longer than two months if the client is traveling in the U.S. and no longer than three months if the client is traveling abroad.

Holding period: The length of time restricted securities must be held before being eligible to be sold.

Holding the market: Sufficient buy orders in a security to sustain the current price.

Home run: A large gain in an investment in a short period of time.

HOMES: An acronym for Homeowner Mortgage Eurosecurities.

Horizon analysis: An analysis based on reinvestment of returns during a specified time period so that comparisons may be made of like securities.

Horizontal price movement: A term describing the price of a security that stayed relatively the same during fairly active trading.

Horizontal spread: The simultaneous purchase and sale of an equal amount of options of the same type with the same strike prices but with different expiration months. (Example: The purchase of 10 XYZ Feb 40 calls and the sale of 10 XYZ May 40 calls.)

Hospital revenue bond: A municipal bond issue with the proceeds used to finance a hospital facility and the revenues from the facility used to pay the principal and interest. A type of industrial development revenue bond.

Hostile merger: The unfriendly merger of one company by another, usually accomplished in such a way as to circumvent the wishes and desires of the current management.

Hostile takeover: The acquisition of a company accomplished in an unfriendly manner against the wishes of the current management, usually accomplished by offering to purchase shares at a price higher than the current market.

Hot issue: A new offering of a stock that is expected to sell at a premium above the public offering price on the first day of trading.

Hot stocks: 1) Stolen securities. 2) Securities that rise rapidly in price on the initial public offering date.

House: 1) A firm or individual engaged in the business of being a broker-dealer. 2) The nickname for the London Stock Exchange.

House account: An account at a brokerage firm handled at the main office or managed by an executive of the firm.

House maintenance call: The demand for additional funds or securities due to an adverse change in the value of a margin account in order to bring the total account value back up to the minimum ratio of debt to equity.

House maintenance requirement: The brokerage firm requirement of minimum equity that a client must maintain in a margin account, usually higher than the New York Stock Exchange requirements.

House of issue: The investment banking firm that underwrites a new issue.

House rules: A brokerage firm's internal rules and regulations, usually more strict than are required by the various industry and governmental rules and regulations.

Housing and Urban Development (HUD): A department of the federal government that encourages lower-to-middle-income housing in the U.S. by various economic means, such as lower interest rates and subsidation of payments.

Housing bond: A bond issued by a local housing authority to finance housing facilities with the mortgage payments pledged to pay the principal and interest.

Housing starts: A compilation of new houses beginning construction, used as one of the 12 leading economic indicators as any changes can severely affect many industries.

HUD: U.S. Department of Housing and Urban Development.

Hulbert rating: A rating by the "Hulbert Financial Digest" of how well various investment advisory newsletters' recommendations have performed.

Hung up: The term used to describe a portfolio that has dropped in value substantially below the purchase price that, if sold, would create a substantial loss.

Hybrid annuity: A combination fixed and variable annuity with the percentage invested in each chosen by the annuity owner.

Hypothecation: The pledging of securities used as collateral.

Hypothecation agreement: A signed statement by a client agreeing to the rules of a margin account (i.e., securities pledged as collateral will be held by the brokerage firm. Those securities may be repledged by the brokerage firm to finance the account and the brokerage firm may sell the securities if needed to protect its financial interest in the account.).

IBRD: International Bank for Reconstruction and Development.

ICC: Interstate Commerce Commission.

Illegal dividend: A dividend declared by the board of directors of a company even though not allowed by the company's charter or state laws.

Illiquid: An investment that, once bought, is difficult or impossible to sell or turn into ready cash.

Imbalance of orders: A situation whereby only buy or sell orders are entered for a security as the result of drastic unexpected news. Often trading is halted until there is a balance of orders established, usually through an adjustment of bid and asked prices for the security. (Example: The top key executive of a company dies suddenly and a large percentage of stockholders want to sell their stock but there are no buyers.)

IMF: International Monetary Fund.

Immediate annuity: An insurance annuity contract purchased for a lump sum that provides an immediate income to the annuitant.

Immediate family: Parents, spouse, children, brothers, sisters, father-in-law, mother-in-law, brother-in-law and sister-in-law are defined as the immediate family of an insider by the National Association of Security Dealers Rules of Fair Practice regarding the trading of a hot issue by a person or the immediate family of a broker-dealer or buyer or seller for institutional accounts.

Immediate- or-cancel (IOC): An order placed for a security that instructs the floor broker to execute as much of the order as possible and cancel any remaining balance.

Immediate payment annuity: An insurance annuity contract purchased for a lump sum that provides an immediate income to the annuitant.

Impaired capital: The capital of a company that is worth less than the stated par value of a company's capital stock.

Import duty: A government imposed tax on imported articles.

Imputed value: Logical estimate of value for a statement when the actual figures are not yet available.

Inactive asset: Assets that aren't earning dividends or changing value.

Inactive bond: A bond that is traded so infrequently as to be considered illiquid. Usually has a wide spread between bid and asked and is generally avoided by the small investor.

Inactive bond crowd: The section of the New York Stock Exchange in which inactive bonds are traded. *(See also: CABINET CROWD)*

Inactive post: A trading post on the New York Stock Exchange that trades inactive stocks in increments of ten shares rather than the usual round lot number of 100 shares. *(See also: POST 30)*

Inactive stock: A stock that is traded so infrequently as to be considered illiquid. Usually has a wide spread between bid and asked and is generally avoided by small investors.

Inactive trading: The situation existing when there are very few orders to buy or sell an individual security or the market as a whole. Usually results in price volatility as well as wide spreads between the bid and asked quotes.

In-and-out trader: An individual who speculates in stocks, options and/ or commodity futures markets by buying and selling positions on the same day or overnight. Also known as "scalper" or "day trader."

Incentive fee: A bonus given to managed account managers based on above-average results.

Incentive stock option: An executive compensation that allows for the exercise of an option for the company's stock, usually at an exercise price lower than the current stock price.

Incestuous share dealing: The buying and selling of shares between two companies resulting in beneficial tax or financial advantages for one or both of the companies.

Income bond: A bond that will pay principal but will pay interest only when earned. Could accumulate interest as a claim against the corporation when the bond becomes due or may be issued in lieu of a preferred stock.

Income fund: A mutual fund designed to provide income through investments in bonds, preferred stocks and/or high paying dividend stocks.

Income limited partnership: A partnership that is formed to invest in items such as equipment leasing or real estate. Generates income rather than growth or tax benefits.

Income property: Real estate that generates a positive cash flow.

Income shares: Those shares of a dual purpose fund issued by a closed-end investment company that offers income as opposed to the shares that offer growth.

Income statement: A financial statement that summarizes a corporation's revenues and expenses for a specific fiscal period.

Income tax: Federal and some city and state government annual assessment against earnings of an individual or a company.

Incorporation: The process followed by a company to obtain a state charter in order to legally operate as a corporation.

Incremental cash flow: The total amount of income and outgo attributable to a corporate investment project.

Indemnify: A clause in an insurance policy stating the agreement by the insurer to compensate the insured for damages or losses incurred up to the limits as specified in the insurance contract.

Indenture: The written agreement of a bond or debenture outlining maturity date, call dates and terms, interest rate and/or other items.

Independent broker: A member of the floor of an exchange who executes orders for other brokers who have more business than can be handled at the time. Also known as "two dollar brokers," dating back to the time the independent broker made $2.00 per transaction per hundred shares.

Index: A statistical standard expressed as a percentage of a base year or years, not an average. (Examples: The Standard and Poor's 100 and 500 Indexes, Major Market Index, New York Stock Exchange Index, etc.)

Index fund: A mutual fund that invests in the same securities in the same percentage of a given index to match the performance of the index.

Indexing: The compilation of a portfolio to match the types and percentages of investments as found in a broad based index.

Index option: Call and put options on stock indexes such as the Standard & Poor's, Major Market, Gold & Silver and Value Line Composite Indexes.

Indicated yield: The earnings rate expressed as a percentage of an investment calculated by dividing the annual dollar amount of earnings by the price.

Indication: The expected adjusted price of a stock, when trading is halted by the exchange officials because of an order imbalance.

Indication of interest: A conditional indication by an investor of interest in buying a forthcoming new issue upon review of a preliminary prospectus. Not a firm order.

Indicator: A technical measurement used by a security analyst to forecast the market's direction.

Indirect obligation: A debt obligation issued by an agency or subsidiary of an entity such as the U.S. government with the payment of interest and the repayment of principal paid by the agency rather than the entity.

Individual retirement account (IRA):   A tax advantaged retirement account for the benefit of an individual with maximum investment limits as set by law. (Caution: Tax laws change constantly and it would be advisable to check with the IRS, a tax attorney or other qualified individual as to the current investment limitations and other pertinent rules and regulations concerning an IRA.)

Individual segregation: The system of identifying and separating a brokerage firm client's fully paid securities held in street name from margined securities.

Industrial: The classification of a company that produces and distributes goods and services.

Industrial development revenue bond: A bond issue with the proceeds used to develop an industrial project such as multifamily housing, which is expected to generate enough income to pay principal and interest payments as specified in the indenture. May be allowed to be issued as a municipal rather than a corporate bond if qualified under the current tax laws.

Inefficiency in the market: Poor investment decisions being made by the buying public when information as to the relative strength or weakness of a company is not available.

Infant industry argument: The enactment of a tariff on goods produced by a well-developed foreign company when the country exacting the tariff is "in its infancy" in producing comparable goods. Used to promote the production of locally produced goods.

Inflation: The persistent and appreciable rise in the general level of prices.

Inflation accounting: A financial statement adjusted for the effect of inflation.

Inflation rate: The rate of rise in the general level of prices.

Infrastructure: A nation's network of communication and utilities, including roads, bridges, transportation and sewage disposal.

Ingot: A metal bar, usually of precious material such as gold or silver, that generally has an engraved stamp indicating weight and purity.

Inheritance tax return: The tax return of a decedent's estate required by the state of the executor to determine the amount of state tax due.

Inheritance tax waiver: A form (required in some states) issued by the state's comptroller office stating inheritance taxes, if due, have been paid. One of the documents possibly required to transfer ownership of cash or a security from the decedent to the estate.

Initial margin requirement: The amount of equity required to be deposited by an investor when making a new purchase or short sale in a margin account according to Regulation T of the Federal Reserve Board, NYSE and NASD.

Initial public offering (IPO): The original sale of a company's securities to the public.

Inside market: Bid or asked quotes between dealers for the purpose of trading for their own inventories.

Insider: Anyone who has nonpublic material knowledge about a corporation. Includes directors, officers, stockholders and their immediate families who own more than ten percent of any class of securities.

Insider information: Corporate news not yet known by the general public, which, if known, usually would have an impact on the price of the corporation's stock.

Insider trading: The illegal trading of a security using material knowledge not known to the general public, which if known, would result in a substantial price change in the security.

Insolvent: Unable to pay debts.

Installment sale: A securities contract with proceeds paid in installments over a period of time and, generally, with the gains or losses taxed on a prorated basis.

Instinet: An acronym for Institutional Networks Corporation. A registered computerized subscriber service stock exchange which allows for direct large block trading among institutional investors to save brokerage commissions. Also known as the "fourth market."

Institution: An established principal, law, usage, corporate body, establishment or well known person or thing.

Institutional broker: A broker who trades securities in large volumes for institutions such as mutual funds, insurance companies and pension plan managers.

Institutional buyer/seller: A buyer or seller of securities who trades in exceptionally large quantities. Also known as "big boy."

Institutional buy/sell program: Very large volume orders to buy or sell securities entered by one or more institutional traders. Buy programs generally tend to drive the whole market up and sell programs tend to drive the whole market down.

Institutional investor: An organization whose primary purpose is the management and investment of assets of its own or those held in trust for others. Includes mutual funds, insurance and investment companies, pension plans, universities and banks, among others. Billions of investment dollars are controlled by institutional investors. Also known as "the big boy."

Instrument: A legal document such as a contract, agreement or stock/bond certificate.

Insurance: The payment of premiums by a large number of individuals or companies to an organization in return for the assurance of financial protection against events as covered in the insurance contract. (Example: An insurance contract may cover such events as accidents, health, death, dismemberment, theft, fire or other catastrophies.)

Insured account: An account in a financial institution in which the assets held are insured up to the amounts specified in the insurance contract against insolvency of the institution.

Intangible asset: An asset that is not physical in nature and cannot be held in the hand, such as a copyright or good will.

Intangible drilling expense: A nonrecoverable expense in the drilling for oil and/or gas, such as labor or fuel.

Inter-bank rate: The interest rate charged between banks in the buying and selling of excess reserves.

Intercommodity spread: A long and a short position in related commodities. (Example: The purchase of live cattle and the sale of live hogs.)

Interdelivery spread: A long and short position of a commodity or option in the same security but in different delivery months.

(Example: The purchase of a contract expiring in January and the sale of a contract expiring in April.)

Interest: Payments a borrower pays to a lender for the use of the lender's funds. (Example: The payments received by a bond holder from the issuer.)

Interest coupon: The amount of interest paid annually on a debt security whether the security is registered or bearer (coupons attached).

Interest rate risk: The risk an investor takes when purchasing a fixed rate instrument in which the interest rate atmosphere changes to such a degree that the resale value of the security changes substantially.

Interim dividend: A dividend declared and paid by a corporation before actual earnings have been determined.

Interim statement: The financial statement covering only a portion of the fiscal year, usually on a quarterly basis.

Interlocking directorate: Membership on more than one board of directors. Only legal if the companies are not in competition.

Inter-market spread: Interdelivery spread.

Inter-market trading system (ITS):   The electronic communications network that links the trading floor of major exchanges that enables any broker or market maker on the floor of a participating exchange to execute an order in whichever exchange shows the best price available.

Intermediary: A specialist empowered to make financial decisions for others hoping to make a higher than average turn on invested dollars.

Intermediate term: The difference in time between a short-term and a long- term investment according to the type of security. Commodities, options and stock terms are normally measured in months and debt instrument terms are in years.

Intermediation: The deposit of money made to a financial intermediary for investments that hopefully will achieve a higher than average rate of return.

Internal control: A company's system to assure policy implementation, promote efficiency and protect assets.

Internal expansion financing: Asset growth financed with company funds rather than assuming a debt obligation or borrowing of money.

Internal rate of return (IRR):   The discount rate at which the future cash flows of an investment equals the cost.

Internal Revenue Service (IRS):   The U.S. agency enpowered to collect federal taxes including personal, corporate, social security, excise and gift taxes.

International arbitrage: The trading of securities in a special international arbitrage account on a national exchange for the sole purpose of taking advantage of price differences between U.S. markets and those not under U.S. jurisdiction.

International Bank For Reconstruction and Development (IBRD):   Bank organized in 1944 to help finance the reconstruction of Europe and Asia after World War II. Now used to finance a nation's infrastructure provided loans are backed by the borrowing country's government. While the IBRD may not compete with local banks, it may be a participating consortium member.

International Monetary Fund (IMF):   Organized in 1944 to lower trade barriers, stabilize currencies and help developing nations pay their debts, funded mostly from treasuries of industrialized nations.

International Monetary Market (IMM):   A division of the Chicago Mercantile Exchange that provides a marketplace for the trading of futures contracts in foreign currencies, coins and U.S. Treasury bills and notes.

International mutual fund: A mutual fund that trades in many different foreign stock exchanges to take advantage of worldwide currency and market fluctuations.

Interpolate: To estimate an unknown number based on known numbers. (Example: The value of a bond with a seven percent coupon due March 15, 2015 is estimated to be 95 percent when compared to the known values of bonds with seven percent coupons due in January and May, 2015 to be 94.3 percent, respectively.)

Interpositioning: The addition of another broker in a securities transaction used to facilitate the execution of a trade. Illegal when used solely to generate additional commissions.

Interstate Commerce Commission (ICC):   The federal agency empowered to insure that carriers and transportation service firms involved in interstate commerce give the public fair and reasonable rates and services.

Inter vivos trust: A trust established between living persons. (Example: A trust established by a parent for the benefit of a child.)

Interrogation device: Slang for the computer terminal that provides such market information as last sales price, bid and asked quotes, volume and other pertinent information relating to a security.

In the money: A put or call option that has intrinsic value. (Example: A call in which the exercise price is at 60 and the underlying security is at 55 or a put in which the exercise price is 50 and the underlying security is at 55.)

In the pipeline: Securities that are in the process of being underwritten for an offering are said to be "in the pipeline."

In the tank: A slang expression describing a security or market that is losing value very quickly.

Intracommodity spread: The purchase and sale of the same commodity on the same exchange but for different months. (Example: The purchase—(long position)—and the sale—(short position)—of June soybeans.)

Intraday: Within the day, usually in reference to the high and low price of a security in one business day of trading.

Intrastate exemption: The exemption from the requirement to register with the Securities and Exchange Commission due to the company offering the securities for sale only in the state in which the company is incorporated.

Intrastate offering: An offering of unregistered securities within the state where the company conducts business. The securities are being offered provided they are sold only to residents of that state.

Intrinsic value: The dollar difference between the exercise and current price of an option. (Example: The underlying stock is 60, but an option has an exercise price of 65, so the option will have an intrinsic value of $5.00 per share.)

Inventory: Assets owned by a company, individual, securities dealer or specialist.

Inventory turnover ratio: A ratio that measures the efficiency with which a company can sell and replace its inventory, calculated by dividing the net sales by the inventory.

Inverted scale: A serial bond offering in which the earlier maturities have higher coupon rates than the later maturities.

Inverted yield curve: A rare situation in which short term interest rates are higher than long term interest rates.

Invested capital: The total amount of a company's long term debt, capital stock and all surplus.

Investment: Money used for the purpose of making more money by capital growth, income or a combination of both.

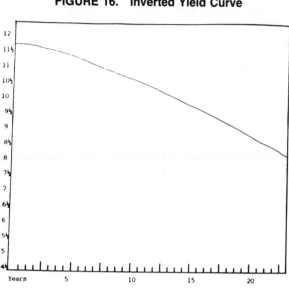

FIGURE 16.   Inverted Yield Curve

Investment advisor: A person who offers financial advice for a fee.

Investment Advisors Act of 1940:   Law designed to protect the public from fraud or misrepresentation by investment advisors. Requires all investment advisors to register with the Securities and Exchange Commission (SEC) and abide by the rules and regulations of the act and the commission.

Investment banker: A financial organization that acts as underwriter or agent serving as intermediary between the issuer of a security and the buying public.

Investment banking: The business of underwriting security issues, buying and/or selling securities as a dealer or for the benefit of others as a broker.

Investment club: An organization formed by a group of people for the purpose of pooling funds, making joint investment decisions and sharing proportionately any gains or losses.

Investment company: A company or trust that uses its own capital to invest in other companies. Is either closed-end or open-end (mutual fund) as described in the Investment Company Act of 1940.

Investment Company Act of 1940:   Legislation passed to define and regulate investment companies.

Investment counsel: A person whose principal business is counseling and advising investors and/or rendering investment supervisory services.

Investment credit: A direct federal tax credit, when allowed by law, given on a percentage of value for business asset investments, usually allowed in periods of faltering economy to encourage business expansion.

Investment grade: A bond which has been rated by a rating service such as Standard & Poor's in the top four categories. AAA, AA, A and BBB are considered investment grade. Also known as bank quality.

Investment history: The investment practices of an individual or firm as established by actual trades.

Investment income: Income which has been generated from investments rather than wages.

Investment letter: A letter of intent between the issuer of a private placement of new securities and the buyer stating that the securities are for investment only and not for resale. Used to avoid having to register the new issue with the Securities and Exchange Commission (SEC). Resale may be accomplished by adherence to the SEC Rule 144.

Investment manager: The manager of one or more portfolios of securities. Usually compensated by a set fee rather than commissions.

Investment objective: The reasons for and the desired results of an individual's investments.

Investment program: An investment plan in which buys and sells are generated by specific guidelines.

Investment strategy: The allotment of assets between various investment vehicles designed to accomplish the investment objectives in order to meet an investor's needs, such as retirement, education or estate growth.

Investment tax credit (ITC): When allowed by law, a direct federal tax credit given on a percentage of value for business asset investments, allowed usually in periods of a faltering economy to encourage business expansion.

Investment trust: A closed-end mutual fund which, like a corporation, has a fixed number of outstanding shares that are traded like stock.

Investment value of a convertible security: The value of a convertible (CV) security as if there were no convertible feature attached.

Investment vehicle: A phrase used in the investment community to mean a type of investment (such as annuity, corporate or municipal bonds, options, utility stocks, etc.) rather than the individual security (such as XYZ Company preferred stock, Ourtown municipal bond due in 2001, etc.)

Investor relations department: The department in most major public companies responsible for investor public relations (PR).

Investors Services Bureau: A public service of the New York Stock Exchange that responds to all written requests concerning securities investments.

Invisible supply: A term referring to uncounted commodities in the hands of wholesalers, manufacturers or ultimate consumers.

Involuntary bankruptcy: The legal state in which one or more creditors have petitioned to have a debtor judged insolvent by a court.

IPO: Initial public offering.

IRA: Individual retirement account.

IRA rollover: The transfer of an individual retirement account from one trustee to another as the result of a qualified retirement plan distribution.

IRA transfer: The transfer of an established IRA from one trustee to another.

Irredeemable bond: A bond that may not be called by the issuer or redeemed by the holder.

Irrevocable trust: A trust that cannot be changed or terminated without the express written agreement by the beneficiary.

IRS: Internal Revenue Service.

Issue: 1) An offering of stocks or bonds for sale to the general public. May be new (initial public or private offering) or secondary (an offering of previously issued securities offered by holders of a large amount). 2) Direct descendants.

Issued and outstanding: The shares of a corporation that have been authorized by the corporate charter, issued (sold) and are, therefore, outstanding.

Issued date: The date a new issue of bonds officially begins accruing interest to be paid to the purchaser.

Issued stock: Stock of a corporation that has been sold to the public.

Issuer: 1) The corporation or municipality that offers its securities for sale. 2) The creator of an option.

Issuing authority: The government entity, corporation or municipality that offers a security for sale through an underwriter. In the case of a debt security, the issuing authority is responsible for the payment of interest and the repayment of principal.

ITC: Investment tax credit.

JAJO: An abbreviation of the cycle for options that expire in January, April, July and October. *(See also: FMAN, MSJD)*

Jobber: A London Stock Exchange term for a market maker.

Joint account: An account in which two or more individuals act as co-owners. May be as joint tenants in common or joint tenants with rights of survivorship.

Joint account agreement: A form required by financial institutions that must be signed by all parties agreeing to the terms of a joint account.

Joint and several bond: A bond that is backed or guaranteed by one or more obligators or guarantors.

Joint and survivor annuity: An annuity contract that makes payments to an annuitant and, should the annuitant die, continues to make payments to the survivor, commonly the spouse of the annuitant.

Joint bond: A bond that is backed or guaranteed by one or more obligators or guarantors. Also known as double barreled bond.

Jointly and severally: Legally, a debt obligation that may be enforced upon all obligators either singly or jointly.

Joint tenancy with right of suvivorship (JTWROS): A legal term for assets owned by two or more persons. Should one of the owners die, the assets pass to the remaining owners rather than the heirs of the deceased.

Joint venture: An agreement by one or more partners formed to work on one project. All members of a joint agreement are considered general partners and share proportionately any gains, losses and liabilities.

JTWROS: Joint tenancy with right of survivorship.

Jumbo certificate of deposit: A certificate of deposit (CD) with a minimum investment of $100,000.

Junior issue: An issue of a stock or debt security that is subordinate to another issue in claims on dividends, interest or principal in the event of liquidation.

Junior refunding: The refinancing of a one to five year government debt by issuing another debt security that matures in five years or more.

Junior security: A security that is subordinate to another issue in claims on dividends, interest or principal in the event of liquidation.

Junk bond: A bond with a fairly high risk regarding the repayment of principal and the payment of interest. Rated BB or lower by Standard & Poor's rating system. Not allowed as an investment by those with fiduciary responsibilities.

Jurisdiction: The right of a regulatory body or court to hear and pass judgment on a case.

Jury of executive opinion: A panel of experts given the same information is asked to make market forecasts based on the information, collectively review the results, make changes based on group decisions, then publish the resulting forecast. Known as the "delphi forecast." Believed to be a more realistic forecast than any given by an individual.

Justified price: The current or fair market value of a security determined by supply and demand.

Kaffirs: A term used in Great Britain that refers to South African gold mining shares.

Kansas City Board of Trade (KCBT): A commodity exchange where wheat and value line stock index futures are traded.

Keogh plan: A money purchase, profit sharing or defined benefit plan available to self-employed individuals. Limited by law as to the percentage and dollar amount allowed to be deposited in any plan or combination of plans. (Caution: Keogh rules and regulations are subject to change. Check with a qualified tax consultant for current rules and regulations.)

Key industry: An industry of prime economic importance to a nation.

Keynesian economics: The theories of John Maynard Keynes (1883–1946), who believed that an orderly economy was accomplished only through government control and intervention.

Kickback: An illegal payment made to someone of influence to ensure the awarding of a contract or other type of favor.

Kicker: An added feature of an investment to make the security more attractive to an investor. (Example: Rights or warrants attached to a new issue of stock used to entice investors.)

Killer bees: Someone who aids a company in fending takeover attempts by devising strategies to make the takeover target less attractive.

Kiting: 1) Driving the price of a stock up by manipulation. 2) The use of checks to transfer funds between financial institutions in order to take advantage of the time required for a check to clear (float), thus drawing interest or having the use of the funds for a longer period of time.

Know your customer: A synopsis of the New York Stock Exchange Rule 405, which is the securities industry's ethics rule, both stated and implied, requiring registered representatives to make investment recommendations based on the experience, financial holdings and needs of the client.

Kondratieff wave theory: Soviet economist Nikolai Kondratieff claimed to have predicted the crash of 1929 based on his theory that the economy of the western capitalist world moves in "supercycles" lasting 50 to 60 years. The crash of 1929 was predicted to follow the crash of 1870.

Krugerrand: A solid bullion coin minted by the Republic of South Africa with weights of full and fractional ounces.

L

Labor-intensive: An industry requiring large pools of workers in which labor costs are more important than capital costs.

Laffer curve: Named for the U.S. economist Arthur Laffer, postulator of the theory that noninflationary growth is spurred when marginal taxes are cut, encouraging productivity and investment.

Laissez-faire: French for "allow to do." The philosophy that interference of government in business and economic affairs should be minimal, leaving businesses free to pursue profitable opportunities as they see fit.

Lapsed option: An option contact that has surpassed the expiration date and is no longer tradable or exercisable.

Last in, first out (LIFO): The accounting method that assumes the last assets acquired are the first assets to be sold or distributed.

Last sale: The latest price at which a security was traded.

Last trade: The last price at which a security traded on a business day.

Last trading day: 1) The last day a commodity futures contract may be offset before being subject to receipt or delivery of the actual commodity. 2) The final trading day that an option may be offset or exercised before expiring worthless.

Late tape: A term used to signify an exchange tape is several minutes behind in the reporting of transactions.

Leg: One side of a hedged position in options or commodities.

Legal: The name of the computerized file of a NYSE member firm that includes customer complaints, enforcement information and the findings of audits by exchange examiners of the firm's records and activities.

Legal age: The age, determined by state law, at which a minor reaches majority and is deemed legally responsible for any of his or her actions.

Legal investments list: A state's list of investments suitable for certain institutions and fiduciaries. Often restricted to high quality securities meeting the state's required specifications.

Legal opinion: A statement of counsel regarding the issuance of municipal bonds that, in the opinion of the counsel, are exempt from federal taxes, permitted by legislation and no restrictive covenants on prior issues are violated by the new issue.

Legal transfer: Transfer of a security from the seller to the buyer that requires more paperwork and signatures than the usual stock or bond power. (Example: The transfer of stock from a decedent's account.)

Legend: The statement printed (usually in red) on a certificate stating restrictions concerning the selling of the security. Only after certain conditions are met may the securities be cleared for the purpose of selling or transferring. *(See also: RULE 144/145)*

Lender: An individual or firm who loans funds or securities to a borrower.

Lending at a premium: The charge (in dollars per 100 shares per business day) to the borrower (short seller) of securities for the loan of the securities.

Lending at a rate: The payment of interest on the money received in connection with securities loaned to short sellers.

Lending securities: Securities borrowed for the account of a short seller to deliver to the buyer of the securities sold short.

Lessee member: A person who has leased a seat from an exchange member for a stated fee for a stated period of time, usually one year.

Letter bond: A bond that is not registered with the Securities and Exchange Commission and sold to a purchaser who has signed a letter stating the bonds were purchased as an investment and not for resale.

Letter of authorization: Authority, either full or limited, giving an agent power of attorney over buy or sell transactions in a brokerage account.

Letter of credit (LOC): A document issued by a financial institution guaranteeing payments up to a specified amount for a specified period of time.

Letter of intent (LOI): 1) A letter signed by the purchaser of mutual fund shares stating the intent to purchase additional shares within a specified length of time in order to qualify for breakpoint sales (lower sales charges). The letter is not a firm commitment and should the purchaser not be able to fulfill the terms of the letter, the sales charge would be adjusted to the original sales charge amount. 2) Any letter expressing the intention to take (or not take) a specific action, such as granting a loan, the merging of two companies or the granting of a contract.

Letter stock: A security which is not registered with the Securities and Exchange Commission and sold to a purchaser who has signed a letter stating the security was purchased as an investment and not for resale.

Level debt service: The clause in a municipality's charter stating that municipal debt shall be approximately equal each year in order to better estimate the amount of tax revenue needed.

Level I Service of NASDAQ: A service that gives highest bids and lowest offers on an electronic screen of NASDAQ traded securities to subscribers. Does not identify the market maker.

Level II Service of NASDAQ: The services of Level I Service as well as indicating the market makers.

Level III Service of NASDAQ: The services of Level II Service as well as allowing market makers to enter competitive bids and offers, in effect, making the service an electronic exchange.

Leverage: 1) The effect earnings have on a company with bonds and/or preferred stock outstanding. (Example: A company with 1,000,000 common shares outstanding with earnings growing from $2,000,000 to $3,000,000 would show a 50 percent increase in earnings per share. The same company that has an additional expense of $1,000,000 in dividend expense would have a 100 percent growth in earnings per share.) 2) The use of borrowed capital to increase earnings.

Leveraged buyout: Using borrowed funds in order to take over another company, usually with the assets of the company being taken over used as collateral and the cash flow used to repay the loan.

Leveraged company: Any company that has loans or debt securities outstanding in addition to equity in its capital structure. Is generally used to denote companies that have a much higher than normal percentage of debt to equity.

Leveraged lease: A lease contract for equipment that is financed almost totally with a nonrecourse loan.

Leveraged stock: Stock that is used as collateral for a loan, usually within a margin account.

Liabilities: All the claims against a company including accounts, wages, salaries, declared dividends, accrued taxes payable and any loans outstanding such as debentures, bonds and bank loans.

LIBOR: London Interbank Offered Rate.

License: A certificate representing completion of requirements needed to qualify for certain permitted actions. (Example: Stock, bond, commodity and option brokers must be licensed prior to soliciting and accepting orders from clients.)

Lien: A creditor's claim against property, may be granted by a court to satisfy judgment.

Life expectancy: 1) The period of time a pool of debt mortgage securities is expected to last before being completely paid back due to prepayments, defaults or liquidations. 2) The age to which a person is expected to live. May be different ages when various factors are considered such as health, sex, age at computation and heredity.

Life of delivery: The period between the first and last day of trading in any futures contract.

Life insurance: An insurance company contract, such as term, whole life, universal life and single premium whole life policies, that provides for payment to the beneficiary upon the death of the contract owner.

LIFO: Last in, first out.

Lifting a leg: The closing of one side of an option or commodity hedge position, such as a spread, straddle or combination.

Limit: The maximum daily price change allowed in a specific commodity. May be changed by the exchange during periods of unusually high market activity.

Limit down: The daily maximum downward price movement on a commodity futures contract as established by the exchange in which the contract is traded.

Limited company (LTD): The British equivalent to a U.S. corporation.

Limited discretion: An agreement between a broker and a client giving the broker limited discretion in the trading decisions of the client's account, such as the time to enter an order.

Limited partnership: A type of business organization in which the general partner(s) makes all business decisions and assumes all liabilities while the limited partners make no business decisions and are liable for only the amount of dollars actually invested. Each type of partner receives specified tax benefits and cash flow as outlined in the partnership agreement. May be a public or private limited partnership.

Limited power of attorney (LPOA): A power of attorney granting control of an account limited to placing buy or sell instructions. Does not include the withdrawal of cash or securities.

Limited risk: An investment in which capital risk is limited to the amount invested, in contrast to unlimited risk in which there is no limit to the amount of additional capital required to maintain a position. (Example: The risk involved in the purchase of an option is limited to the amount paid for the option while the risk of selling a security short is only limited in how high the price of the security may rise.)

Limited tax bond: A municipal bond backed by the full faith of the issuing municipality but only by a limited or special tax base.

Limited trading authority: Power of authority given to an agent which allows the agent to place buy or sell orders in a brokerage account. Does not allow the agent to withdraw funds or securities.

Limit move: The maximum daily price movement of a commodity futures contract as established by the exchange on which the contract is traded.

Limit-or-better order: A limit order placed reminding the floor broker that the current price might be better than the limit amount.

Limit order: Instructions for a security to buy no higher or sell no lower than the amount stated on the order.

Limit order information system: An electronic system that gives information on bid and asked prices and quantities available on the various exchanges allowing subscribers to take advantage of the best prices available.

Limit price: The price at which a limit order is placed.

Limit up: The maximum daily upward price limit a commodity futures contract may move as established by the exchange on which the contract is traded.

Line of credit: The maximum amount of money a borrower may obtain in a given period of time.

Lipper Gauge: The common term used for the Lipper Mutual Fund industry average.

Lipper Mutual Fund Industry Average (Lipper Gauge): The average performance of mutual fund types such as growth, income, money market, tax free, government bond, etc. as reported by Lipper Analytical Services of New York.

Liquid asset: An asset of cash or an item that is easily convertible to cash.

Liquidating dividend: A dividend that is a distribution of the assets of a company in the process of bankruptcy or liquidation.

Liquidating value: The estimated value of an asset that is subject to liquidation as the result of a company going out of business.

Liquidation: 1) The process of turning assets into cash for the purpose of paying creditors and, if possible, distributing the remaining funds on a pro rata basis to the shareholders. 2) A transaction made in reducing or closing out a long or short position.

Liquidity: 1) Enough buyers and sellers of securities at reasonable prices to maintain an orderly market. 2) A measure of a company's ability to meet its current obligations.

Liquidity diversification: A portfolio consisting of short and long term debt securities (bonds and debentures) to help protect against sharp interest rate fluctuations.

Liquidity ratio: A measure of a firm's ability to meet maturing short term obligations.

Liquid Yield Option Notes (LYONs):   A convertible bond that pays no current interest but is issued at a discount to face value with the yield figured by calculating the difference between the purchase and maturity prices as relates to the purchase price and length of maturity.

Listed: A security such as a stock, bond or option that is allowed to be bought and sold on the listing exchange(s).

Listed bond: A bond that can be bought and sold on a major exchange.

Listed option: An option that can be bought and sold on an option exchange.

Listed stock: The stock of a company that is traded on one or more exchanges.

Listing requirements: Rules that must be met before a security can be listed for trading on an exchange.

Living trust: A trust established between living persons. (Example: A trust established by a parent for the benefit of a child.) Also known as "inter vivos trust."

LMV: Long market value.

Load: The sales charges involved in the purchase (front load) or sale (end load) of shares of a mutual fund. Mutual fund shares bought or sold without sales charges are called "no load."

Load fund: A mutual fund that charges a fee for either the purchase or sale of shares, but not for both.

Loan consent agreement: A form required of the holders of a margin account that gives the brokerage firm permission to loan the client's securities.

Loan crowd: The congregation of stock exchange members who lend or borrow securities for brokerage firms' clients who sell short.

Loaned flat: Securities loaned to short sellers without an interest charge.

Loan prices: The prices at which commodity producers may obtain loans from the government for their crops.

Loan value: The amount of funds able to be borrowed using a security as collateral. Different securities will have different loan values according to price and/or safety of principal as well as the loan policy of the lending firm.

LOC: Letter of credit.

Local safekeeping (LSK): Securities deposited in a client's brokerage account that are registered in the client's name and held in the safety deposit box of the brokerage firm. *(See also: STREET NAME)*

Locked in: An investor who owns shares of stocks with such a large gain that the sale of the shares would subject the investor to immediate capital gains tax.

Locked market: The market condition where the bid is exactly the same as the asked price. The entrance of more buyers and sellers unlocks the highly competitive condition.

LOI: Letter of intent.

London Interbank Offered Rate (LIBOR): The rate international banks of high credit standing who deal in Eurodollars, Eurocurrency and other mediums charge each other for loans. Similar to the "prime rate" at U.S. banks.

Long: 1) Signifies ownership of a security. 2) The buying side of an open commodity futures contract. 3) A trader whose net position in the futures market shows an excess of open purchases over open sales. *(See also: SHORT)*

Long bond coupon: 1) The first interest payment of a new bond issue that becomes due after the usual six months period of time. 2) A bond that matures in ten years or more.

Long hedge: 1) The purchase of a futures commodity contract to protect the buyer against a rise in prices of the actual commodity. (Example: A poultry producer may purchase soybean meal futures contracts to protect against the cost of the meal rising.) 2) The purchase of a futures contract or call option as protection against interest rates dropping as a direct result of the price of the debt security going up.

Long leg: The purchase side of an option or commodity spread.

Long market value (LMV):   The value of securities owned.

Long position: Assets owned by an investor.

Long-term: The length of time if allowed by federal law an asset must be held prior to selling in order for the gain or (loss) to be taxed at a favorable rate. (Caution: Federal laws change regarding taxes. Check with a tax attorney, accountant or other qualified adviser regarding the current federal tax laws.)

Long-term capital gain or (loss):   The taxable gain or loss of a capital asset that has been held for longer than the current law specifies and subject to favorable tax treatment. (Caution: Federal law changes occur quite often. Check with a tax attorney, accountant or other qualified adviser for the current rules regarding long term capital gain or [loss].)

Long-term debt: 1) Liability that is not due to be paid off for a year or more. 2) A bond that matures in 10 years or more.

Long-term gain or (loss):   The taxable gain or loss of a capital asset that has been held for longer than the current law specifies and is subject to favorable tax treatment. (Caution: Federal law changes occur quite often. Check with a tax attorney, accountant or other qualified adviser for the current rules regarding long term gain or [loss].)

Long-term trading: A trading strategy involving the purchase of securities to be held for longer than six months.

Long-term trend: A trading trend that has been evident or is expected for an extended period of time. (Example: The market "is" in a long term trend on the upside.)

Loophole: A technicality that makes it possible to circumvent the intent without violating the letter of a law.

Loss: The net difference between the purchase and the selling price of an asset or other security when the purchase price is higher than the selling price.

Loss carryover: The capital loss that is carried over to subsequent tax years for use as a capital loss deduction. (Caution: Federal law changes occur quite often. Check with a tax attorney, accountant or other qualified adviser for the current rules regarding Loss Carryover.)

Lot: Any number of goods or services that are needed for a transaction. *(See also: ODD LOT, ROUND LOT)*

Low: The bottom price of a security over a specified period of time, usually within the previous 12 month period.

LPOA: Limited power of attorney.

LSK: Local safekeeping.

LTD: Limited company.

Lump-sum distribution: The distribution of assets from a retirement plan given to the recipient in a single payment. May be subject to ten-year forward averaging or IRA Rollover.

Luxury tax: The tax assessed on goods considered to be "luxury" or nonessential.

LYONs: An acronym for Liquid-Yield Option Notes, or zero-coupon convertible bonds.

M: 1) An abbreviation for 1,000 2) On the daily pink sheets that list all publicly traded companies, signifies the security is eligible to be margined. 3) Designates stocks that are traded on the Midwest Stock Exchange. 4) Designation of the nation's money supply, followed by a number and/or a letter.

M1: The narrow definition of the money supply that includes money in circulation, including coins, currency and demand deposits (money in checking accounts).

Macroeconomics: The analysis of a nation's economics as a whole. *(See also: MICROECONOMICS)*

Maintenance call: The demand for additional funds or securities (due to an adverse price change in the value of a margin account) in order to bring the total account value back up to the minimum ratio of debt to equity.

Maintenance excess: The equity value in a margin account above the minimum requirement.

Maintenance fee: An annual fee charged by custodians of certain special accounts, such as individual retirement accounts and Keogh accounts.

Maintenance requirement: The minimum equity value required in a margin account. Should the value go below the minimum value, a margin call will be generated requiring an additional deposit of cash or securities to bring the account back up to the required minimum.

Majority shareholder: One or more shareholders who own and control a higher percentage of the outstanding shares of a company than any other shareholder.

Make a market/price: The section of a brokerage firm that buys and sells a particular over-the-counter stock for its own portfolio and at its own risk.

Maloney Act: Legislation enacted in 1938 to include over the counter securities regulations to those covered in the Securities Exchange Act of 1934.

Managed account: An account funded by one or more investors in which the manager makes all investment decisions for a fee with the investors sharing gains or losses on a pro rata basis.

Management company: An investment company that manages portfolios, including various types of securities for a fee. May be at the total discretion of the management company or with the input of the owner of the portfolio, according to the terms of the contract.

Management fee: A fee (usually a fixed annual percentage of asset value), charged for the management of a portfolio of a mutual fund or other managed account.

Manager, the: The entity responsible for a) the investment decisions of a mutual fund. b) the issuance of a new or secondary offering or c) the investment decisions of a managed account.

Managing underwriter: The leading (and usually original) member of an underwriting group organized for the purpose of distributing a new issue of securities such as stocks, bonds, mutual funds or limited partnerships.

Mandatory remedial action: The requirement of immediate additional deposit of cash or securities as mandated by federal Regulation T margin requirements.

Manipulation: The illegal buying or selling of a security for the purpose of creating a false impression of trading activity.

MAPS: An acronym for Market Auction Preferred Stock.

Margin: 1) The brokerage industry name for "loan." 2) The amount of money or securities that must be deposited by a client at the time a purchase is made in a margin account. 3) Cash or equivalents posted as a guarantee of fulfillment of a futures contract (not to be considered a partial payment of purchase).

Margin account: An account at a brokerage firm that allows a client to borrow money using securities in the account as collateral. Usually used as a leverage.

Margin agreement: A signed statement by a client agreeing to the rules of a margin account (i.e., securities pledged as collateral will be held by the brokerage firm. Those securities may be repledged by the brokerage firm to finance the account and the brokerage firm may sell the securities if needed to protect its financial interest in the account.)

Margin call: The requirement demanded of a client to deposit additional funds or securities in order to maintain the minimum ratio of debt to equity as required by the exchange or brokerage firm.

Margin department: The department within a brokerage firm that computes on a daily basis the status of margin, cash and any special accounts.

Margin of profit: A ratio used to determine the operating efficiency of a business, calculated by dividing the operating profit by net sales.

Margin requirement: The amount of cash or securities, (based on a percentage of the trade) required by a brokerage firm when a client purchases long or sells short a security in a margin account. Usually a higher percentage than is required by Regulation T.

Margin risk: The risk involved in a margin account in which the client may be required to deposit additional funds or securities in order to maintain the minimum ratio of debt to equity.

Margin security: A security that may be purchased and/or sold in a margin account according to Regulation T. Only those securities that qualify according to Regulation T are eligible for margin. All others must be traded on a cash basis.

Mark down: The difference between the current bid price among dealers and the actual price paid to a client.

Marketability: Enough buyers and sellers of a security at reasonable prices to maintain an ordinary market.

Marketable securities: Securities which are easily bought and sold.

Market analysis: A technical or fundamental security research report. Usually outlines the past performance and lists future plans in order to draw a conclusion about the growth possibilities.

Market arbitrage: The simultaneous purchase and sale of a security on separate exchanges or markets to take advantage of any price difference.

Market Auction Preferred Stock (MAPS):   A fund or trust that is comprised of preferred stocks trading on auction markets such as the New York Stock Exchange.

Market hours: The hours during a business day an exchange is open to buy and sell securities. Each exchange sets its own hours of operation.

Market-if-touched order (MIT):   An order to buy or sell a security at the market (best possible price) should the price indicated on the order be "touched" or attained.

Market index: The weighted value of the components that comprise an index, such as the Standard & Poor's 500 Index.

Market letter: Any publication that is distributed to an organization's clients that makes remarks on the outlook and performances of the market in general, industries or individual companies.

Market maker: An individual or firm that buys and sells particular over-the-counter stocks for its own portfolio and its own risk.

Market order: An order to buy or sell a security at the best price possible after the order is presented to the trading crowd. Usually filled immediately. (Caution: In order to complete a transaction, there must be an opposite side. Even a market order does not guarantee execution if there is no one willing to be on the opposite side.)

Market out clause: The clause in an underwriting contract that relieves the underwriter of its commitment under unusual circumstances, such as unexpected bad news about the issuer prior to the offering.

Marketplace: The exchange, network or location where securities are bought and sold, either directly or through intermediaries.

Market price: The last price or current quote of a security.

Market research: A technical analysis of stock movement including volume, price advances and declines as well as market breadth.

Market risk: The risk of the day to day fluctuations in the price of securities.

Market share: The percentage of sales by an individual company as compared to the entire related industry.

Market, the: 1) Generally used to mean securities as a whole, such as stocks, bonds, options or commodities. 2) Synonym for the Dow Jones Industrial Average.

Market timing: Purchase and sell decisions based on such factors as interest rates, Dow Jones Industrial Average and the economy, hopefully timed to take advantage of the highest prices on selling and the lowest prices on buying.

Market tone: The general strength and vigor of the securities market.

Market value: The current value or price of a security at any given time, determined by the effects of supply and demand.

Market value-weighted index: An index whose components are weighted according to the total market value of the index's total outstanding shares. Constantly fluctuates according to the price movements of the stocks.

Marking: The execution of an option trade at the close of the business day at a price not representative of the true value in order to enhance the client's equity position. A manipulative maneuver.

Mark to the market: 1) The assessment of the value of securities held long or short in a margin account in order to evaluate the compliance to maintenance requirements. If a negative figure, the owner of the account must deposit additional funds or securities.

Mark up: The difference between the current price among dealers and the actual price that is charged to a client.

Marry a put: The simultaneous purchase of a stock and the purchase of a put against the stock specifically identified as to a hedge position.

Master limited partnership: A publically traded limited partnership in which all earnings are passed on to the shareholders. All earnings are taxed by the Internal Revenue Service as belonging to the individual partners (shareholders).

Match: In an auction market dispute, such as on the New York Stock Exchange, the flipping of a coin to decide which floor broker wins the bid or offer.

Matched and lost: The losing result of the flip of a coin to decide which floor broker wins a bid or offer.

Matching orders: The simultaneous entering of identical orders to buy or sell a security to give an appearance of active trading in the security. An illegal maneuver.

Material information: Any information that, if known by an investor, would influence the investment decision.

Matrix trading: A bond swap technique to take advantage of a temporary yield spread difference in bonds of different classes or ratings.

Mature economy: A nation's economy that is stagnant or declining and no longer robust and growing.

Maturity or maturity date: The date on which a bond is scheduled to repay the principal to the bondholder.

Maximum capital gains fund: A mutual fund that invests in companies expected to grow rapidly. The selling of the stocks within the portfolio produces capital gains or (losses).

Maximum corporate tax rate: The maximum federal rate at which a corporation must pay taxes.

Maximum loan value: The maximum amount of money that may be borrowed using the security as collateral. The inverse of the Regulation T requirement. (Example: If Regulation T is 75 percent, the maximum loan value would be 25 percent.)

May Day: May 1, 1975, the date brokerage firms were allowed to start setting their own commission structures rather than have a fixed rate. The beginning of the era of discount brokers and the expansion of full service brokerage firms to include a wide range of financial services.

Mean return: The average of the expected return of a portfolio.

Meat complex: Commodities contracts issued on meats, including feeder cattle, live cattle, pork bellies (bacon) and live hogs.

Medium-term bond: A bond that matures in two to ten years.

Member: 1) One of the 1,366 individuals who owns a seat on the New York Stock Exchange. 2) Any broker-dealer admitted to membership in the National Association of Securities Dealers (NASD).

Member bank: A bank that is a member of the Federal Reserve System.

Member corporation: A brokerage firm, organized as a corporation, with at least one member of the New York Stock Exchange who is an officer or an employee of the corporation.

Member firm: A brokerage firm, organized as a partnership, with at least one member of the New York Stock Exchange who is a general partner or employee of the partnership.

Member organization: Any New York Stock Exchange member corporation or firm.

Member short sale ratio: The comparison of the number of shares of stock sold short by New York Stock Exchange members to the total number of shares of stock sold short. Said to be a market trend indicator. The higher the ratio, the more bearish; conversely, the lower the ratio, the more bullish.

Member takedown: When a syndicate member buys a portion of bonds in an issue at the "takedown" or member's discount price, then sells the bonds to the client at the public offering price.

Merchant bank: A large-scale European financial institution that specializes in the counseling and negotiations involved in financial banking, such as mergers, acquisitions, portfolio management and participation in commercial ventures.

Merger: The combining of two or more companies, usually with one of the companies being the surviving entity.

Mezzanine level: A private company's development stage just prior to going public with a syndicated new issue offering.

Microeconomics: The study of basic economics as applied to industries within a nation, rather than the overall view of a nation studied in macroeconomics. (*See also: MACROECONOMICS.*)

Midwest Stock Exchange (MSE): One of the regional stock exchanges.

MIG: Moody's investment grade.

Mini-manipulation: The price manipulation of a stock underlying an option in order to cause a dramatic price change in the option. As the leverage afforded by option trading is much higher than stock trading, the potential for gain is much greater. Any type of manipulation is an illegal practice.

Minimum maintenance: The minimum equity value required in a margin account. Should the value go below the minimum maintenance level, a margin call will be generated, requiring an additional deposit of cash or securities to bring the account back up to the required minimum.

Minimum variation: The usual minimum change in the price of a security, may be in terms of fractions, percentage points or cents, according to the type of security. (Example: Stock ordinarily has a $\frac{1}{8}$th point minimum move, U.S. Treasury bill securities are $\frac{1}{32}$nd and cattle trade at a minimum of 2½ cents.)

Mini-tax: The minimum tax that is levied against tax preference items.

Mini-warehouse limited partnership: A limited partnership that invests in "mini" warehouses that are leased to individuals. Income, depreciation and capital gains are the usual benefits desired by the limited partners. May or may not have tax benefits.

Minor: A person who has not yet reached the age of majority in the state of residence.

Minority interest: Ownership of a company in which the aggregate shareholders own less than 50 percent of the shares of the company. Usually not a wholly owned subsidiary of another company.

Minus symbol (–): The designation in the reporting of the price change of a security that indicates the price is less than the previous price.

Minus tick: A transaction made at a price lower than the preceding transaction. Also known as a down tick.

Missing the market: A limit order that stays unexecuted because the current price is just above a buy order or just below a sell order.

MIT: Market-if-touched order.

Mixed account: A margin account in which there are both long (owned) and short (borrowed) positions.

MJSD: Short for the quarterly option expiration cycle consisting of March, June, September and December. (*See also: JAJO, FMAN.*)

MM: The abbreviation for million.

Mobile home certificate: Issued by the Government National Mortgage Association (GNMA). Backed by mobile home mortgages, usually shorter in term than the regular single-family GNMA certificate.

Momentum: The rate of acceleration in an economy, price or volume.

Monetarist: Someone who believes the money supply (M1) is the key to the economy rather than the government's fiscal policy.

Monetary policy: The policies of the Federal Reserve Board that determine the size of the money supply and the level of interest rates.

Money center bank: A major financial center that buys money market instruments and securities and makes loans of international importance and scope. Includes banks in New York, Los Angeles, London, Paris and Tokyo. Within the U.S., the ten largest banks comprise the money center banks.

Money market fund: A mutual fund that invests in high-quality, short term, high-yielding debt instruments.

Money purchase plan: A type of KEOGH account (retirement plan) in which the employer contributes a specific percentage of salary for its employees.

Money spread: An option strategy involving the simultaneous purchase and sale of put or call options with the same expiration dates but with different strike prices.

Money supply: The total supply of money in a nation, measured by components made up of money in circulation and the different types of money on deposit, such as demand, savings, CDs, time, etc.

Monopoly: The major control of price, production and distribution of goods or services due to lack of competition.

Monthly investment plan: A constant dollar plan in which a set dollar amount is invested on a monthly basis to take advantage of dollar cost averaging and systematic investing.

Moody's investment grade (MIG): The rating given by Moody's Investors Service to certain short-term municipal bonds.

Moody's Investors Service: One of the two best known rating agencies in the U.S. Rates such items as bonds, commercial paper, preferred and common stocks and municipal short-term bonds. *(See also: STANDARD AND POOR'S).*

Moral obligation bond: A tax-exempt municipal bond backed by a moral (but not legal) obligation pledge of a state government.

Moral suasion: The effort by the Federal Reserve Board to restrain or expand credit by the persuasive use of influence rather than coercion.

Mortgage: A debt instrument in which the borrower gives the lender a lien on property being held as collateral until the loan is repaid.

Mortgage-backed certificate security: A pool or trust of mortgages issued by government agencies or mortgage lenders in which the investor receives periodic interest payments and the principal is returned as the mortgages are prepaid, paid or defaulted.

Mortgage banker: A company or individual who deals in the issuance, sales and servicing of mortgages.

Mortgage bond: A debt instrument (bond) that is secured by a mortgage on a property owned by the issuer.

Mortgage pool: A group of mortgages with similar characteristics, such as type of structure, interest rate and maturity.

Mortgage REIT: A real estate investment trust. Usually chartered to return as much as 90 percent of the earnings to the shareholders.

Most active list: The list of stocks that have had the highest volume shares traded on a particular day.

Moving average: The average price of a stock or commodity based on a specific number of previous trading periods. May be days, weeks, months or years. As the latest period price is added, the earliest period is subtracted, thus giving the name "moving average."

MSRB: Municipal Securities Rulemaking Board.

Multinational corporation: A corporation that has facilities in at least one foreign country and makes decisions based on global considerations.

Multiple: The common term used for the price-to-earnings ratio in which the price of a share of stock is divided by the annual earnings per share.

Multiplier effect: 1) The doctrine that investments increase national income by a multiplying factor. 2) The effect that "new money" deposits multiply the money supply by making the amount not needed as reserves available as a loan, thus creating more "new money," starting the process over again or having a "multiplier effect."

Municipal bond: A bond issued by a state or political subdivision such as a city, state, country or village. Interest paid from municipal bonds are exempt from federal tax as well as state and local income taxes in the state of issue.

Municipal bond calendar: A list of soon to be issued bonds and their expected offering dates.

Municipal bond fund: A mutual fund that invests in municipal bonds to generate tax-free income for the investors.

Municipal bond insurance: A policy underwritten by a private insurer(s) that guarantees the timely payment of interest and principal should the issuing municipality default. Insured municipal bonds carry the highest ratings and are considered as safe as the insurer.

Municipal improvement certificate: A debt certificate issued in lieu of a bond to finance improvements or services. Repaid by a special tax assessment against those who benefit from the improvement.

Municipal investment trust (MIT): A unit investment trust (self-liquidating portfolio) consisting of muncipal bonds, passing the tax-free income to the investors.

Municipal note: A short-term municipal debt obligation.

Municipal revenue bond: A municipal bond issued in order to finance a revenue producing project, with the revenues used to pay the interest and repay the principal of the bonds.

Municipal Securities Rulemaking Board (MSRB): The proposer of rules and provider of arbitration facilities to dealers in municipal securities.

Mutilated security: A certificate of ownership which does not have enough detail necessary to identify the issue, the issuer or the ownership.

Mutual company: A corporation owned by its membership who receive their proportionate share of profits. May or may not have voting and/or management rights.

Mutual exclusion doctrine: The federal doctrine that says states and other municipalities must not tax federally owned properties and the federal government will not tax property owned by states or other municipalities.

Mutual fund: An open or closed-end investment company or trust which uses its own capital to invest in other companies as described in the Investment Company Act of 1940.

Mutual fund custodian: The trustee who physically safeguards the securities of a mutual fund. Makes no management or investment decisions.

Mutual improvement certificate: A debt certificate issued in lieu of a bond to finance improvements or services, repaid by a special tax assessment against those who benefit from the improvement.

N: 1) Trading accomplished on the New York Stock Exchange (upper case); 2) Newly listed on an exchange (lower case); 3) A note rather than a bond in the U.S. government securities bid-offer tables (lower case).

Naked call writer: The seller or writer of a call option who does not own the underlying security.

Naked option: An option position that is not offset by an equal and opposite position in the underlying security.

Naked position: A securities position, either long or short, which is not hedged or covered (protected from dramatic loss) in any way.

Narrowing the spread: The bid and asked price of a security coming closer together as the result of more active trading.

Narrow market: A commodities or securities market with low volume and resulting volatile prices. Also known as "thin market" and "inactive market."

NASD: National Association of Securities Dealers.

NASDAQ: National Association of Securities Dealers Automated Quotations.

NASD Business Conduct Committee: A committee appointed from the membership of the NASD to act in accordance with the by-laws, Rules of Fair Practice and the Code of Procedure to handle trade complaints.

NASD bylaws: The body of laws that describes how the NASD functions, defines it powers and determines the qualifications and registration requirements for stock brokers.

NASD Form FR-1: A certification form required of nonsyndicate members who are desiring an allocation of a hot issue that binds the receiver of the allocation to abide by the rules of the National

Association of Securities Dealers (NASD) regarding the distribution of a hot issue.

National Association of Securities Dealers (NASD):   An association of brokers and dealers in the over-the-counter securities business.

National Association of Securities Dealers Automated Quotations (NASDAQ):   The automated information network that provides brokers and dealers with price quotations on over-the-counter securities.

National bank: A U.S. Comptroller of the Currency chartered commercial bank, required to be a member of the Federal Reserve System, belong to the Federal Deposit Insurance Corporation and purchase stock in the Federal Reserve Bank in its district.

National Crime Information Center: A computerized information center under the authority of the Securities and Exchange Commission (SEC) where securities may be checked or reported for theft or misplacement.

National debt: The total amount of debt owed by the federal government, including Treasury notes, bills and bonds.

Nationalization: The governmental takeover of a private company.

National Market Advisory Board (NMAB):   A board appointed by the Securities and Exchange Commission (SEC) to study and advise on a national exchange market system (NEMS). A system envisioned to provide continuous auction markets while still preserving the individual exchanges.

National Market System (NMS):   The current marketing system that provides price and security information for over the counter and auction market trading, including such information as bid and asked prices, last trade, PE, dividend information and where traded.

National Quotation Bureau: A subsidiary of the Commerce Clearing House that provides subscribers with a daily service of a collection of bid and offer quotes in stock and bonds.

National Securities Clearing Corporation (NSCC):   A securities clearing organization that functions as a medium through which brokerage firms, exchanges and other clearing corporations complete transfers among members electronically.

Natural: A match of corresponding buy and sell orders for securities. Also known as "clean."

NAV: Net asset value.

NC: Noncallable.

Nearest month: The closest month to the present in which an option or commodity contract is available for trading.

Near money: Assets that are easily convertible to cash.

Negative amortization: The repayment of a debt, usually a mortgage, in which the monthly interest is higher than the payment actually increasing the debt owed. No principal is paid off.

Negative carry: A before-tax situation that exists when the cost of borrowing money is more than the yield or income from the item purchased with the borrowed money. Not necessarily a loss situation after taxes have been taken into consideration.

Negative cash flow: The situation that exists when a business spends more cash than it receives.

Negative pledge clause: A promise in an indenture that states the issuer will not pledge any of its assets if doing so would result in less security to the debtholders covered by the indenture agreement. Also known as "covenant of equal coverage."

Negative working capital: A situation in which the income of a company is not sufficient to pay its liabilities that, unless corrected, could result in bankruptcy.

Negative yield curve: A rare situation in which short term interest rates are higher than long term interest rates. Also known as inverted yield curve.

Negotiable: Anything that can be sold or transferred by proper delivery of title, required paperwork and signatures.

Negotiable certificate of deposit: A negotiable debt security issued by a financial institution, usually a bank or a savings and loan, with a stated maturity date and interest rate.

Negotiable security: A security certificate that has been properly endorsed and has any necessary paperwork attached in order to transfer ownership.

Negotiable warehouse receipt: A document issued by a warehouse that guarantees existence and usually specifies the grade of a commodity being stored. Used to facilitate transfer of ownership by the endorsement of the receipt by the owner.

Negotiated: A bargaining between individuals in order to reach a mutually acceptable decision.

Negotiated marketplace: A market, such as the over the counter, in which bids and offers are negotiated rather than auction marketplaces such as the New York Stock Exchange.

Negotiated underwriting: An underwriting in which a brokerage firm consults with the issuing authority and arrives at a concensus regarding the most suitable price and timing of a forthcoming securities offering. *(See also: COMPETITIVE BIDDING)*

Net: The figure remaining after all deductions have been made.

Net assets: The difference between a company's total assets and total liabilities.

Net asset value (NAV): A valuation on a per share value figured by taking the total net worth of assets and dividing the resulting figure by the total number of shares outstanding.

Net capital requirements: The term used for SEC Rule 15c3-1 that mandates the ratio of net assets to debt of broker-dealers.

Net change: The difference in the price of a security from the close on one business day to the close on the next business day.

Net current assets: The difference between a company's current assets and current liabilities.

Net estate: The total value of a deceased person's estate after all liabilities have been deducted.

Net income/earnings: The income remaining after all expenses have been deducted.

Net income per share of common stock: The amount of income available on a per share basis, figured by taking the total income, deducting all expenses and dividing the resulting figure by the number of common shares outstanding. Also known as "earnings per share (EPS)."

Net investment income per share: The income on investments that, after all fees and expenses have been deducted, are available for distribution to the investors on a pro-rata basis.

Net lease: A lease stipulating that the user shall pay all costs associated with the use of the leased facility or equipment. May or may not have escalator clauses.

Net liquid assets: The difference between a company's cash plus readily marketable securities and its current liabilities. The most stringent test of a company's ability to meet its current debt obligations.

Net loss: The amount of loss sustained when the selling price of an asset is lower than the purchase price.

Net operating loss (NOL): A loss by a corporation taken as a result of more expenses than revenues, does not include income from other sources or deductions before income.

Net position: The difference between the open long and short contracts held in any one stock, option or commodity account.

Net proceeds: The net amount received from the sale of an asset or security after all costs and expenses have been deducted.

Net profit: The income remaining after all expenses have been deducted.

Net quick assets: A stringent test of a company's liquidity calculated by adding the sum of cash, cash equivalents and accounts and notes receivable then dividing that sum by the total current liabilities. Also known as the "acid test ratio."

Net realized capital gains per share: An investment company's capital gain realized on the sale of an asset or security after all expenses have been deducted, divided by the number of outstanding shares then distributed to the shareholders on a pro-rata basis.

Net sales: The total amount of sales of a company after all returns and allowances have been deducted.

Net transaction: A transaction in which the client pays a net amount with no fees or commissions attached. (Example: A new issue is a net transaction. If the new issue price is $30 per share, the buyer pays a total of $30 per share.)

Network A: A tape display of the round lot transactions on the New York Stock Exchange.

Network B: A tape display of the round lot transactions on the American Stock Exchange.

Net worth: The residual claims that stockholders have against a company's assets. Calculated by subtracting the total liabilities from the total assets. Also known as "stockholder's equity."

Net yield: The rate of return after all costs associated with the transaction have been taken into consideration.

New account report: A report required to be filed on all new accounts by the broker involved detailing financial information as well as past investment experience. Used to determine whether a client is financially able or experienced enough to trade in various securities.

New issue: The initial public offering of a stock or bond.

New issues act: Another name for the Securities and Exchange Act of 1933.

New money: 1) An amount of additional long-term financing provided by a new issue offering or maturation of debt. 2) Preferred stock issued after October 1, 1942 in which the dividend is 85 percent tax excluded to corporations. 3) The deposit of cash made to a financial organization over and above reserve requirements and, therefore, eligible to be loaned. *(See also: MULTIPLIER EFFECT)*

New York Coffee, Sugar and Cocoa Exchange: One of the commodity futures trading exchanges.

New York Curb Exchange: The slang term for the American Stock Exchange, which started doing business on the curb of a New York street in Manhattan.

New York Futures Exchange (NYFE): The subsidiary of the New York Stock Exchange that engages in the business of trading commodity futures contracts.

New York Mercantile Exchange (NYMEX): One of the commodity futures trading exchanges.

New York Stock Exchange (NYSE): Founded in 1792, the largest U.S. securities exchange, a not-for-profit organization made up of 1,366 members, governed by a board of directors and formed to provide a place for the orderly trading of securities.

New York Stock Exchange Index: A weighted index based on all stocks traded on the New York Stock Exchange.

Niche: A company has a "niche in the market" when it is a supplier of such a specialized product or service that the company is able to command a price that will assure a high profit.

Nifty Fifty: The 50 companies that are the most highly favored investments by institutional buyers.

Nine-bond rule **(Rule 396):** The New York Stock Exchange rule that requires orders for listed bonds in quantities of nine bonds or less to be sent to the floor of the NYSE for possible execution before being sent to the over-the-counter market.

No brainer: The term used to describe a market condition that takes "no brains" to figure out the obvious direction.

NOL: Net operating loss.

No-load fund: A mutual fund that does not change the investor a sales charge when buying or selling shares of the fund. *(See also: FRONT-END LOAD FUND, BACK-END LOAD FUND)*

Nolo contendere: A legal term of Latin origin meaning "I do not wish to contest the action." Usually the preliminary step to an out-of-court settlement.

Nominal exercise price: The adjusted exercise price of a Ginnie Mae mortgage pool option contract multiplied by the unpaid principal balance of the pool to determine the nominal exercise price. (Example: A Ginnie Mae pool with a balance of $76,000 and an adjusted exercise option price of 72 percent has a nominal exercise price of $54,720.)

Nominal interest rate: The interest rate that is stated on the face of a bond.

Nominal price: A price quotation given on a commodity future for a period in which no actual trading occurred.

Nominal quotation: A courtesy quote from a market maker. Not a firm bid or offer. Used when establishing a value for a security.

Nominal yield: The interest rate that is stated on the face of a bond. *(See also: COUPON RATE)*

Nominee: The role of the brokerage firm when securities are registered in the firm's name (street name).

Noncallable (NC):   A bond that cannot be redeemed by the issuer prior to maturity.

Nonclearing member: A member firm of an exchange that does not have the facilities necessary to settle securities for transfer and thus must pay a fee to a clearing member to have the service performed.

Noncompetitive bid: A bid for a minimum of $10,000 Treasury bills entered by smaller investors through a Federal Reserve Bank, the Bureau of Federal Debt or certain commercial banks.

Noncumulative preferred stock: A type of preferred stock that, should any dividend not be declared by the board of directors, the dividend would not be declared or paid at a later date. *(See also: CUMULATIVE PREFERRED STOCK)*

Noncurrent asset: An asset that is not readily convertible or expected to be converted to cash.

Nondiversified management company: A management company that has no restrictions in its choices of or concentrations in a security.

Nonguaranteed municipal bond: A municipal bond issued on the full faith and credit of the issuing authority that is not backed or guaranteed by any specific tax or income.

Nonmarketable security: A security for which no buyers can be found.

Nonmember firm: A brokerage firm that is not a member of any organized exchange and must execute transactions through a member firm.

Non-negotiable item: A securities certificate that has not been properly endorsed or lacks legal paperwork in order to make the certificate eligible for transfer to a new owner.

Nonparticipating preferred stock: Preferred stock that pays only the stipulated dividends. The most common type of preferred stock. *(See also: PARTICIPATING PREFERRED STOCK)*

Nonproductive loan: A type of commercial loan that does not lead to increased output but does increase spending power. (Example: a loan for the purpose of taking a public company private.)

Nonpublic information: Corporate news not yet known by the general public and usually, if known, would have an impact on the price of a corporation's stock. Also known as "insider information."

Nonpurpose loan: A loan collateralized by securities but not used for the purpose of purchasing other securities.

Nonqualifying annuity: An annuity that is not qualified under Federal IRS retirement plan rules and regulations.

Nonqualifying stock option plan: An employee stock option plan that does not qualify for favorable tax treatment. Any gain is fully taxed in the tax year in which the option is exercised.

Nonrecourse loan: The terms of a loan that states only the assets used as collateral for the loan are at risk in case of default and there shall be no further recourse allowed by the lender.

Nonrecurring charge: A one-time extraordinary charge, expense or write off in a company's financial statement.

Nonrefundable: A provision in a bond indenture that limits or prohibits the issuer from the use of retiring the bonds with proceeds of another bond issue (refunding issue).

Nonvoting stock: A class of company stock that does not have voting privileges attached for the shareholder.

No par value: A stock that has been issued without a stated (par) value.

Normal investment practices: The trading history of a brokerage client's account. Used to determine allocation requirements of a "hot issue."

Normal trading unit: 1) The usual number of units traded of a security. 2) The normal trading unit of stock is called a round lot, consisting of 100 shares of stock (an odd-lot is less than 100 shares). 3) The normal trading unit of a bond is $5,000. For options and commodities are contracts against underlying quantities, such as 5,000 bushels of wheat or an option contract on the Standard and Poor's 500 based on the performance of 500 stocks.

Note: A loan in which the borrower promises to repay the principal and pay the specified interest on demand or on a specified date, usually within two to ten years.

Not for profit: An organization that has no shareholder, trustee or custodian that shares in profits or losses, formed to provide goods or services (usually on a nonprofit basis). A not for profit group is exempt from corporate income tax but is subject to taxes on income producing properties or enterprises. (Examples: charitable hospitals, foundations and health care societies.)

Not held (NH): A term used to describe an order placed to a floor broker or market maker that permits limited discretion as to time or price while not holding the floor broker or market maker responsible for any errors in judgment.

Not rated (NR): A company or securities issue that has not been rated by a major rating service as to its financial stability (ability to pay its debts), has neither positive nor negative implications.

Novation: The replacement of one debt or obligation with another.

NOW account: An acronym for Negotiable Order of Withdrawal, a checking account combined with the features of a savings account to permit interest being paid on average balances.

NR: Not rated.

NSCC: National Securities Clearing Corporation.

Numbered account: An account titled with other than the owner's name, such as a number, symbol or special title. A "two or more" form must be signed by the owner designating ownership of the account.

Numbers only: The response given to a request for a nominal quotation used for valuation only that does not obligate the one giving the evaluation to make a transaction.

NYFE: New York Futures Exchange

NYSE: New York Stock Exchange.

NYSE composite index: A weighted index comprised of all common stocks traded on the New York Stock Exchange based on the close of trading December 31, 1965 as 50.00, weighted according to the number of shares listed for each issue and converted to dollars and cents in order to provide a meaningful measure of the average price changes.

NYSE maintenance call: The demand for a client to deposit additional funds or securities should equity in the client's margin account fall below NYSE minimum maintenance requirements.

NYSE maintenance requirement: The minimum amount of equity that must be maintained in a margin account at all times according to NYSE rules.

NYSE Rule 396:   The New York Stock Exchange rule that requires orders for limited bonds in quantities of nine bonds or less to be sent to the NYSE floor for possible execution before being sent to the over the counter market.

O: The newspaper's abbreviation for a security that trades over-the-counter.

OAR: Original accretion rate.

OB: Or better.

Obligation bond: A type of mortgage bond in which the securing property is valued less than the face amount of the bond. Used to compensate the seller for costs over and above the mortgage value.

Obligor: The entity, such as the issuer of a bond, who is responsible for the repayment of a debt when due, including interest.

OBO: Order book official.

OCC: Options Clearing Corporation.

OCC disclosure document: A document published by the Options Clearing Corporation that must be provided to each potential option trader prior to the time the investor is approved for option trading.

Odd lot: Shares of stock less than the established round lot number of 100. (Example: 1,347 shares of stock represent 13 round lots and an odd lot number of 47.)

Odd lot dealer: A dealer who executes odd lot orders for the commission plus the odd lot differential.

Odd lot differential: The additional amount, usually ⅛th of a point or 12.5 cents, that is often added per share on an odd lot execution.

Odd lot theory: The buyers and sellers of odd lots are usually the general public rather than "traders" or institutional buyers. The odd lot theory is an unproven, contrarian theory that recommends an action opposite of odd lot trading activities. (Example: If odd-lot sales are up, the theory says "sell," and if odd lot sales are down, the theory says "buy.")

Off-board: A transaction executed over the counter or executed but not on a national exchange.

Offer: The price of a security at which the owner is willing to sell. Also known as "asked." (*See also: BID*)

Offering: A primary or secondary offering of a security.

Offering circular: The official selling document highlighting the registration statement filed with the Securities and Exchange Commission.

Offering date: The date on which a new issue of securities will be available for sale to the public.

Offering price: The price per share of a new or secondary offering of securities that will be offered for sale to the public.

Offering scale: The prices at which serial bonds will be offered for sale to the public. Usually expressed as yields to maturity.

Offering statement: A document restricted to Regulation A offerings that contains information about a corporation's issue of securities similar to, but briefer than, information available in a prospectus.

Offer wanted (OW): An indication by a market maker or potential buyer of a security who is looking for a seller of the security.

Off-floor order: An order to buy or sell a security that is originated off the floor of an exchange, usually by the client of a broker-dealer. Exchange rules state all off floor orders are to be executed before a floor broker's orders for his or her own account.

Office of Management and Budget (OMB): The Office of the President agency responsible for: a) preparation and presentation of the presidential budget; b) development of a fiscal program for administration of resulting Congressional appropriations, developed jointly with the Council of Economic Advisers and the Treasury Department; c) reviewing of administrative policies and performance of government agencies; and d) the advising of the president on legislative matters.

Official notice of sale: A notice, often published in the "Daily Bond Buyer," inviting investment bankers to submit competitive bids for an upcoming municipal bond issue.

Official statement: A document, much like a prospectus, published by municipal bond issuers giving pertinent facts about the issue. The document, or a summary thereof, is required to be sent to purchasers of the issue.

Offset: 1) An equal and opposite transaction resulting in a flat position. (Example: The purchase of shares of stock originally sold short.) 2) A transaction initiated as a hedge to protect against or lessen the risk of loss of capital.

Offshore: 1) Drilling for oil and gas that is done in seawater. 2) Any financial organization domiciled outside the United States.

Off the shelf: An initial or secondary offering that has been preregistered and is available for purchase.

OID: Original issue discount.

Oil and gas limited partnership: A partnership including one or more general partners and one or more limited partners engaged in the business of: a) finding, b) drilling and/or c) marketing oil and gas.

Oil and gas lottery: A lottery run by the Bureau of Land Management at the U.S. Department of the Interior, permitting anyone filing an application to be selected for the right to drill for oil and gas on selected parcels of federal land. The winner of a lottery may sublet the property to an oil drilling company.

Oil depletion allowance: A percentage of income from the gross revenues generated by the sale of gas and oil from a producing property that, when allowed by federal law, is tax-free to the investor.

Old money: Dividends of preferred stock of domestic companies that, if issued prior to October 1, 1942, qualify for a 60 percent dividend exclusion, if held by another domestic company. "New money" on preferred stock issued after that date is eligible for an 85 percent dividend exclusion, if held by another domestic corporation.

Oligopoly: A situation in which all providers of the same goods or services work together in controlling the supply which in turn controls prices. (Example: Airline companies flying the same air routes.)

Oligopsony: A situation in which all buyers of the same goods or services control the demand which in turn controls the price. (Example: Oil processors who purchase the output of small producers.)

OMB: Office of Management and Budget.

Omitted dividend: A dividend that was scheduled but was not declared by the board of directors of a company.

On a scale: An order to buy or sell a security at specified price variations. (Example: A broker-dealer client places an order to sell 5,000 shares of stock, 1,000 at a time at ⅛th point intervals.)

FIGURE 17.   On-Balance Volume

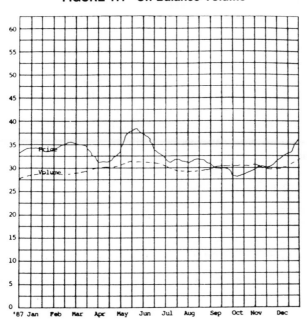

On-balance volume: A technical analysis that superimposes the volume line on the price line. Is said to be a buy signal when accumulation is detected and a sell signal when disbursement is detected. Figure 17.

One cancels the other: Two simultaneous orders given to a registered representative by a client for the purchase or sale of a security with instructions to cancel one order should the other execute.

On-floor order: An order originated by and for the account of a floor broker, so designated because off floor orders take precedence over on floor orders.

Ongoing buyer or seller: An order to purchase or sell a large quantity of a security that is accomplished over an extended period of time in order to keep the price from changing dramatically.

On margin: A long purchase or short sale in a margin account.

On the sidelines: Said of an investor that is not actively trading in any security and is waiting "on the sidelines" for what is felt to be a better trading opportunity.

OPD: An indication on the ticker tape which is: 1) A term used to designate trading in a security has been delayed beyond the normal opening time. 2) A change of more than $1.00, if under $20.00, or $2.00, if over $20.00, in the price of a security from the previous day's close.

Open: To establish or begin a position.

Open-end management company: A mutual fund management company that continually issues new shares of the mutual fund for purchase by the investing public. (Caution: Even though an open end management company is allowed to continually issue new shares, there is always a possibility the fund may close to new investors and continue open only to current shareholders.This situation is because a large amount of money is being invested in the fund so that a "cap" must be implemented in order to continue proper management.)

Open-end mortgage bond: A mortgage bond in which the indenture permits the issuance of other bonds, using the same property as collateral. All bondholders would have equal and proportionate claims in the case of default.

Opening: 1) The price at which a stock, option or commodity starts trading at the start of a business day. 2) A short term opportunity to take a desired action. Also known as a "window of opportunity."

Opening transaction: The execution of a transaction that creates a new or additional position for the client and does not close or hedge any other position of the client.

Open interest: The number of outstanding option or commodity futures contracts that have not been offset, exercised or expired.

Open market operations: The Federal Open Market Committee buying and selling of government securities for the purpose of increasing or decreasing the money supply.

Open market rates: The interest rates on various debt instruments that are bought and sold in the open marketplace and priced as a direct result of supply and demand.

Open order: An order to buy or sell a security that is to stay in effect until executed or cancelled by the client. Also known as a "good till cancelled order."

Open outcry: The method of trading in a pit on a commodity exchange. (Example: A trader enters the live cattle trading pit, shouts out a particular price to buy a number of contracts, another trader shouts back acceptance of price constituting the consummation of a contract.)

Open repo: An unspecified repurchase date of a repurchase agreement that can be terminated at any time by either party.

Operating lease: A type of lease in which the term is usually much shorter than the average life of the equipment and usually specifies that the maintenance and servicing is the responsibility of the lessor. (Example: Copiers, computers and cars normally are leased on an operating lease.)

Operating leverage: The use of borrowed capital to increase earnings.

Operating profit or (loss): The difference between business revenues and expenses, not including income from other sources or deductions before income.

Operating ratio: The ratio of operating expenses to net sales.

Operations department: The back office personnel of a brokerage firm where all clerical functions are performed for security executions—clearance, settlement, record keeping and monitoring of margin accounts.

OPM: Other people's money.

OPOSSMS: An acronym for Options to Purchase Or Sell Specific Mortgage-backed Securities.

Opportunity cost: The estimated dollar difference of the expected results between two investments. (Example: A bond with an annual yield of eight percent, compared to a stock that pays an annual dividend of three percent where the price is expected to increase substantially, would have an opportunity cost of five percent. The client would give up the additional five percent yield on the bond in order to speculate on the growth of the stock.)

Opposite side: An order to a) buy a security that is being sold or b) sell a security that is being bought. Also known as a "match."

OPRA: Options Price Reporting Authority.

Option: The right to buy or sell a quantity of a security at a specified price within a specified period of time. *(See also: CALL OPTION, PUT OPTION)*

Option agreement: A brokerage firm form requiring the details of a client's financial position and outlining the rules and regulations of option trading that must be completed and signed by the client, then approved by the brokerage firm, prior to any option trading activity.

Optional dividend: A dividend that may be paid either in cash or in additional stock at the option of the shareholder.

Optional payment bond: A bond that the interest and/or the principal are payable in one or more foreign currencies at the option of the holder.

Option credit spread: An option strategy where the premium difference of the purchase and sale of the two option positions results in a credit to the client.

Option debit spread: An option strategy where the premium difference of the purchase and sale of the two option positions results in a debit to the client.

Option holder: Someone who has bought a put or a call option that has not yet been sold, exercised or expired.

Option mutual fund: A mutual fund using put or call option trading techniques in order to increase the return of the fund.

Option premium: The amount per underlying security that is paid for the purchase or sale of a put or call option. (Example: A premium of $2.00 for an option on 100 shares of stock would have a total cost, not including commissions, of $200.)

Options Clearing Corporation (OCC):   The exchange-owned corporation that handles all clerical and mechanical duties of options trading, such as record keeping, exchange of money and issuance of option contracts. Also includes guaranteeing payments to both sides of an option transaction.

Option series: All put or call options on the same underlying security with the same strike price and expiration date. (Example: An option series would include all XYZ January 25 calls.)

Option spread: The simultaneous purchase and sale of options of the same class (put or call). A spread may have different expiration dates and/or different strike prices. (Example: The buy of an XYZ May 25 call and the sale of an XYZ August 30 call.)

Options Price Reporting Authority (OPRA):   The subscription service that provides option transactions and quotations.

Option writer: The seller of a put or a call option.

Or better (OB):   A limit order placed to remind the floor broker that the current price might be better than the limit amount.

Order: An instruction by a client to buy or sell securities.

Order book official (OBO):   An employee of the Chicago Board Options Exchange or of the Philadelphia or Pacific stock exchanges who accept orders for options that cannot be executed immediately. Once the order can be filled, the OBO notifies the member firm the order was executed on an agency basis.

Order department: The brokerage firm department responsible for the transmittal of an order to its proper destination.

Order ticket: A form completed by a broker that lists all information necessary to execute an order for a client, such as buy or sell, trading exchange, number of units desired, name of security, price, time in force and account number.

Ordinary income: Income that is not qualified by the federal government as long-term capital gains.

Ordinary interest: Simple interest based on a 360-day year (12 months times 30 days per month), rather than the "exact interest," based on a 365-day year.

Organization chart: The chart showing the interrelationships of positions within an organization.

Original accretion rate (OAR): The percentage rate set at issue at which a zero coupon bond accrues.

Original issue discount (OID): A bond issued at a discount from par (face) value. An OID issued without coupons is a "zero coupon" bond. (Caution: Federal tax rules are very complicated concerning OID and zero coupon bonds. Consult a tax attorney, accountant or other qualified financial adviser regarding tax consequences.)

Original maturity: The interval of time between the date a bond is issued and the date it matures. Also known as "current maturity."

Originator: The entity that originally arranged a loan, such as a mortgage or equipment loan.

OTC: Over-the-counter.

OTC margin stock: OTC stock which is marginable.

OTC option: A put or call option that is not listed on an options exchange, but is traded over the counter.

Other income: Income listed on a balance sheet not derived by the distribution of goods or services but by other means, such as profit from sale of assets or interest from investments.

Other people's money (OPM): Slang used when funds are borrowed by an individual or company, using "other people's money" to make higher returns.

Out for a bid: Municipal bonds that are being solicited for sale from a dealer through a broker to a client.

Out of favor: A security or industry that is not a currently favored investment. (Example: Transportation stocks would be "out of favor" during periods of extremely high energy costs.)

Out of line: The price of a security that is out of proportion to others in the same general category.

Out-of-the-money: A put or call option that has no intrinsic value, but may have time premium. (Example: A July 50 call option against a stock currently selling at 48 would be out of the money.)

Outright purchases or sales: An expression that refers to the net purchases or sales of government securities by the Federal Open Market Committee. Does not include any repurchase or reverse repurchase agreements.

Outside director: A member of the board of directors but not an actual employee of the company.

Out-sourcing: The business practice of shopping the world for the cheapest supplier of parts, manufacturing processes or other products and services.

Outstanding stock: Issued stock of a company that is in the hands of the public. Does not include any treasury stock held by the company itself.

Out the window: A term used to describe a new issue that has substantially risen in price. Also called a "blowout" and a "hot issue."

Overall market price coverage: An indication of the extent the market value a particular class of securities is covered in the event of bankruptcy or liquidation.

Over alloting: The sale of more shares of a new issue than are offered for purchase, resulting in a net short position of the selling dealer.

Overbanked: A phrase used to describe the situation where more shares of a new issue than are being offered for sale have been alloted to members of the selling team. A procedure used to ensure the complete distribution of the shares even should a selling member drop out of the syndicate.

Overbooked: A term used to describe a new issue with more indications of interest than there are units available to be purchased.

Overbought: A phrase used to indicate that, due to an excessive amount of buy orders, a security or the market as a whole is "too high" and is quite likely to have a correction on the down side.

Overhang: A large block of securities that, if bought or sold, would put pressure on prices. (Example: An option block nearing expiration that needs to be sold. But if the entire block were to be sold at the same time, the price would go down substantially.)

Overhead: The costs of a business not directly attributed to the production of the goods or services. Also called "indirect costs."

Overheated: An economic term used to describe the situation where too much money chases too few goods. Usually a forerunner of inflation.

Overissue: The issuance of more shares of stock than are authorized by a company's charter.

Overlapping debt: Municipality residents that are subject to be taxed by more than one taxing authority or district.

Overnight position: The net long or short positions held at the end of a business (trading) day.

Overnight repos: An overnight repurchase agreement. (Example: A financial institution with excess cash will buy interest bearing instruments with the understanding the institution will sell them back the next day.)

Oversold: A term used to indicate that, due to an excessive amount of sell orders, a security or the market as a whole is "too low" and is quite likely to have a correction on the up side.

Oversubscribed: A term used to describe a new issue with more indications of interest than there are units available to be purchased. Also known as "overbooked."

Over-the-counter (OTC): A highly sophisticated telephone network among dealers set up for the purpose of executing transactions for clients in securities that are not listed on any exchange. All mutual funds, government bonds and all other nonlisted stocks and bonds are traded on the over-the-counter network.

Overtrading: The excessive buying and selling of securities in a client's account. Also known as "churning."

Overvalued: A security in which the high price is not justified by the present earnings outlook, PE ratio or financial strength.

Overwriting: A speculative technique used by an option seller who believes a security price is too high and writes a large quantity of put or call options, hoping the price of the underlying security will correct and the options won't get exercised.

OW: Offer wanted.

Owner: The individual or group having possession of an asset and/or debt security.

p: Used to designate put options being reported (lowercase).

P&L: Profit and loss statement.

P&S: Purchase and sales department.

Pacific Stock Exchange (PSE): One of the regional stock exchanges with trading floors both in Los Angeles and San Francisco that trades stocks and options listed on that exchange as well as many stocks and options listed on other exchanges.

Pac-Man strategy: The strategy used as a takeover defense that involves the target company starting to "eat up like a Pac-Man" or buy shares of stock in the potential acquirer's company to thwart the takeover efforts. Named after a computer game that tries to consume others but can also be consumed itself.

Paid-in capital/surplus: The portion of stockholders' equity that has been generated through the issuance of stock above its stated value or through assets acquired as gifts.

Painting the tape: The frequent buying and selling of a security (could be but not necessarily the result of manipulation), that results in repeated appearances on the ticker tape.

Paired stock: Common stock of two companies under the same parent company or manager that are sold as one unit, usually with one certificate being issued with the information on one company on the front and the other company on the back. Also called "Siamese stock" and "stapled stock."

Paper: Slang for short-term debt securities.

Paper profit (loss):   Unrealized profit or loss on securities or assets still owned or held.

Paper tiger: An investment that looks outstanding on paper but in reality has no merit.

Par: 1) Common stock: A dollar amount assigned on a per share basis by the company charter. Has no relationship to market value. 2) Debt securities (bonds and/or preferred stock): The amount that signifies the dollar value upon which dividends are figured. Also known as "face value."

Par bond: A bond that is selling at 100 percent of face value.

Parent company: A company who owns the securities of another, usually with voting control.

Paris club: Belgium, Canada, France, Italy, Japan, the Netherlands, Sweden, the United Kingdom, the United States and West Germany, who organized to try to coordinate monetary and fiscal policies to promote a more stable world economic system. Also known as "the group of ten."

Parity price: The price or ratio by which two items are compared or pressed to each other. (Example: 1) U.S. farm crop prices are pegged to farmer's purchasing power prices in order to determine the percentage of parity, if any, the government will subsidize or 2) The price of a stock that, should a convertible bond be converted, would equal the value of the conversion.)

Parking: 1) The placement of assets in a safe investment, such as a savings account, while other investments are being considered. 2) The transfer of the registration of an individual from one employer to another so, at a later date, the employee may be rehired by the original employer without having to go through new registration examinations. 3) An illegal practice in which a dealer sells securities to another dealer to reduce its net capital requirements and in which the securities are later brought back at a price to compensate the other dealer for the cost of carrying the security.

Partial delivery: The term used when only a portion of the required amount is delivered. (Example: A brokerage firm client sold 1,000 shares of stock and only made a partial delivery of 500.)

Partial fill: An order to buy or sell a security in which only a portion of the number requested was executed. (Example: An order was placed to buy 25 call options, 15 were bought leaving a balance of ten not executed.)

Participate but do not initiate:　An order placed with the floor broker to buy or sell a large order that states "do not initiate a new price," to let the price be determined by market action.

Participating preferred stock:　An unusual issue of preferred stock that offers the holder a share of the earnings remaining after all senior securities have been paid in a form of "additional dividend." May be cumulative, noncumulative or convertible.

Participating trust:　A unit investment trust (plan company) that issues shares representing an interest in an underlying mutual fund investment to form the basis for a contractual-type mutual fund. Investors receive a prospectus for the plan company and a prospectus for the mutual fund shares.

Participation certificate:　A certificate representing ownership in a pool of funds or other instruments. (Example: A Ginnie Mae mortgage pool is a participating certificate.)

Partnership:　An organization in which two or more participants are equally and personally liable for the debts of the organization and share equally in the profits or (losses).

Par value (PV):　1) Common stock—a dollar amount assigned on a per share basis by the company charter. Has no relationship to market value. 2) Debt securities, including bonds and/or preferred stock—the amount that signifies the dollar value on which dividends are figured. Also known as "face value."

Par value of currency:　The ratio of one foreign currency to another, defined by the official exchange rate between the two companies.

Passed dividend:　A dividend not declared by the board of directors even though it was expected or regularly declared in the past.

Passive activity:　Any activity involving the conduct of a trade or business in whose operations the taxpayer does not "materially participate" on a regular and continuous basis, such as a limited partnership.

Passive assets:　Assets that produce no income.

Passive bond:　A bond that yields no interest. Usually used when raising money for charity.

Passive income (loss):　Gain or (loss) realized as the result of activities not "materially participated" in by the investor. Passive (loss) may be offset against taxes only by passive income.

Pass-through security:　A bond or other type of investment that takes all net income and passes the amount on a pro-rata basis to all investors. (Example: A mortgage bond passes all net income received from mortgage payments, prepayments and foreclosures from the trustee to the bondholders.)

Payback period: The amount of time required to recoup the cost of a capital investment.

Paydown: The amount saved by the refunding of a bond by a company through the issuance of a smaller new bond issue, usually issued at a smaller interest rate than the original. (Example: The paydown is the amount saved when a company issues a $50,000,000 bond with a seven percent yield in order to refund a $75,000,000 bond with a 12½ percent yield.)

Paying agent: A trustee who receives funds from the issuer of a security in order to pay the principal, interest or dividends to the security holder. (Example: Money is received by a bank (trustee) from a bond issuer in order for the trustee to pay the interest due on the bonds.)

Payment date: The date on which a periodic payment is due to be paid, such as bond interest or stock dividend.

Payment versus delivery (PVD):   The trading situation by which the certificate of a security sold and the net proceeds of the sale switch hands in a simultaneous transaction.

Payout ratio: The percentage of a company's profits that are paid out to shareholders in the form of a dividend.

Pay-through bonds: A mortgage debt security backed by a pool of mortgages owned by the issuer. Payback is accomplished by distribution of the interest and principal from the pool of mortgages much like a pass-through certificate.

Pay up: 1) A term said to an investor who must pay additional funds as the result of a purchase cost exceeding the proceeds of a sale. 2) Term used when borrower must pay higher than prevailing interest rates. 3) The situation that occurs when an investor misses the purchase of a security at a desired price and must pay a higher price in order to buy. 4) Said of an investor who pays what is considered a premium for a security in order to buy shares in what the investor feels is a solid company.

P/E: Price-to-earnings ratio.

Pegging: Trading in a new security for the purpose of stabilizing its price above the established offering price. Also known as "fixing."

Penalty plan: Slang used by critics of a contractual mutual fund plan in which an investor is subject to severe penalty should the contractual plan not be completed.

FIGURE 18:   Pennant

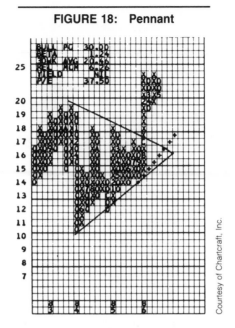

Courtesy of Chartcraft, Inc.

Penalty syndicate bid: A price stabilizing bid offered by the syndicate manager to the syndicate members with the stipulation that selling concessions will be withheld and penalties assessed against any members whose customers reoffer the shares to the manager.

Pennant: A technical chart pattern formed by prices becoming less volatile (considered to be consolidating), characterized by diminishing trade volume. Supposedly after a pennant pattern form is completed, prices should rise or fall sharply. Figure 18.

Penny stock: A security priced at under $1 per share, considered speculative. (Caution: Penny stocks are usually fairly new ventures and may not be "blue skied" or registered by the Securities and Exchange Commission. It is best to check with an investment broker as to the status of penny stocks.)

Pension Benefit Guaranty Corporation (PBGC): A federal corporation established in 1974 to guarantee basic pension benefits in covered plans by administering terminated plans and placing liens on corporate assets for certain pension liabilities that were not funded.

Pension fund: A fund set up by a corporation, organization or business owner to pay the pension benefits of retired workers.

Per capita debt: Total bonded debt of a municipality as divided by its population. Used to determine the expected probability of the municipality's debt repayment.

Percentage order: An order placed by a client to a broker to buy or sell a security at a limit or market price only after a certain number of the securities have been traded.

Perfect competition: A theoretically ideal situation in which no buyer or seller of goods or services has the power to change the market price.

Perform: To act, carry out, execute, achieve or fulfill. Usually used to mean a company, security or the market as a whole is expected to grow or rise in value.

Performance fund: A mutual fund that invests in growth or performance stocks that are expected to grow rapidly in value and pay little or no dividends. Considered to have investment risk in direct proportion to the amount of growth projected.

Performance stock: A stock that is expected to have a substantial rise in value. Usually pays little or no dividend as profits, if any, are used for expansion. Also called a "growth stock."

Periodic payment plan: A plan to accumulate shares of a mutual fund through the use of fixed periodic investments, usually monthly or quarterly, in order to take advantage of dollar cost averaging.

Periodic purchase deferred contract: An annuity contract in which the owner makes periodic payments (premiums) over a period of time and in which the contract does not begin paying out (annuitize) until a future date as specified by the owner. The premiums may or may not cease at the time of annuitization.

Period of digestion: The period of time following the issuance of a new security in which the price becomes "digested" or fairly stabilized.

Perpendicular spread: The simultaneous purchase or sale of put or call options with the same expiration date but with different strike prices.

Perpetual bond: A bond with no maturity date that pays interest perpetually. A very rare security—the only notable issue in existence is one used to refund smaller issues that were used to finance the Napoleonic Wars in 1814.

Perpetual warrant: A warrant that gives the holder the right to purchase a specific number of shares of the underlying security at a specific price with no expiration date.

Personal property: Assets other than real estate that are owned by an individual.

Petrodollars: Dollars paid to worldwide oil producing companies and deposited in Western banks.

Phantom income: Income that is accrued but not paid and that, if not sheltered, is subject to income tax.

Phantom stock plan: An executive bonus plan in which future bonus compensations are tied to the dollar value increase of a company's stock and paid in the form of stock options or in cash as if the executive actually owned the stock.

Philadelphia Stock Exchange (PHLX):   A regional stock exchange.

Physical commodity: An actual commodity that is delivered to the buyer upon completion of a commodity contract in either the spot or futures market. (Example: Gold, live cattle, soybeans, frozen concentrated orange juice and lumber are all physical commodities.)

Pickup: The value gained as the result of a bond swap.

Pickup bond: A bond with a high coupon rate that is relatively close to a call date having a redemption premium. (Example: A bond callable in six months at 103 percent of face value with a coupon rate four percent higher than rates currently being offered will likely be called by the issuer resulting in a gain for the bondholder if the bond is called.)

Picture: A term used when requesting bid and asked information from a market maker or specialist. (Example: "What's the picture on XYZ company?")

Piggyback registration: A securities offering in which a secondary, as well as a new issue, is offered. The offering prospectus includes all details of the offering, including the holders of the shares being offered as secondary.

Pink sheets: The daily quotation sheets publishing the interdealer wholesale quotes for over the counter stocks.

Pipeline: Securities that are in the process of being underwitten for an offering are said to be "in the pipeline."

Pit: An octagonal platform on the trading floor of a commodity's exchange, consisting of steps upon which traders and brokers stand while executing futures trades.

Place: The distribution of a public or private placement or new issues. (Example: Almost 50 percent of the new issue was "placed" to one institutional investor.)

Placement ratio: Compiled by the "Daily Bond Buyer," a ratio of the percentage of municipal bond new issues of $1 million or more that have been purchased during the previous week from underwriters.

Plan company: A Securities and Exchange Commission designated company registered as a participating unit investment trust sales organization that sells contractual-type funds on behalf of the fund's underwriters.

Plan completion insurance: A decreasing term insurance policy used to ensure completion of an investment plan, such as a contractual plan or private placement.

Plato: A system developed by the Control Data Company to provide computerized instruction and testing procedures. Many of the various tests required of security dealers are given on the Plato system.

Pledge: The transfer of property to a lender or creditor used as collateral. (Example: Securities are pledged to the brokerage firm by the holder of a margin account as collateral for positions held.) *(See also: HYPOTHECATION)*

Plow back: The reinvestment of a company's earnings into the business rather than being used to pay dividends.

Plus symbol (+): 1) Indicates a price that is higher than the previous trade. 2) Indicates the closing price of a security is higher than the previous day's closing price. 3) Indicates a Treasury bond quote including one additional 64th. (Example: A quote of 97 $^{12}/_{32}$ + indicates an actual quote of 97 $^{25}/_{64}$.)

Plus tick: A term used to signify a security has traded at a price higher than the previous trade.

Plus tick rule: The Securities and Exchange Commission regulation that states a short sale may only be executed at a price equal to or above the previous trade price. *(See also: UPTICK)*

POA: Power of attorney.

Point: The full (not fractional) change in the value of a security. (Examples: 1) Common stock: one point equals a one-dollar move. 2) Bond: one point equals a one percent move. 3) Market average: one point equals a full one point move. [On 1), 2) and 3), changes usually occur in fractions of points.] 4) Commodity futures contracts: any minimum unit in which changes in futures prices may fluctuate. Commodities may fluctuate in 32nds, fractions of cents, cents or multiples thereof, according to the trading terms of the individual commodity.)

Point and figure chart: A technical analysis using a graphic technique to follow the up and down movements in the price of a security. An X is placed on the chart on the next square up from the last square each time the price goes up and an 0 is placed on

FIGURE 19: Point and Figure Chart

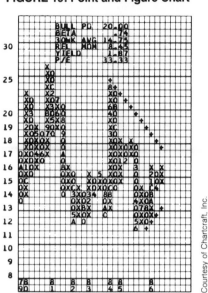

Courtesy of Chartcraft, Inc.

the next square down on the chart each time the price goes down. The resulting figure is used to indicate price movement patterns and momentum. Figure 19.

Poison pill: A strategy used by a takeover candidate to discourage a takeover attempt. (Example: a company might issue a type of preferred stock that, should a takeover occur, would be redeemable at a very high premium.)

Policy loan: Any loan by an insurance company using the contract's cash value as collateral. The amount available for borrowing, as well as the interest rate to be applied, are stated in the insurance contract.

Pool: A combination of like items or securities for a common purpose or benefit, such as a portfolio of bonds used to form a unit trust, a group of investors to combine resources to take over ownership of a company or a selection of mortgages combined for the issuance of pass-through certificates (Example: Ginnie Mae certificates).

Pooling of interests: Combining like items for a common purpose.

Pork bellies: Processed pork (bacon) traded in the cash and futures commodity markets.

Portfolio: The entire holdings, including debt and equity positions, of an individual or institution.

Portfolio BETA score: The volatility of an individual portfolio as a whole in comparison to the average of the BETA coefficients of the securities comprising the portfolio.

Portfolio construction financial risk: The risk of loss of principal or income that must be considered in the construction of a portfolio.

Portfolio manager: The individual responsible for the fiduciary functions in the management of a portfolio. Could be the manager of a mutual fund, individual portfolio, institutional portfolio or retirement plan. Usually manages for a set fee, a percentage of assets under control and/or percentage of gain.

Portfolio theory: Portfolio investment decisions based on four factors: a) security valuation, b) asset allocation, c) portfolio optimization, the rate of return as compared to the inherent risk and d) performance measurement. Shifts security analysis from individual issues to the portfolio as a whole.

Position: 1) The total holdings of an individual or group including all assets and/or securities owned (long) and borrowed (sold short). 2) To acquire a net long or short position. (Example: The client was trying to position XYZ company for addition to a portfolio.)

Position building: The purchase or selling of additional securities in order to increase a long or short position.

Position limit: The limit on the number of futures commodity or option contracts any one person may hold. Established by the exchanges on which the contracts are traded.

Position trader: A commodities trader who takes positions in contracts six months or more away from expiration.

Positive carry: The situation that occurs when the cost of borrowing to purchase securities is lower than the yield received on the securities.

Positive cash flow: The situation that exists when a company has more income than is required to pay liabilities.

Positive yield curve: The usual interest rate situation in which long term yields are higher than short term yields. *(See also: NEGATIVE YIELD CURVE)* Figure 20.

Post: 1) The transfer of information from one source to a recordkeeping source. (Example: When an investment broker "posts" trade information from confirmations to a client's account card.) 2) The horseshoe-shaped trading area in an exchange where specialists and floor brokers trade specific securities. An exchange consists of a number of trading posts that, when all securities traded in each

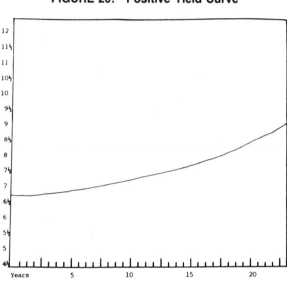

FIGURE 20:   Positive Yield Curve

post are added together, comprise the total securities listed for trading on the exchange.

Post 30:   A numbered post on the New York Stock Exchange floor where inactive listed preferred stocks are traded in ten share round lots rather than the usual 100 shares.

Pot: An underwriting term used to denote the number of securities returned by an investment banker to the managing underwriter to facilitate sales to institutional bankers.

Pot is clean: A managing underwriter's announcement to the underwriting group members that the securities held for institutional investors have all been sold.

Power of attorney (POA):   A written document that authorizes one person to act on behalf of another (the originator of the POA). May be a full or limited power of attorney.

Precedence: The ranking of auction bids and offers according to the time the order is entered then by size (number of shares to be bought or sold).

Precious metal complex: A classification of commodities, which are traded in the cash and futures market, consisting of such precious metals as gold, silver and platinum.

Preemptive right: The legal right of stockholders to purchase the number of shares of a new issue required to sustain proportionate ownership before the new issue is offered to the public.

Preference: An exchange floor term for the one who goes first in an auction impasse. Settled first by time then, if the brokers entered the crowd at the same time, by a flip of a coin.

Preference item: Tax preference item.

Preference shares: Previously issued preferred stock.

Preferred dividend coverage: A ratio used to determine how many times over a preferred dividend requirement is covered by current earnings. Figured by dividing the amount of preferred stock dividends by the net income after interest and taxes but before common stock dividends.

Preferred stock: An issue of stock that has qualities of both the debt and equity securities. Preferred stock has claims against assets before common stock but after lienholders and may or may not have voting rights attached. Dividends due on preferred stock must be paid before any dividends may be declared for common stockholders. Preferred stock may also be cumulative, participating or convertible.

Preferred stock ratio: The percentage of capitalization represented by preferred stock. Figured by dividing the total par value of the preferred stock by the total capitalization of a company.

Prefunding: The use of proceeds from the maturity of a second bond issue to pay the principal of a first bond issue at first call date.

Preliminary prospectus: The initial selling document that is distributed prior to final registration by the Securities and Exchange Commission (SEC) that includes all essential facts about a new issue with the exception of the underwriting spread, final public offering price and the date the securities will be delivered. *(See also: RED HERRING)*

Premature distribution: The paying of funds to an individual out of a qualified retirement account prior to the age of 59½. Subjects the individual to taxes and penalties.

Premium: 1) The amount by which a debt security is selling over and above its face value, expressed as a percentage (Example: A bond valued at 103 percent is selling at a three percent premium over par.) 2) The amount a stock's price exceeds that of comparable stocks. 3) The per-unit price of a put or call option times the number of units of the underlying security. (Example: An option with a premium of two on 100 shares of stock has a total cost, not including commission or fees, of $200.) 4) The amount by which the trading price of a new issue exceeds the offering price. 5) The amount by which a given futures quality of a spot commodity sells over another futures quality of spot price. 6) In general, an added amount over and above the normal.

Premium bond: A bond selling at a price higher than the par (face) value expressed as a percentage. (Example: A bond selling at 103 percent has a three percent premium.)

Premium income: Income received by an investor as the result of the writing (selling) of a put or call option in which the option either expires or is bought back at a lesser price.

Premium over bond value: The value of a convertible bond, when higher, as compared to the straight bond issued by the same company.

Premium over conversion value: The amount by which the market price of a convertible security exceeds the price at which it is convertible.

Premium raid: A surprise attempt to acquire control, but not ownership, of a company by the offer to purchase outstanding shares at a premium over market value. Any takeover attempt must be disclosed; therefore, only a desire to control can be accomplished by surprise.

Prepaid charge plan: Another name for a contractual mutual fund in which the total sales charge is paid in the early years of the plan.

Pre-payment: Payment of a debt before the actual maturity date.

Pre-payment penalty: A fee that must be paid by the borrower in the event of prepayment of a debt, as and if stipulated in the loan contract.

Presale order: An order to purchase a portion of a new municipal bond issue prior to the public offering. A legal maneuver as municipal bond issues are exempt from SEC registration.

Present value: The value of a future payment or amount expressed in today's dollar value after inflation has been taken into account. (Example: The value of a $100 bill in 20 years may only be $23.00 after the effects of inflation have been taken into consideration.)

President: The company officer higher in rank to any other officer excluding the Chief Executive Officer (CEO). The CEO is usually either chairman of the board or president of the company.

Presidential election cycle theory: A theory by some investment advisors that major stock market moves can be predicted, based on the four year presidential election cycle. Supposedly, the first few months of a newly elected or re-elected president sees lower market prices because of unpopular presidential actions and decisions. During the following two years the stock market should show a general rise in the economy, followed by a recession during the time remaining before the next election, which starts the cycle over again.

Presold issue: An issue of government or municipal bonds that have been completely sold prior to a public announcement of the next issue. Corporate bonds may not be presold as corporate bonds must be registered by the Securities and Exchange Commission (SEC) and must adhere to the rules stating the presale of registered securities is illegal. Municipal and government bonds are exempt from SEC registration requirements.

Pretax earnings/profits: Net income before federal taxes have been taken into consideration.

Pretax rate of return: The yield or capital gain before federal taxes have been taken into consideration.

Price (PX):   The amount of money or goods for which an asset, security or other item is bought or sold.

Price change: The difference in the price of a security either from the last trade, the closing price from the previous business day or other reference point.

Price gap: A term used if one day's price range does not overlap the price range of the previous day. (Example: A stock with a price range of 15 to 16 on one day and 16½ to 17 the next day is said to have a "price gap.")

Price limit: The price at which a limit order is placed.

Price range: The high and low prices of a security as traded over a period of time.

Price spread: The simultaneous purchase and sale of two options on the same security with the same expiration date but with different exercise price. *(See also: MONEY SPREAD; TIME SPREAD; VERTICAL SPREAD)*

Price support: A government-set price floor of produce or goods that, should the price drop below the floor level, the government guarantees to subsidize the difference to the producer.

Price talk: 1) An informal discussion among underwriters about the price range that will be offered on a negotiated issue or bid on a competitive issue. 2) The maximum offering price of a first-time public sale of a security as stated in the preliminary prospectus.

Price-to-earnings ratio (P/E):   The price of a share of stock divided by the annual earnings per share. Used to compare stocks selling at various price levels. (Example: A stock that has earnings per share of $1.25 currently trading at 18¾ has a PE of 15.)

Price-weighted index: An index in which the components are weighted by their price. The higher the price, the greater percentage impact on the index.

Pricey: An unrealistic bid or offer considering the market value of the security at the time the bid or offer is made. (Example: An order placed to buy a stock at $25.00 when the stock is currently selling at $42.00.)

Primary dealer: One of the banks authorized by the Federal Reserve Bank to buy and sell government securities.

Primary distribution: The original public offering of a company's securities, with the total net proceeds going to the issuing company.

Primary earnings per (common) share: Net earnings divided by the number of outstanding common shares.

Primary market: The market in which new issues of stock, option, government securities and futures contracts are bought and sold.

Primary movement: An initial strong movement, either up or down, in the price of a security or the market as a whole.

Primary offering: The initial offering by a company of an issue of securities to the buying public with the use of an underwriter.

Prime paper: Commercial paper of the highest quality as rated by an independent rating service. Considered investment grade and is therefore eligible for investment by those with fiduciary responsibilities.

Prime rate: The lowest possible interest rate a lending institution will charge its most creditworthy customers. Other loan rates at the lending institution are usually tied to its prime rate.

Principal: 1) The amount of invested capital. 2) The person for whom a broker executes an order. 3) Dealers trading for their own accounts.

Principal amount: The face value of a debt instrument that must be repaid to the holders upon maturity.

Principal stockholder: A stockholder who owns ten percent or more of the voting stock of a corporation and must be registered with the Securities and Exchange Commission is considered an insider and must report any trading activity in the company's stock.

Print: Slang used to denote the records of securities transactions that appear on exchange tapes.

Priority: First person in an auction to bid or offer at a given price.

Prior lien bond: A bond that has prior claim over all other bonds issued by the company. Usually issued as the result of a reorganization due to insolvency or bankruptcy.

Prior preferred stock: A class of preferred stock that has prior claim over all other preferred stocks issued by the company.

Private limited partnership: A partnership that is exempt from registration by the Securities and Exchange Commission (SEC) by limiting the amount of accredited investors (those investors who meet certain financial and experience qualifications). (Caution: The number of investors as well as the qualification rules are subject to change. Consult with a tax attorney prior to the formation or investment in a "private limited partnership.")

Private placement: A conditional offering of nonregistered securities, the requirements of the offering must be strictly followed. (Caution: The various laws pertaining to private placements change fairly often. Check with a tax attorney prior to the offering of or investment in a private placement.)

Probate: The judicial process by which the will of a deceased person is presented to the court and an executor(trix) or administrator is appointed to carry out the instructions of the decedent.

Proceeds: Money received by a borrower or a seller after all fees or charges have been deducted.

Proceeds sale: The simultaneous sale and purchase of a security accomplished as one transaction. The proceeds of the sale are used to pay for the purchase in order to accomplish a "swap" and establish a gain or loss in a tax year.

Producer Price Index (PPI): A monthly report issued by the U.S. Department of Labor Statistics that measures the change in wholesale price. Formerly called the "wholesale price index."

Production rate: The coupon rate of a Government National Mortgage Association (Ginnie Mae) pass through certificate.

Profit: The net difference between the purchase and the selling price of an asset or other security when the selling price is higher than the purchase price.

Profitability: The ability of a company to generate sufficient income to pay expenses and liabilities while having excess funds as profit.

Profit and loss statement (P&L): A summary of the income and operating expenses of a company during an accounting period, usually quarterly or annually.

Profit center: A segment or subsidiary of a company or corporation that is profitable on its own. (Example: A company manufactures three items of which two are profitable or profit centers.

Profit margin: A ratio that is used to determine the operating efficiency of a business, calculated by dividing the operating profit by net sales.

Profit-sharing plan: A type of KEOGH (retirement plan) fund set up by a company, organization, business owner or other entity funded from profits to pay the pension benefits of retired workers.

Profit taking: 1) The sale of an asset in order to realize a gain. 2) An explanation given when there is a general downtrend in the marketplace after a period of high prices.

Profit zone: The estimated area of profitability after all expenses have been taken into consideration.

Pro forma: Latin for "as a matter of form or custom." Refers to a presentation of figures based on hypothetical facts and figures. (Example: A group of investors are presented with a pro forma balance sheet on a proposed limited partnership offering.)

Program trading: A systematic or computerized system of buying and selling investments.

Progressive tax: A tax that takes increasingly larger percentages of the income of individuals as their income levels increase.

Projection: An estimate of future performance by an expert in the field being analyzed. (Example: A securities analyst bases a projection of possible earning power of a particular company on research of the company.)

Project link: An econometric model linking all world economics used to forecast the effects a change in one country's economy will have on the economy of another.

Project note (PN): A type of municipal short-term security issued to provide temporary funds. These include anticipation notes on taxes (TANs), bonds (BANs) and revenue (RANs).

Promissory note: A loan in which the borrower promises to repay the principal and pay the specified interest on demand or on a specified date.

Properly executed assignment: A security certificate that is endorsed exactly as the certificate is registered.

Proprietorship: A business organization in which only one person has total ownership and control over the business and makes all business decisions.

Pro rata/pro rata basis: Calculated proportionately, usually for payment as to percentage of ownership.

Prospectus: The official selling document highlighting the registration statement filed with the Securities and Exchange Commission.

Protective covenant: The promise to perform all duties as required in a trust endenture or formal debt agreement.

Provision: A measure taken in advance against a future need. (Example: A cattle grower places a hedge position in order to make a provision against lower cattle prices.)

Proxy: The written authorization given by a shareholder to someone else for the purpose of representing the shareholder's voting privilege at the shareholders' meeting.

Proxy department: The department within a broker-dealer firm responsible for the distribution of proxy materials to owners of shares being held in street name.

Proxy fight: The technique used by an acquiring company to gain control of a company by soliciting enough proxy votes of shareholders to select a board of directors favorable to a takeover or merger.

Proxy statement: The information given to shareholders in connection with the solicitation of a proxy.

Prudent man rule: The state rule regarding investments by a fiduciary that requires investments be made in securities (according to state statute) of either: a) Those on a legal list provided by the state, or b) Investments a "prudent and intelligent" person would choose.

PSE: Pacific Stock Exchange.

Public housing authority bonds: The technical name for an issue of municipal bonds guaranteed by the full faith and credit of the U.S. government. Used to finance the construction of public housing.

Public limited partnership: A partnership registered with and subject to the rules and regulations of the Securities and Exchange Commission (SEC), consisting of one or more general partners and many limited partners. Formed to provide investment capital for such ventures as real estate, oil and gas, equipment leasing and others.

Publicly held: A corporation that has issued shares available to be bought and sold by the general public.

Public offering: The initial offering by a company of an issue of securities to the buying public with the use of an underwriter.

Public offering price: The price at which a new issue is offered to the public as established in the issuing corporation's prospectus.

Public Securities Association (PSA):   An association representing underwriters of municipal, U.S. government and federal agency debt securities, as well as dealers in mortgage backed securities.

Public Utility Holding Company Act of 1935:   Legislation that re-organized the financial structure and regulated the debt and dividend policies of holding companies in the gas and electric utility industries.

Purchase acquisition: The takeover of one company by another for cash or treasury stock purchased within the previous two years. When the cost exceeds the net tangible assets of the acquired corporation, the excess is considered goodwill and is amortized against future revenues over a 40-year period.

Purchase and sales department (P&S):   The brokerage firm department responsible for the computation of commissions and taxes, as well as the delivery of client confirmations.

Purchase and sale statement: A statement of account sent to a commodity futures trader upon the completion of a closing transaction showing the futures contract purchase price, selling price, commission charged, exchange fees and profit or (loss).

Purchase fund: A provision in a preferred stock contract or bond indenture requiring the issuer to provide at a maximum price or par value voluntary, but not mandatory, tender offers by which the holders may elect to redeem all or part of their holding.

Purchase group: A group of investment bankers formed to underwrite and distribute a new or secondary issue of securities. Also known as a "syndicate."

Purchasing power: 1) The dollar amount of additional securities that may be purchased using the balances in a margin account, including Special Miscellaneous Account (SMA), cash and other security values. 2) A measure of the amount of goods or services that a dollar can buy in relation to a prior period of time.

Purchasing power risk: The risk that a certain amount of money will not purchase the same amount of goods at some point in the future as could be purchased today.

Pure play: Slang for a company that provides only one product or service.

Purpose loan: A loan collateralized by securities with the proceeds used for the purpose of purchasing other securities under the Federal Reserve Board margin and credit regulations.

Purpose statement: A form required when a borrower uses securities as collateral. The purpose of the loan must be stated as well as an attestment that the loan will not be used to purchase, carry or trade securities.

Put: 1) A type of option contract giving the buyer the right to sell and the seller the obligation to buy a specific number of the underlying security at a specific price on or before a specific date. 2) The right by the holder of a debt security to redeem the security on a date specified by the indenture before the actual maturity date.

Put bond: A type of bond issue that allows the holder the option to redeem the bond at par (face) value at a time(s) specified in the bond indenture.

Put option: 1) The right by the buyer to sell and the obligation by the seller to buy a specific number of the underlying security for a specific price within a specified period of time. 2) The right by a bondholder to redeem a bond before maturity at face value at a time specified in the bond indenture.

Put to the seller: A term used when the buyer of a put option exercises the option and "puts" the underlying security to the seller at the exercise price of the option.

Putting on the crush: A commodity phrase used when soybean contracts are bought, and soybean meal and soybean oil contracts are sold. Usually a crush is put on by the producer of soybean meal and oil. *(See also: REVERSE CRUSH)*

PV: Par value.

PVD: Payment versus delivery.

PX: Abbreviation used to denote price.

Pyramid: A graphic illustration used in financial planning that shows the proportionate relationships of low, medium and high risk investments and approximate portions of funds which would ideally be invested in each. Low risk investments, shown as the base of the pyramid includes insurance, fixed income securities, CDs, savings and other safe items. The middle portion of the pyramid includes assets and investments in which there could be fluctuations in values, such as real estate and stocks. The top, and least proportionate share, of the pyramid includes investments, such as commodities and options of the highest risk in which all or more of the amount invested is at risk. Figure 21.

Pyramiding: 1) The use of leverage to increase possible gains (or losses). 2) The addition of more long positions as prices are drop-

FIGURE 21:   Pyramid

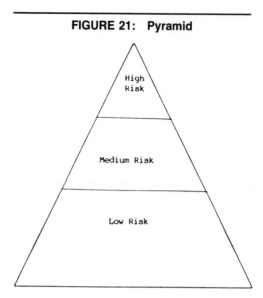

ping or more short positions as prices are rising in order to increase possible gain (or loss) potential. 3) A legal business marketing procedure in which distributorships are sold in conjunction with the sale of goods or services in order to increase market potential. 4) An illegal scheme by which new money being received as an investment is used to pay "earnings" to old money received as an investment.

Q: Signifies a company operating under federal bankruptcy law that will eventually be reorganized or liquidated.

QT: 1) Acronym for questioned trade, used when a detail of a securities transaction is unclear. 2) Abbreviation for fiscal quarter.

Q-tip trust: Acronym for qualified terminable interest property trust, which permits assets to be transferred between spouses. Usually used to provide for the welfare of a spouse while keeping the assets out of the estate of another (for instance, a future marriage partner) should the grantor die first.

Qualified opinion: Language that calls attention to a limitation or exception an auditor takes to items in a financial statement, presented as part of the accountant's opinion accompanying the financial statement.

Qualified retirement plan: A retirement plan that is qualified under Sections 401 and 501 of the Internal Revenue Code set up by an employer for the benefit of an employee upon retirement.

Qualifying annuity: An annuity approved by the Internal Revenue Service for the inclusion in a qualified retirement plan such as a Keogh or IRA.

Qualifying coupon rate: The current coupon rate of Ginnie Mae (Government National Mortgage Association) securities that determines whether previously issued Ginnie Maes shall be delivered at a premium or discount when settling a cash, forward (commodity) or option contract.

Qualifying share: The share of common stock required to be owned in order to qualify as a director of the issuing corporation.

Qualifying stock option plan: A stock option plan offered to employees that permits the purchase of a limited number of the company's stock at a special price under conditions spelled out in the Internal Revenue Service Code.

Qualitative analysis: An analysis of items of a company that cannot be precisely measured, such as morale, caliber of management and labor relations. *(See also: QUANTITATIVE ANALYSIS)*

Quality of earnings: The description of a corporation's earnings that are directly attributable to increased sales and cost controls rather than inflation or deflation.

Quantitative analysis: An analysis of items of a company that can be precisely measured, such as earnings, assets, costs and liabilities. *(See also: QUALITATIVE ANALYSIS)*

Quarterly: 1) A three-month period of time. 2) The usual time frame of dividend payments. 3) Basis of time on which earnings reports are made to shareholders.

Quarterly report: A financial statement covering a three-month period of time.

Quarter stock: Stock with a par value of $25.00 per share.

Quasi-public corporation: A privately run corporation that has publicly traded stock, some sort of public mandate and usually has the government's backing in issued debt securities. (Example: Federal National Mortgage Association and the Student Loan Marketing Association.)

Quick assets: Current assets minus inventory.

Quick ratio: A liquidity ratio figured by taking the total of cash, marketable securities and accounts receivable and dividing the figure by current liabilities. Also called "acid test ratio."

Quid pro quo: Latin for "something for something" a type of barter in which one party provides a good or service for which is received another good or service in return. (Example: A portfolio evaluation is provided at no cost if the client affects trades based on recommendations of the evaluation through the firm providing the service.)

Quotation board: An electronic reporting service to brokerage firms and others that displays current price quotation and other pertinent financial data such as dividend information, annual and daily price ranges as well as current trading volume.

Quote: The highest bid to buy and the lowest offer to sell a security at a given time on a given market.

Quoted price: The actual price at which a security or commodity last traded.

R&D: Research and development.

Radar alert: Close watch by senior company managers of unusual trading patterns that might indicate a takeover attempt.

Raid: An endeavor to take over the controlling interest of a company to simplify a takeover or merger attempt.

Raider: An individual or corporate investor who tries to gain controlling interest so that a management team friendly to a takeover or merger will be installed. (Caution: Any investor who owns five percent or more of a company's voting stock must register with the Securities and Exchange Commission, the listing exchange and the company itself.)

Rally: A sharp rise following a decline in the general price trend of the market or of an individual security.

RAN: Revenue anticipation note.

Random walk theory: A theory first hypothecated in 1900 by Louis Bachelier that stock and commodity futures past prices are no indication of future prices as prices reflect reaction to news and are therefore "no more reliable than the random walk of a drunken person."

Range: The difference between the high and low price of a security or commodity futures contract during a given period of time.

Rate base: The cost base of a utility, as regulated by the appropriate utility commission, on which the utility is allowed to earn a particular rate of return.

Rate covenant: A provision in a municipal revenue bond indenture that addresses the method of adjustment for the rates charged to the users of the project in order to provide for repair and maintenance, as well as the payment of interest and the repayment of principal on the bond issue.

Rate of exchange: The amount of currency of one country needed to convert to another country's currency.

Rate of inflation: The rate of rise in the general level of prices. *(See also: CONSUMER PRICE INDEX)*

Rate of return: The return on investment, whether in the form of dividends or interest, based on the price paid for the security.

Rating: 1) An evaluation of the financial worthiness of a company or a security issued by the company by an independent, disinterested third party. 2) The statistical analysis required to establish the premium for an insurance policy.

Ratio analysis: The comparison of figures taken from a balance sheet and/or financial statement by which conclusions are drawn. (Example: Acid test ratio, bond ratio, capitalization ratio, cash to equity ratio, dividend payout ratio, price to earnings ratio and return on equity ratio.)

Ratio spread: A hedging strategy in which the buyer of long call options sells more call options than are held. May be a bullish or bearish technique.

Ratio writer: An owner of a security who sells more call option contracts than are covered by the underlying security. (Example: An owner of 300 shares of XYZ Company sells five call options, three of which are covered (owned) and the remaining two are naked or not owned.)

Reaction: The downward price movement of a security or commodity as the result of adverse news or a sell program being implemented.

Reading the tape: The analysis of an individual security or the market as a whole by monitoring information as it is given on the ticker tape. *(See also: DON'T FIGHT THE TAPE)*

Real estate: Land, all physical attachments such as buildings, plants and fences as well as the air above and earth below. Any items not attached are considered personal property.

Real estate investment trust (REIT):   An organization with investments in real estate. The formation charter usually calls for as much as 90 percent of the earnings to be returned to the shareholders.

Real estate mortgage investment conduit (REMIC):   An entity formed to hold a fixed pool of mortgages secured by interests in real property. Created by the 1986 Tax Reform Act to clarify the tax treatment of entities that invest in multiple-class, mortgage-backed securities.

Real income: Income of any entity adjusted for changes in purchasing power due to inflation.

Real interest rate: The current interest rate less the inflation rate. (Example: An interest rate of eight percent less the inflation rate of three percent gives a real interest rate of five percent.)

Realized profit or (loss): When a profit or (loss) is realized either by a liquidating sale or the repurchase of a short sale.

Real property: Land and anything that is erected on, growing or affixed to the land.

Real rate of return: The rate of return of a security after tax liability has been taken into consideration.

Recapitalization: The alteration of a company's capital structure in order to improve cash flow, tax status or other adjustments. Accomplished by such means as preferred stock tenders, convertible bond tenders or exchange of capital stock for bonds.

Recapture: 1) A clause in some contracts allowing a party to recover a portion of assets. 2) An IRS rule that states depreciated assets sold for more than the depreciated value subjects the owner to gains tax.

Receivables: Money owed to a company by customers for goods and/or services charged on an open account.

Receiver: A court appointed trustee who takes over management responsibilities of a business or estate that is in receivership due to bankruptcy or one that is the subject of a legal battle.

Receivership certificate: A debt instrument issued by a receiver to finance continued operations of a company in receivership. Constitutes a lien on the property and is senior to all other secured or unsecured debt instruments.

Receive versus payment: Delivery of securities made to a buyer's account simultaneously in exchange for cash. Also known as "delivery versus payment," "cash on delivery" and "delivery against sale."

Recession: A downturn in the economy and economic activity. *(See also: ECONOMIC GROWTH RATE)*

Reciprocal immunity: The federal doctrine that says states and other municipalities must not tax federally owned properties and in return the federal government will not tax property owned by states and other municipalities. Also known as "mutual exclusion doctrine."

Reclamation: A corrective measure to recover a loss or correct a mistake.

Recommendation: Advice given by an authority or specialist regarding an investment.

Record date: The date on which a shareholder must be registered as the owner in order to receive a declared dividend, vote on company affairs or other ownership benefits.

Recourse loan: A loan that is backed, guaranteed or collateralized by more than the assets upon which the loan is based. *(See also: NONRECOURSE LOAN)*

Recovery: A period of time in which general prices and the economy pick up after a period of lower prices.

Redeem: To submit a debt security to the issuer for repayment of principal at par or premium at maturity or before according to the bond indenture.

Redeemable bond: A bond that may be redeemed by the issuing authority at a stated date(s) in the future prior to the maturity date listed on the face of the bond.

Redemption: The repayment of a debt security on or before the maturity date at par or a premium.

Redemption notice: A notice issued by the issuing corporation or municipality that a certain issue of bonds is being called (redeemed).

Redemption price: The price at which a bond may be redeemed prior to maturity at the option of the issuer as stated in the bond indenture.

Red herring: Slang for preliminary prospectus (the initial selling document) of a new issue that is distributed prior to final registration by the Securities and Exchange Commission. Called a red herring because a disclaimer statement is printed in red on the face of the document. *(See also: PRELIMINARY PROSPECTUS)*

Rediscount: The use of eligible collateral received by a member bank of the Federal Reserve System and pledged to the Federal Reserve, used by the member bank to secure borrowed funds.

Refinancing: The replacement of an old debt by the use of a new one. *(See also: REFUNDING)*

Refunding: The replacement of an old debt with a new one, usually accomplished when the new debt is able to be issued at a much lower rate than the issue being retired. (Example: A company issues bonds with a coupon rate of seven percent to retire a bond issue at 12 percent.)

Regional exchanges: The Boston, Cincinnati, Intermountain, Midwest, Pacific, Philadelphia and Spokane securities exchanges located outside New York City.

Regional fund: A mutual fund that limits its investments within a specified single industry or group of related industries. Also known as a "specialized mutual fund."

Registered bond: A bond issue in which each new and successive owner is registered in the books of the issuing authority.

Registered company: A company that has registered with and is subject to the rules and regulations of the Securities and Exchange Commission in connection with a public offering.

Registered competitive market maker: A member of the New York Stock Exchange who trades on the floor for his or her own or firm's account and who must, upon the request of a NYSE official, offer bid or offers from and for his or her own account in order to narrow a quote.

Registered competitive trader: A New York Stock Exchange member who trades for his or her own account, pays no commissions, but must abide by all exchange rules.

Registered coupon bond: A bond in which ownership is registered on the books of the transfer agent regarding the principal only. The coupons are not registered and must be presented to the transfer agent for interest payments.

Registered equity market maker: An American Stock Exchange (ASE) member who trades stock and options on the floor of the ASE.

Registered investment company: A company or trust that uses its own capital to invest in other companies. Is either closed end or an open end mutual fund, as described in the Investment Company Act of 1940.

Registered options principal (ROP): An officer or partner of a brokerage firm responsible for written approval of accounts that engage in certain types of option trading.

Registered options representative: A broker-dealer employee licensed to solicit clients and accept option trading orders.

Registered representative (RR): A person who has passed the General Securities Examination 7, registered with the exchanges on which trades are to be executed, is an employee of a firm licensed as a broker/dealer and who solicits orders for the purchase or sale of securities for the employer's clients, including subscriptions for investment management services furnished by the employer. Also known as "stock broker," "investment broker," "investment adviser," "RR," "broker" and "account executive."

Registered secondary offering: The offering by prospectus of a large block of previously issued securities.

Registered security: 1) A security such as a stock or bond in which the owner is registered on the books of the company, the company's registrar or transfer agent. 2) A security registered with the Securities and Exchange Commission as a new or secondary offering.

Registered trader: A member of an exchange who primarily trades for his or her own account and at his or her own risk.

Registrar: The entity responsible for the keeping of records of the names and addresses of holders of a security for the issuer and verifies transfers have been accomplished correctly. Usually a registrar is separate from the transfer agent.

Registration: 1) Required by the Securities Act of 1933 of securities offered for sale to the general public. Only after completion of specific requirements will the Securities and Exchange Commission register a security. 2) Required by the Securities Exchange Act of 1934 before a security may be traded on a natural exchange. The issuing company must file an application for registration with both the exchange and the SEC.

Registration fee: The fee charged by the Securities and Exchange Commission for the registration of a public offering.

Registration statement: A document detailing the purpose of a proposed public offering outlining financial, business and management details as well as any information of importance to potential investors.

Reg T call: The initial deposit of funds for an opening transaction in a margin account as required by Regulation T of the Securities and Exchange Commission.

Regular-way settlement: Stocks, mutual funds and some bonds must be delivered to the buying broker and payment made to the selling broker on the fifth business day after the transaction unless otherwise specified. Some bonds and all options settle the next business day.

Regular-way transaction: Settlement and delivery on or before the usual settlement date for the security involved. *(See also: REGULAR-WAY SETTLEMENT)*

Regulated commodities: All commodities traded in organized contract exchanges that are under control of the Commodities Futures Trading Commission established to police matters of information and disclosure, fair trading practices, registration of firms and individuals, protection of customer funds, record-keeping and the maintenance of orderly futures and options on futures markets.

Regulated investment company: A mutual fund company eligible by IRS rules to pass through capital gains, dividends and earnings directly to its shareholders.

Regulation A of the Securities and Exchange Commission: A provision requiring a shorter form of the prospectus for simplified registration of small issues.

Regulations of the Federal Reserve Board (Regulations A, G, T, U, W and Z): A) Means and conditions under which Federal Reserve Board banks made loans to member and other banks at what is called "the discount window." G) Regulates financial lending institutions that extend credit to individuals to purchase or carry securities. T) Covers the extension of credit to clients by securities brokers, dealers and members of national securities exchanges, establishes initial margin requirements and defines registered, unregistered and exempt securities. U) Limits the amount of credit a bank may extend a customer for purchasing and carrying margin securities. W) Governs commercial credit including down payments and maturity dates. Z) Covers the Truth in Lending Act of the Consumer Protection Act of 1968.

Rehypothecation: The pledging of a client's securities by a broker dealer to a bank as collateral for broker loans under a general loan and collateral agreement.

Reinsurance: A consortium of insurance companies organized to spread the risk of insurance among many companies in exchange for a portion of the premium paid by the insured.

Reinvestment privilege: The right of a shareholder of a mutual fund to reinvest dividends in order to purchase additional shares.

Reinvestment rate: The rate of return as a result of reinvestment from an income producing security.

REIT: Real estate investment trust.

Rejection: The refusal to accept a security presented to complete a trade, usually due to a lack of proper endorsement or other problems.

Relative value: The comparison of one security against another as a possible investment.

Remargining: The deposit of additional cash or eligible securities to correct an equity deficiency in a brokerage margin account.

REMIC: Real estate mortgage investment conduit.

Remit: The payment for purchased goods or service.

Reopen an issue: A term used when the Treasury sells more of an issue than is already outstanding and another issue of the same terms and conditions is reopened in order to not have to auction a new issue.

Reorganization: The financial restructuring of a firm, usually as a result of bankruptcy, seeking protection from creditors while trying to work out a plan to recover financially.

Reorganization bond: A debt security issued by a company in reorganization proceedings. Generally issued to the company's creditor. Pays interest only if earned and is senior to any other debt issue(s) of the company.

Reorganization department (REORG):   The department within a broker-dealer firm that is involved in the exchange of one security for another, such as tender offers, mergers, acquisitions and conversions.

REPO: Repurchase agreement.

Repurchase agreement (REPO, RP):   1) Purchase by the Federal Reserve of money market instruments from nonbank dealers who simultaneously agree to repurchase the securities at a stated price, date and interest rate. 2) An agreement between two or more entities stating purchase and repurchase terms of financial instruments.

Required rate of return: The rate of return on a portfolio required to avoid a loss in the value as a result of systematic risk.

Rescind: The cancellation of a contract or trade with all parties restored to their original positions. (Example: A registered representative transacts a trade in the wrong security, the trade is rescinded and the client's account is adjusted to correct the error.)

Research: An analysis of a company or industry using any and/or all information available, including written reports and personal interviews.

Research analyst: A person who studies particular stocks or groups of stocks and makes recommendations based on the findings. Some analysts have enough credibility and followers as to influence the price of stocks based on their recommendations.

Research and development (R&D):   The departments of a company involved in the scientific research and marketing requirements of a new product or service.

Research and development limited partnership: A limited partnership formed to finance the research and development of a new product. May be either a public or a private limited partnership.

Research department: The division within a brokerage firm or other financial institution responsible for the analysis of markets and individual securities.

Research report: The analysis (and sometimes recommendations) of a company or industry usually written to enable investors to make better informed investment decisions.

Reserve requirement: The amount of cash that a member bank of the Federal Reserve System must keep on deposit with a Federal Reserve Bank.

Reserves: 1) Money on deposit with the Federal Reserve as required by banks to maintain certain minimum percentages for every $100 of deposits. The main tool used by the Federal Reserve to control the money supply. 2) Retained earnings set aside for payment of dividends, retirement of preferred stock, contingencies and/or improvements. 3) Valuation reserve to provide for charges to a profit and loss statement. 4) Understatements of balance sheet values.

Residual security: A security such as a right, warrant, convertible bond or preferred stock that has the potential of diluting earnings per share. (Example: Should the exercise of rights cause an addition of one million shares of stock added to ten million already outstanding, earnings of $11-million would mean earnings per share of $1.10 before dilution and $1.00 after dilution.)

Residual value: The net value of an asset after all charges and/or depreciation. Also known as "salvage value."

Resistance level: A technical term used to describe the top of a security's trading range. (Example: A broker may say "If the stock were to go higher than $73, it would be breaking its resistance level and stands a good chance of going higher.") Figure 22.

Resolution: An expression of desire or intent, usually a formal declaration of intent and purpose, such as a corporate resolution or a bond resolution.

Resting order: Instruction to buy or sell at a price away from the current level.

Restricted account: A margin account that has less equity than required by Regulation T of the Federal Reserve Board.

Restricted list: A list provided to the registered representatives of a broker-dealer of the names of issues that may not be traded or that have trading restrictions.

FIGURE 22:   Resistance Level

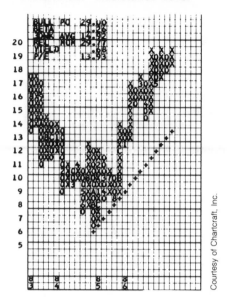

Courtesy of Chartcraft, Inc.

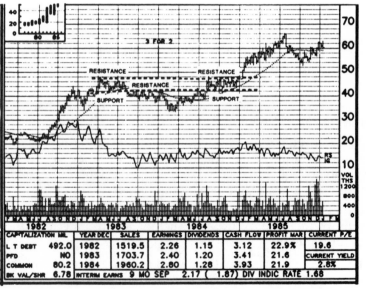

Courtesy of Standard & Poor's Corporation.

Restricted stocks: Stock that is restricted from being sold until certain conditions have been met. (Example: Stock received by the seller of a company may have a legend stating the shares may not be traded for a period of two years, making it restricted stock.)

Restricted surplus: Any portion of retained earnings not legally available for the payment of dividends. (Example: A corporation has cumulative preferred stock with dividends due but not paid. The company may have retained earnings but not enough to pay the divided arrears.)

Restrictive covenant: The pledge by an issuer of debt securities to perform all duties as required in a trust indenture or formal debt agreement.

Resyndicated limited partnership: A public or private real estate limited partnership formed to purchase properties that have already been fully depreciated—properties that no longer give the previous owners or partnership any tax advantage—in order to start the depreciation process over again.

Retail house: A full service brokerage firm (wire house) or small firm (boutique) that specializes in retail trade rather than institutions.

Retail investor: An investor who trades for his or her own account more than for a client's accounts.

Retail transaction: A trade in which a client buys or sells an over the counter stock from or to a broker/dealer.

Retained earnings: The amount of net income remaining after all dividends have been paid to common and preferred shareholders.

Retained earnings ratio: The ratio of retained earnings to the net income available for common stock. The complement of the dividend payout ratio.

Retained earnings statement: A detail of changes in the retained earnings of a company including the beginning and ending balances.

Retention: The amount of securities of a new issue kept by an underwriter for selling to its own clients.

Retention requirement: The amount that must be retained if anything is withdrawn from a restricted margin account.

Retirement: 1) Removal from service. 2) The redemption by tender, call, purchase or maturation of a stock or debt security. 3) Repayment of a debt. 4) The cessation of working by an employee for one of several reasons, including age and health.

Retirement account: An account that is qualified under Sections 401 and 501 of the Internal Revenue Code to be set up by an employer for the benefit of an employee on retirement.

Retirement plan: 1) A formal plan qualified under Internal Revenue Service rules for contributions to be made for the benefit of the individual upon retirement. Qualified retirement plans include individual retirement accounts (IRAs), profit sharing, money purchase, deferred compensation and defined benefit plans. (2) An informal goal and/or guideline set by an individual of retirement needs and how to attain them.

Return: The earnings and/or profit made on an investment in the form of capital gains, interest, dividends and/or other income.

Return if exercised: The amount of profit realized when an investor owns stock, sells a covered call and the call is exercised, thus selling the underlying stock.

Return if unchanged: The amount of profit realized when an investor owns stocks, sells a covered call and the call expires worthless without being exercised.

Return on capital/principal: A distribution not the result of earned income treated as a return of the investor's own money from the sale of assets or other causes, thus reducing the base cost of the investment.

Return on equity: The amount earned on a company's common stock, expressed as a percentage.

Return on investment (ROI):   The amount earned on a company's total capital (common and preferred stock equity plus its long term debt) expressed as a percentage.

Return on sales: The net profits before taxes expressed as a percentage of net sales.

Revaluation: An increase in the value of a country's currency based on the decision of a nation's authorities rather than on fluctuations in the market.

Revenue anticipation note (RAN):   A municipal debt issue of which the payment of interest and the repayment of principal is to be paid out of anticipated revenues of the municipality.

Revenue bond: A type of municipal issue that is used to finance an income producing project with the interest and principal payments being payable only from the revenue generated by the project.

Reverse a crush: The simultaneous selling of soybean commodity contracts and the purchase of soybean meal and soybean oil contracts. *(See also: PUTTING ON THE CRUSH)*

Reversal: The change in price direction of a security, commodity or the market as a whole.

Reverse a swap: A transaction that reestablishes an original bond portfolio position.

Reverse conversion: A legal technique by which a brokerage firm earns interest on its customers' stock holdings.

Reverse split: A technique used by a company to reduce the number of shares outstanding while raising the price per share. Accomplished by trading all outstanding shares for a smaller percentage of the same stock. (Example: A company with five million outstanding shares valued at $2.00 per share declares a one for five reverse split and ends up with one million outstanding shares, valued at $10.00 per share.) Also known as a "split down."

Revocable trust: A trust agreement entered into by a grantor to provide income from assets held for an heir that also allows for changes or even cancellation. Upon the death of the grantor, the assets held in the trust pass directly to the heir, avoiding probate yet still counts in estate tax valuations. *(See also: IRREVOCABLE TRUST)*

Revolver: A slang expression for a revolving line of credit, issued by a bank for a fee to be used if and as needed.

Rich: A term referring to a stock, bond or other security that is priced too high in relation to a similar security or element of risk.

Rigged market: The illegal buying or selling of a security for the purpose of creating a false impression of trading activity. Also known as "manipulation."

Right: When a company wants to raise more funds by the issuance of additional securities, a paper called "a right" is given to current shareholders offering them the opportunity to retain percentage ownership through the purchase of additional shares. Rights usually must be tendered or traded within a relatively short period of time.

Right of redemption: The right to recover property at or before foreclosure by paying off the mortgage or lien.

Right of rejection: The right to reject a bid or offer a negotiated price.

Right of rescission: 1) The right given by the Consumer Credit Protection Act of 1968 to void any contract by formal notice within three business days and receive a full refund of any monies given. 2) The right to cancel a contract should any part of the contract be illegal or fraudulent.

Rights of accumulation: In order to meet the terms and conditions of a mutual fund letter of intent, any distributions of dividends and capital gains are allowed to be added to new purchases and applied toward the total purchase amount.

Rights offering: An offering that gives each shareholder an opportunity to maintain a proportionate ownership in the company before the shares are offered to the public.

Rights of survivorship: A legal term that refers to assets owned by two or more persons. Should one of the owners die, the assets pass to the remaining owners rather than the heirs of the deceased.

Ring: A circular platform on the trading floor of a futures commodity exchange upon which traders and brokers stand while executing future trades.

Rising bottoms: A technical chart pattern that indicates a progressively rising trend in the low prices of a security signifying rising and higher support levels. Figure 23.

Risk: The measurable loss potential of an investment.

Risk and reward: The amount of return on an investment relative to the risk factor. *(See also: DOWNSIDE RISK)*

Risk arbitrage: A risky arbitrage strategy. (Example: The simultaneous purchase of call and put options in a volatile market, subject to gains on both transactions. In the worst case scenario, the market flattens and both the call and put options expire worthless.)

Risk averse: The assumption that a knowledgeable investor analyzes the risk to reward factors, then invests accordingly.

Riskless transaction: An over-the-counter transaction is which a brokerage firm buys or sells a security in order to fill an order previously entered from a client for the same security. "Riskless" as the buy and sell orders are consummated almost simultaneously.

ROI: Return on investment.

Roll down: An option strategy involving the closing out of an option position and the opening of another position with a lower strike price than the original.

Roll forward: An option strategy involving the closing out of one option position and the opening of another position with an expiration of a later date than the original.

Rolling stock: Equipment that moves on wheels, such as trucks, railroad cars and tractor-trailers.

Rollover: The change of custodianship for a qualified retirement plan, usually as the result of a distribution from an employee retirement plan upon retirement or termination of the employee.

Roll up: An option strategy involving the closing out of one option position and the opening of another with a higher strike price than the original.

FIGURE 23:   Rising Bottoms

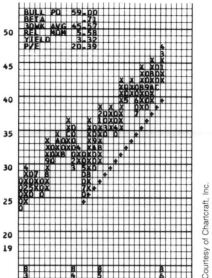

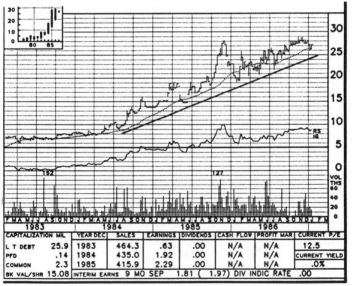

ROP: Registered options principal.

Rotation: The system whereby options are assigned bid and asked prices on a rotating basis at the opening of the market based on the opening price of the underlying security.

Round lot: The usual trading unit or multiple thereof. (Example: The stock round lot is 100, a bond round lot is $5000 and in some inactively traded stocks a round lot is ten. Options and commodities are traded per contract.)

Round trip trade: The opening and closing (purchasing and selling) of a security or a commodity on a very short term basis, possibly even a day-trade.

Round turn: The completion of a purchasing and a selling transaction of the same commodity for the same number of contracts. Commissions on futures trading are generally charged on a round turn basis.

Royalty trust: A spin-off of producing property by an oil or gas company to shareholders.

RP: Repurchase agreement.

RR: Registered representative.

RTD: 1) Rated. 2) Returned.

Rule of 45:   A vesting rule stating that when the sum of an employee's age and numbers of years employed reaches 45, that employee must be 50 percent vested in the company's employee retirement plan and must be vested at ten percent per year for five additional years.

Rule of 72:   A rule-of-thumb formula used to find the length of time needed for an investment to double or the interest rate needed to double an investment in a given number of years when the interest is being compounded. FORMULA: X = Compound Interest Rate, Y = Number of years, 72 divided by $X = Y$, 72 divided by $Y = X$. (Example: 72 divided by an interest rate of nine percent equal eight years to double, 72 divided by ten years equal 7.2 percent, so, 7.2 percent interest is needed to double the investment in ten years.)

Rule 144/145:   Covers the selling of two kinds of securities—control securities and restricted securities—stating the rules and regulations required prior to the removal of restrictions and the selling or transferring of the securities.

Rule 405:   The New York Stock Exchange rule that requires every member organization to exercise due diligence in learning the essential facts about every customer. Also known as the "know your customer" rule.

Rule 406:   The New York Stock Exchange rule that states no member organization may carry an account designated by number or symbol unless a customer has signed a written statement attesting to the ownership of such account and that the form must be on file with the member organization.

Rules of fair practice: Rules established by the National Association of Securities Dealers' Board of Governors designed to foster just and equitable principals of trade and business, high standards of commercial honor and integrity among members, the prevention of fraud and manipulative practices, safeguards against unreasonable profits, commissions and other charges and collaboration with governmental and other agencies to protect investors and the public interest.

Rumor: Information that is not necessarily fact and is unsubstantiated.

Run: 1) A list of securities available at a broker-dealer for trading, including current bid and asked. 2) The sudden rise in the price of a security. (Example: A broker may say, "The stock has risen two points in the last hour due to the news, it's really on a run.")

Rundown: A summary of serial bonds still available in a new issue.

Runner: A person on the floor of an exchange who physically takes (runs) the order ticket from a member of the exchange to the proper trading post or pit.

Running ahead: An illegal manuever in which a broker enters an order for his/her own personal account before orders for clients.

Running through the pot: The recall of a portion of a new issue by the manager of a syndicate in order for that portion to be included in a "pot" intended for institutional investors.

Runoff: The closing prices listed on the ticker tape after the market has closed.

S: 1) Signifies round lot on the ticker tape (Example: T 5s25 on the ticker tape indicates 5 round lots (500 shares), of AT&T were traded at $25.) 2) Indicates in a newspaper stock report a stock split or stock dividend.

S Corporation: A type of corporate structure that passes gains or losses directly to the owners taxed at their individual tax levels rather than a corporate tax level. Also avoids the double taxation of corporations that pay taxes on income as well as year-end inventory.

Safe harbor: 1) The provision in a law that excuses liability if it can be proved that good faith was demonstrated. 2) A form of defense against an unfriendly or hostile takeover attempt by making the company less attractive to the entity attempting the takeover.

Safekeeping: Securities deposited in a client's brokerage account that are registered in the client's name and held in the safety deposit box of the brokerage firm. Also known as "local safekeeping." *(See also: STREET NAME)*

Salary reduction plan (SRP): A company sponsored plan in which employees may invest a percentage of salary on a before-tax basis; may or may not be matched with company funds.

Sale: An exchange of goods or services for cash.

Sales charge: The commission amount which, when added to the net asset value of mutual fund shares, equals the offering price at which a mutual fund may be bought.

Sales literature: Any material that describes a firm's facilities, research reports, market letters or any other material that is prepared for general distribution.

Sales load: A commission amount added to the net asset value of mutual fund shares that equals the offering price at which a mutual fund may be bought.

Sallie Mae: Student Loan Marketing Association (SLMA).

Same-day substitution: Offsetting changes in a margin account that results in neither a margin call nor a credit. Occurs when a simultaneous purchase and sale of similarly priced securities are made or part of the margin positions go up in value and part go down equally in value.

Saturday night special: A surprise announcement made after market hours or on the weekend that directly effects the price of a security.

Saucer: A technical chart pattern that indicates a gentle dropping of the price of a security, a bottom reached, then a gentle rising in the price. An inverted saucer indicates a price has been going up, topped out, then goes back down. Figure 24.

Savings and loan association: A financial institution that obtains the bulk of its deposits from consumers and holds the majority of its assets as home mortgage loans.

Savings bank: A state chartered stock or mutual company bank that accepts both time and demand deposits. Funds are invested in mortgages, real estate, government bonds and other state banking commissioner approved securities.

Savings bond: A U.S. government bond that is issued either at a discount to face value (pays no current interest) or at par and pays a periodic interest. There are no state or local taxes due and no federal taxes due until the bonds are redeemed. Bondholders of Series EE bonds may defer payment of taxes by exchanging the bonds for Series HH bonds.

SBA: Small Business Administration.

SBI: Shares of beneficial interest.

Scale: The information on a new issue of serial bonds that indicate the number of bonds, when they mature, the coupon rate and the offering price.

Scale order: An order to buy or sell a security at specified price variations. (Example: A broker-dealer client places an order to sell 5,000 shares of stock, 1,000 at a time at ⅛th point intervals.)

Scalper: 1) A day trader who (hopefully) makes many small profitable trades. 2) An illegal maneuver whereby an investment adviser takes a securities position, recommends the security for purchase, watches the stock rise based on the advice then sells the position at a profit. 3) A market maker who takes excessive mark-up or mark-down according to the Rules of fair practice of the National Association of Securities Dealers (NASD).

FIGURE 24:   Saucer

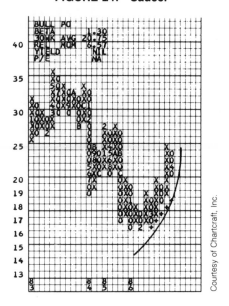

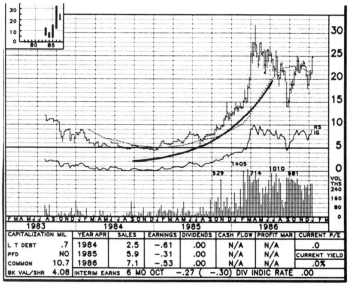

Schedule 13D: The form required within ten business days when acquiring direct or beneficial ownership of five percent or more of any class of securities of a publicly-held corporation. Must be filed with the Securities and Exchange Commission (SEC), the exchange

Inverted Saucer

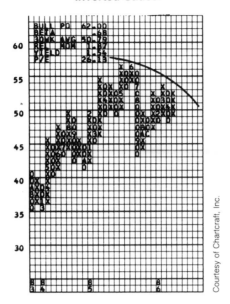

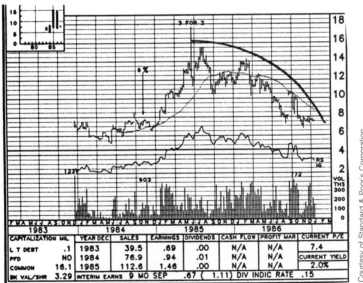

on which the shares are listed (if applicable) and the company itself.

Schedule 13G: The form required to be filed with the Securities and Exchange Commission (SEC) by owners of five percent or more of the voting stock of a company who have received the shares in the ordinary course of business and/or who have no intention of changing or influencing the management of the company. Must be filed prior to 45 days before year's end. A shortened version of Schedule 13D.

Scienter: Latin for "with knowledge." Conviction for fraud in the securities business must be proved to have been accomplished "in scienter" or with full knowledge.

Scorched-earth policy: The procedure a takeover target takes in order to make its shares less attractive to the acquirer. *(See also: POISON PILL, SHARK REPELLENT)*

Screen: The process of finding stocks that meet the same specified requirements, oftentimes with the aid of a computer. (Example: A client would like stocks screened that are at a PE of 12 or better and are selling within ten percent of their annual low.)

Scripophily: The collecting of antique stock, bond and other financial certificates.

SDRs: Special drawing rights.

Seasonal stocks: Stock of any company that provides goods or services that tend to be bought or used in a given season. (Example: A tax preparation company, Christmas decorations company and Halloween supply company are all examples of seasonal companies.)

Seasoned issue: An issue of a company that has gained a reputation as being solid with the investing public.

Seat: A term used to indicate an exchange membership.

SEC: Securities and Exchange Commission.

SEC fee: A fee levied by the Securities and Exchange Commission (SEC) usually charged to the seller of securities in the amount of one cent per so many hundreds of dollars of the transaction. Caution: Check with an investment broker for the current rate.

SEC Rule 3b-3:   Defines a short sale as one in which the seller does not own but must borrow the security being sold.

SEC Rule 10a-1   Prohibits short sales of securities except at a price above the last regular-way transaction. Known as the "plus tick" rule.

SEC Rule 10b-2:   Prohibits solicitations for the purchase of securities by those involved in a primary or secondary distribution except through the use of the offering circular or formal prospectus.

SEC Rule 10b-4:   Prohibits the short sale of securities being tendered to the entity making a tender offer.

SEC Rule 10b-6: Prohibits those involved in a distribution from trading in the securities during the distribution.

SEC Rule 10b-7: Governs rules of stabilization activities by issuers or underwriters in securities offerings.

SEC Rule 10b-8: Prohibits price manipulations by those involved in securities offerings.

SEC Rule 10b-10: Governs the minimum information required on securities; confirmations.

SEC Rule 10-b13: Prohibits entities making tender offers from purchases in the securities or convertible to the securities until the tender has expired.

SEC Rule 10b-16: Spells out the terms and conditions involving interest charges on margin accounts.

SEC Rule 11a: Defines rules governing floor trading activities by exchange members.

SEC Rule 13d: Requires the filing of disclosure documents by purchasers of five percent or more in any SEC registered equity security.

SEC Rule 13e: Regulates tender offers and going private transactions by the issuers or their affiliates.

SEC Rule 14a: Sets forth the information and documents required for proxy material distributed to public corporation shareholders.

SEC Rule 14d: Sets forth the rules and regulations covering public tender offers and the related disclosure requirements.

SEC Rule 15c2-1: Regulates the hypothecation and safekeeping of securities held in margin accounts.

SEC Rule 15c3-1: Spells out net equity requirements for broker-dealers in regards to client margin indebtedness.

SEC Rule 15c3-2: States broker-dealers must inform margin account owners that any credit balances may be withdrawn by the account owner upon demand.

SEC Rule 15c3-3: Regulates the handling by broker-dealers of free cash, fully paid securities and excess margin securities.

SEC Rule 17f-1: Requires the immediate notification from broker-dealers of information regarding lost, stolen, misplaced or counterfeit securities to the National Crime Information Center (NCIC), SEC and the appropriate law enforcement agency and to check with the NCIC should any suspicious security come into their possession.

SEC Rule 19b-3:   Prohibits fixed commissions by exchanges on stock transactions.

SEC Rule 19c-3:   Permits exchange members to trade securities on or off the trading floor of the exchange. A step toward an experimental National Market System.

SEC Rule 144:   Sets forth the conditions unregistered securities may be sold without filing a formal registration statement.

SEC Rule 145:   Sets forth the conditions in which shares acquired as a result of reclassification, merger, consolidation or transfer of corporate assets may be sold without an effective registration statement.

SEC Rule 156:   Forbids false and misleading promotional sales material on investment company (mutual fund) securities.

SEC Rule 174:   Outlines the circumstances under which a dealer must continue to provide a prospectus to purchasers of recently registered securities.

SEC Rule 237:   Expands rule 144 to include fully-paid privately placed securities held more than five years that may be sold within one year at a lesser of $50,000 of the value of such securities or one percent of a particular class of the outstanding securities.

SEC Rule 415:   Permits corporations to file a registration for securities that are to be issued when market conditions are favorable.

SEC Rule 433:   Sets forth the conditions under which a dealer may use a preliminary prospectus.

SECO: Securities and Exchange Commission Organization.

Second account: A second account at a brokerage firm in the name of a client. The client must sign a "two or more accounts" form designating ownership of the separate account. *(See also: NUMBERED ACCOUNT)*

Secondary distribution: The redistribution of a block of stock that had already been sold in a public offering and offered for sale by someone other than the issuing company. Also known as a "secondary offering."

Secondary market: The markets and exchanges upon which all securities are traded that are not part of a new or secondary issue.

Secondary mortgage market: The buying, selling and trading of home mortgages, usually for the purpose of gathering for a pool or pass through certificate such as GNMA or FNMA.

Secondary movement: A price movement of a security or the market as a whole following a strong primary movement.

Secondary offering: The reoffering of a block of stock that had already been sold in a public offering and offered by sale by someone other than the issuing company.

Second-preferred stock: A preferred stock issue that ranks below other preferred stock issues in terms of priority of claim on dividends and on assets in liquidation.

Second round: The growth of a company that has passed the stage of seed money (start up) but has not yet reached the level (mezzanine) of a leveraged buyout or initial public offering.

Sector: The corporations that collectively comprise an industry, such as the airlines, toy manufacturers, oil and gas distributors or automobile manufacturers.

Secured bond: A debt issue backed by a pledge of assets or collateral. Unsecured bonds are called "debentures."

Secured debt: A debt obligation that is secured by assets or collateral.

Securities Act of 1933: Federal legislation that requires the full and fair disclosure of all material information about the issuance of new securities.

Securities Act of 1934: Federal legislation that established the Securities and Exchange Commission (SEC) for the purpose of providing regulation of securities exchanges and the over the counter markets and to protect investors from unfair and illegal practices.

Securities analyst: One who analyzes a company for its investment potential.

Securities and Exchange Commission (SEC): A federal agency established by the Securities Exchange Act of 1933 as a regulatory body charged with protection of the public against malpractice in the securities market.

Securities and Exchange Commission Organization (SECO): Any SEC registered broker-dealer who is not a member of the National Association of Securities Dealers (NASD) or a national securities exchange is considered an SECO member in order to give the SEC direct jurisdiction over his or her activities.

Securities Industry Association (SIA): A trade group made up of broker-dealers.

Securities Industry Automation Corporation (SIAC): New York and American Stock Exchange's jointly owned subsidiary that provides automation, data processing, clearing and communications services.

Securities Investors Protection Corporation (SIPC):   A nonprofit organization created by an Act of Congress that provides funds for use, if necessary, to protect clients' cash and securities that are on deposit with an SIPC brokerage member firm in the event the firm fails and is liquidated under the provisions of the SIPC Act.

Securities loan: A loan collateralized by securities. Generally used for margin accounts and between brokerage firms.

Security: 1) A generic term used to indicate stocks, bonds, options, commodities, rights, warrants and any other items traded on stock, commodity and over the counter markets and exchanges. 2) Collateral. 3) A feeling of safety and freedom from danger, risk, care, poverty, doubt, etc.

Security arbitrage: The simultaneous purchase and sale of interchangeable or convertible securities to take advantage of a price disparity existing between the two securities.

Security ratings: The evaluation by a commercial rating agency of the credit and investment risks of a corporation.

Seed money: The first funds used to start up a business. Also known as "venture capital."

Seek a market: The effort to find a buyer or a seller of a security.

Segregate: Fully paid for securities registered in the name of a client but held at the brokerage firm separately from those of other clients. *(See also: LOCAL SAFEKEEPING)*

Segregated account: An account in which a client's securities held in margin are kept separate from other client's securities and may not be commingled with others or borrowed against in excess of the client's debt without prior written permission.

Segregated securities: Customer securities that must be kept separate at a broker-dealer from those that are used as collateral by the client or by the brokerage firm for margin or loan accounts.

Selected dealer agreement: The agreement spelling out the responsibilities of the selling group in a security's underwriting and distribution.

Self-directed IRA: An IRS qualified Individual retirement account (IRA) in which the owner assumes active investment management.

Self-employment: An individual who has earned income from personal services or would have if there had been profits from his or her trade or business. Income from real estate or investments do not qualify as earnings.

Self-liquidating program: A trust made up of assets which, when sold or retired, states the proceeds must be returned to the investor(s) and not reinvested into new assets.

Self-regulatory organization (SRO): Under federal securities laws, agencies registered with the Securities and Exchange Commission (SEC) must be self-policing in monitoring the activities of its members and are therefore termed SROs.

Self-supporting debt: A bond issued to finance a project which will produce sufficient income to pay interest and repay principal of the issue.

Sell: The transfer of ownership of an asset in exchange for cash and/or other consideration.

Sell at best: Instructions in an over the counter order in which other broker-dealers are asked to help sell a market security order at the best possible price.

Seller's market: A market atmosphere in which the prices are so high it is more advantageous to be a seller taking profits than a buyer establishing a cost basis.

Seller's option: An out of the ordinary transaction allowing the seller to deliver the certificate at any time within a period ranging from six to 60 days.

Selling climax: The sudden drop in a security or the market as a whole accompanied by high volume. Called a climax as analysts view this type of activity as the end of a bear market (or the bottoming out of prices) and an indication of the beginning of a bull market.

Selling concession: That portion of the underwriting spread that is paid to the selling group member on the securities it sells during a new or secondary issue offering.

Selling dividends: An unfair practice of inducing clients to buy shares of a mutual fund by implying that a pending distribution will be of benefit. In truth, the net asset value of the mutual fund is adjusted downward by the amount of the dividend.

Selling group: Brokerage firms that sell new and secondary public offerings but are not members of the underwriting syndicate.

Selling off: The selling of long positions under the pressure of further decline in prices.

Selling on the good news: The selling of a security after good news has caused the security to go up and (hopefully) before the price has corrected down.

Selling short: The selling of nonowned securities that must be borrowed in order to deliver the security to the purchaser. *(See also: SHORT SALE)*

Selling short against the box: A technique used by the owner of a security who wishes to sell the shares without giving up control of the security, usually in order to transfer the tax gain or loss from one tax year to another.

Sell order: An order placed by the owner of a security to sell that security at the market or at a limit price.

Sell out: The result of a buyer failing to pay for and accept delivery of securities as stipulated in a contract with any liability incurred as the result of the sell-out being charged to the failing buyer.

Sell-plus: An order placed to sell a security only if the price is higher than the last different preceding price.

Sell program: Sell orders of such volume and of so many different securities that the market as a whole goes down in value, sometimes dramatically, usually implemented by a "signal" when a computerized chart/plot program indicates a sell program is advisable. (Example: The institutional investor's computer generated a sell signal to sell ten million shares of various companies causing the market to go down 21 points in 15 minutes.) Also called "computerized sell program."

Sell stop order: An order to sell a security at market only when and if the price indicated on the order is touched or reached.

Sell the book: An order to sell a large quantity of a security only at the current bid price.

Senior debt: A debt security with a prior claim to assets over any junior securities in the event of failure or bankruptcy.

Senior funding: The retirement of debt securities with maturities of five to 12 years using the funds from a new debt security issue maturing in 15 years or more, usually used to decrease interest costs, consolidate debt or lengthen maturity time.

Senior registered option principal: The officer or general partner who holds responsibility for the supervision of client accounts and options transactions.

Senior security: An equity security having prior claim to any assets over any junior securities. Debt is always senior to equity. Of debt, the descending order of priority is as follows: first mortgage bonds, second mortgage bonds, then any other junior mortgage bonds then debentures, which are unsecured.

Sensitive market: A market in which the price changes easily as the result of positive or negative news, usually accompanied by low volume trading.

Sentiment indicators: Any measure of the mood of investors that would indicate bearish or bullish attitudes.

SEP: Simplified employee pension plan.

Separate account: That portion of an annuity that consists of a mutual fund.

Separate customer: The designation of the Securities Investor Protection Corporation (SIPC) used in allocating insurance coverage. Each individual or combination of individuals is considered a separate customer regardless of how many types of accounts are controlled by the individual or combination of individuals. (Example: All security accounts controlled solely by one individual are added together to comprise one separate customer.)

Serial bond: A bond issue with maturities at periodic stated intervals. (Example: A company may issue serial bonds that come due every year starting in five years.)

Series: The total of all options written on the same security of the same class, strike price and expiration date. (Example: All XYZ May 65 calls comprise a series.)

Series bonds: Bonds with the same priority claim issued by a corporation in a scheduled series of public offerings.

Series EE bond: A nonmarketable U.S. government savings bond that is issued at a discount from par, priced to yield a specific interest rate upon maturity.

Series HH bond: A nonmarketable U.S. savings bond issued at par that pays a periodic stated interest.

Series of option: All put or call options on the same underlying security with the same strike price and expiration date.

Settle: To complete the terms of an obligation.

Settlement date: The date by which a security transaction must be settled (certificate or cash delivered).

Settlement price: The official daily closing price of a commodity futures contract, set by the exchange for the purpose of settling margin accounts.

Severally and jointly: An underwriting term indicating the underwriting group members agree to purchase a new issue and are both individually and jointly responsible for the purchase price of the issue.

Severally but not jointly: An underwriting term indicating the underwriting group members agree to buy a certain portion of an issue while not agreeing to assume joint liability for shares not sold by the other members.

Shadow calendar: A list of securities pending registration with the Securities and Exchange Commission (SEC).

Shakeout: Forced liquidation of positions, even if at a loss, due to market events or conditions usually accomplished by stop orders being triggered.

Share: A unit of ownership interest in an equity security.

Share broker: A discount broker who charges commissions based on the number of shares per transaction, the higher the number of shares involved, the lower the per share commission.

Shareholder: The owner of one or more shares of stock in a corporation.

Shareholder's equity: The total assets minus the total liabilities of a corporation.

Share repurchase plan: A plan by a corporation to buy back shares in the open market. May be to obtain shares for employee stock option plans, take the company private or take advantage of undervalued share prices.

Shares authorized: The number of shares of stock that a corporation is permitted to issue as stipulated in the corporation's state-approved charter.

Shares of beneficial interest (SBI): Shares in the ownership of an investment trust created by a corporation in order to attract capital. The trust includes certain income producing assets of the company in which the income and any gains realized on the sale of the assets are returned to the share owners.

Shares outstanding: The shares of a corporation that have been authorized by the corporate charter, issued (sold) and are, therefore, outstanding.

Shark: An entity in the process of trying to takeover a targeted company.

Shark repellent: Any measure taken by a takeover target intended to "repel the shark" or keep their corporation from being taken over.

Shark watcher: An individual or group specializing in finding and capitalizing on takeover activity.

Shelf registration: A technique permitted by the Securities and Exchange Commission (SEC) that allows corporations to place registration of securities "on the shelf" to be offered for sale to the public during more favorable market conditions for a period of up to two years, accomplished by updating regularly filed annual, quarterly and related reports to the SEC.

Shell corporation: An incorporated company with no significant assets or operations.

Shelter: An investment intended to reduce or eliminate the tax liability of an individual.

Shop: 1) A term used to indicate the office of a broker-dealer. 2) The act of looking for the best possible price of a security.

Shopping the street: A search for a security that is being sought for purchase that is unavailable in the usual marketplace. (Example: A specific bond is desired by a client. The bond department must "shop the street" to try to find that bond.)

Short: 1) The selling of a security as an opening position. 2) A trader whose net position shows more short (sold) than long (bought) positions.

Short against the box: A technique used by the owner of a security who wishes to sell the shares without giving up control of the security, usually in order to transfer the tax gain or loss from one tax year to another.

Short bond: A bond that is: 1) Due to mature in less than two years. 2) Payable in less than one year and is classified as a current liability on a balance sheet. 3) A short term coupon bond.

Short coupon: A bond in which the first interest payment covers less than the usual six month period of time, usually as the result of being a new issue.

Short covering: The buying of a security to pay back that which was previously borrowed in order to make delivery on a short sale.

Short exempt transaction: A short sale that is exempt from the Securities and Exchange Plus Tick Rule, such as an arbitration order, an error correction or a floor broker's order.

Short hedge: Any transaction that limits or eliminates the risk of declining value in a security or commodity that does not entail ownership. (Example: Selling a call against stock owned or selling a futures contract on live cattle against feeder cattle owned.)

Short interest: The sum total of all shares of stock that have been sold short and have not yet been bought back to close out the short position.

Short interest theory: A theory that propounds the larger the short interest in stock, the more likely the stock will go up because short stock must be bought back and heavy buying usually causes prices to rise.

Short leg: A term used to indicate the sell side of a spread position in options or commodities.

Short position: 1) Stockshares that have been borrowed, then sold, but at some time in the future must be bought back to repay those borrowed. 2) Options—Put or call contracts that have been written (sold) in order to hedge a position or for speculation. 3) Commodities—A futures contract sold against future delivery or for speculation. Short positions not being used as hedges are initiated when the investor feels the security is going to go down in value and anticipates the purchase being at a much lower price than the sell price.

Short sale: The sale of a security that is not owned and therefore must be borrowed in order to deliver the security to the purchaser. A short sale results in an open short position. At some point in the future, the security must be purchased in order to pay back the securities which effectively closes the position. Short sales must be transacted in a margin account.

Short-sale rule: The Securities and Exchange Commission (SEC) rule that states short sales may only be accomplished if: 1) the last transaction was at a price higher than the last preceding, or 2) the last preceding price was equal, but higher than the one preceding it. Also called the "plus tick rule."

Short squeeze: A situation when a sudden move up in the price of a security causes short sellers to cover their positions by buying back the securities causing the price to go up even higher forcing still more short sellers to cover their positions, etc., etc.

Short tender: A prohibited practice of borrowing stock to respond to a tender offer.

Short-term: 1) If the law allows long-term capital gain, any period of time an asset is held shorter than long term. (Caution: The laws regarding the holding period and tax benefits are subject to change. Check with a tax attorney, accountant or financial adviser regarding current laws.) 2) Debt—a maturity of less than one year. 3) Equity—generally means less than six months but can mean as short a time as a few hours or days.

Short-Term Auction-Rate Stock (STARS):   A fund or trust that is comprised of preferred stocks trading on auction markets such as the New York Stock Exchange due to mature in three to five years or less.

Short-term capital gain or (loss):   The taxable gain or (loss) on a capital asset that is held for a shorter time than that required to be held for a long-term capital gain or (loss). (Caution: The period of time a security must be held to qualify for short-term capital gain treatment is subject to change. Check with a tax attorney, accountant or financial adviser to determine the correct holding period.)

Short-term debt: Any debt obligation due to be retired within the current accounting period, shown on a balance sheet as current liability.

Short-term gain/loss: The taxable gain (or loss) on a capital asset that is held for a shorter time than that required to be held for a long-term gain (or loss). (Caution: The period of time a security must be held to qualify for short-term capital gain treatment is subject to change. Check with a tax attorney, accountant or financial adviser to determine the correct holding period.)

Short-term trading: A trading technique of holding security positions for a very short time, even as short as minutes or hours.

Short-term trend: Usually indicates a minor correction in an otherwise fairly steady market or security direction.

Shown on front: A phrase used to indicate a signature is required to be signed exactly as is shown of the face of the ownership certificate.

SIA: Securities Industry Association.

SIAC: Securities Industry Automation Corporation.

Siamese stock: Common stock of two companies under the same parent company or manager that are sold as one unit, usually with one certificate being issued with the information on one company on the front and the other company on the back. Also called "paired stock" and "stapled stock."

SIC: Standard Industrial Classification system.

Side-by-side trading: The simultaneous purchase of a security and the sale of an option against that security.

Silent partner: A partner in a business or venture who has no direct role in management. May or may not share any further financial liabilities.

Silver Thursday: Thursday, March 27, 1980, the day the price of silver dropped to the point that a margin call of $100 million was generated on the account owned by the Hunt brothers of Texas. The inability to meet the call caused far-reaching problems and almost resulted in the financial ruin of the firm holding the account, Bache, Halsey, Stuart & Shields (now known as Prudential-Bache Securities).

Simple interest: Interest calculated on the original principal amount only. (Example: A two year $1000 investment earning five percent simple interest will earn $50 per year for a total of $100.) *(See also: COMPOUND INTEREST)*

Simplified employee pension (SEP): A retirement plan for those employers and their employees not covered by a pension or profit-sharing plan in which contributions are made on a before-tax basis and are tax-deferred until withdrawn.

Single option: An option that is not part of a spread, straddle or other hedge position.

Single premium annuity (SPA): An insurance company issued annuity contract in which an investment is made in one lump sum with an income that starts immediately or is deferred until some point in the future. May be tax-deferred within the limits allowed by law.

Single state municipal bond fund: A mutual fund that invests entirely in tax-free debt obligations issued within one state only. States with state income tax do not tax dividends on municipal bonds issued within their own states.

Sinker: A term used to indicate a debt security with a sinking fund.

Sinking fund: A fund required by the indenture or charter of a bond, debenture or preferred stock established for redemption of the securities.

SIPC: Securities Investors Protection Corporation.

Size: 1) The actual number of shares being offered for purchase or sale. 2) Indicates an order of large quantity.

Skip-day settlement: A transaction that settles the second business day following the trade date, usually occurs in the trading of commercial paper but may also include Treasury bills and bankers acceptance paper.

Slam shut: An investment opportunity that is no longer available.

Sld last sale: A ticker tape indication of a greater than normal change in price since the last sale, $1.00 or more on lower priced issues and $2.00 or more on issues priced at $20.00 or more.

Sleeper: A stock that is considered to be considerably underpriced but has great potential for gain once the buying public has been made aware of the company.

Sleeping beauty: A company considered to be a good takeover candidate but has not been made a takeover target.

SLMA: Student Loan Marketing Association.

SMA: Special miscellaneous account.

Small Business Administration (SBA): A government agency formed to provide loans and management assistance to small businesses.

Small investor: An individual (retail) investor who tends to trade in odd lots and small dollar amounts.

Smart money: Investments made by knowledgeable or institutional investors.

Snowballing: The effect of a sudden price change that triggers stop orders, putting further pressure on the price, which triggers more stop orders, etc., etc., etc.

Social and economic risk: The impact that international social events may have on national or world economics.

Social consciousness mutual fund: A mutual fund that invests in only those securities not in conflict with specific social causes, such as war products, out of favor foreign country stocks, etc.

Soft currency: Currency of one country not acceptable as an exchange for currency of another country.

Soft dollars: An agreement whereby no charges will be made for services, provided orders are placed that will result in commissions or fees collected. *(See also: HARD DOLLARS)*

Soft market: A market characterized by low volume, wide bid and asked spreads and volatility on news, a result of more sellers than buyers. Also known as a "buyer's market."

Soft spot: A localized weakness in an industry or individual security in the face of general strength in the market.

Sold-out market: An expression in the commodity market used to indicate a lack of available futures contracts.

Solicited order: An order to buy or sell a security that is solicited or recommended by a registered representative.

Solvency: A long term measure of the ability of a company to pay its debts and have adequate funds for growth and expansion.

Sophisticated investor: An investor with several years of trading experience, usually in many different types of securities who is familiar with the risks, rewards and terminology of the various markets.

Sovereign risk: The risk associated with foreign loans to governments in which there may be a default due to a change in national policy.

SPA: Single premium annuity.

Special arbitrage account: A special margin account in which the securities held are hedged by an offsetting position.

Special assessment bond: A debt security issued by a municipality in which the payment of interest and the repayment of principal is repaid from taxes imposed on those who benefit directly from the project funded by the bond issue.

Special bid: A block trading procedure in which a block of stock is offered for sale after a prior announcement on the broad tape.

Special block sale: The sale of a large block of a security for a specialist's own account. Allowed only when the block cannot be absorbed in the regular market.

Special bond account: A special type of margin account in which eligible debt securities are traded. Debt securities generally have less stringent margin requirements than stock.

Special cash account: The technical term for a cash account in which securities may be bought long and is subject to the five-day-rule. No margin activities may occur in a cash account.

Special convertible security account: The account within a client's margin account that holds any convertible securities margined by the client.

Special deal: An illegal maneuver by an underwriter of a new issue to offer a "gift" of something of value other than the selling concession to an employee of a dealer in conjunction with the sale of the issue.

Special district bond: A debt security issued by a municipality in which the payment of interest and the repayment of principal are repaid from taxes imposed on those who benefited directly from the project funded by the bond issue.

Special drawing rights (SDRs): "Paper gold," issued first in 1970 to maintain stability in the foreign market. More than 140 countries were issued SDRs in proportion to the gross national product of the nation and may be used to exchange with another country for gold or convertible securities. Because of the use of SDRs to stabilize exchange rates, the SDR has been used to calculate the value of private contracts, international treaties and securities on the Eurobond market.

Specialist: A member of a stock exchange with two primary purposes: 1) Maintain an orderly market in the specialists' registered securities and 2) Act as a broker-dealer in those securities.

Specialist block purchase or sale: A transaction in which a specialist buys or sells a large block of a security for his or her own account. Allowed only when the block cannot be absorbed in the regular market.

Specialist unit: A stock exchange specialist authorized to deal as principal and agent for other brokers in maintaining a stable market in one or more particular stocks.

Specialist's book: The record kept by a specialist that includes the personal securities in the specialist's own account, as well as any short sale, stop or limit orders placed by other exchange members with the specialist.

Specialist's short-sale ratio: The ratio of short sales by specialists as compared to the total amount of short sales.

Specialized mutual fund: A type of mutual fund that tries to achieve its investment objectives by concentrating its investments within a single industry or group of related industries.

Special miscellaneous account (SMA):   A separate account operated in conjunction with a general margin account. Funds are credited to the SMA on a memo basis and the SMA is much like a line of credit with the brokerage firm.

Special offering: A block-trading procedure in which a block of stock is offered for sale after a prior announcement on the broad tape.

Special omnibus account: The title of an account owned by one broker-dealer at another broker-dealer firm in order to transact orders without disclosing the names of the clients.

Special situation: A stock that is: 1) Undervalued but expected to rise in value because of favorable impending action, such as a drug company about to launch a miraculous drug. 2) Highly volatile, usually due to takeover rumors and possibilities.

Special subscription account: A type of margin account in which a client is allowed to borrow more than the usual amount allowed in order for the client to exercise a right or warrant. The client must pay the additional margin in four or less quarterly payments and then transfer the securities to the regular margin account.

Special tax bonds: A municipal bond payable only by the proceeds of a special tax.

Spectail dealer: A broker-dealer who spends more time trading his or her personal account than the accounts of clients.

Speculation: An investment strategy in which growth with a fairly large degree of risk is the major factor.

Speculative: A security in which the investor stands to gain (or lose) in proportion to the amount of risk. Some speculative positions expose the investor to a loss greater than the amount of initial investment.

Speculator: A trader who assumes a higher degree of risk in the hopes of a higher gain.

Spin-off: The separation of a division or subsidiary of a corporation from its parent company through the issuance of shares in the newly formed company. Shareholders in the parent company receive their proportionate number of shares in the new company.

Split: The division of the outstanding shares of stock of a corporation into a larger (forward split) or smaller (reverse split) number of shares. *(See also: STOCK SPLIT)*

Split commission: A commission that is: 1) split between two or more brokers. 2) split between the broker executing a transaction and the broker who brought the trade to the executing broker.

Split down: A technique used by a company to reduce the number of outstanding shares while raising the price per share. Accomplished by trading all outstanding shares for a smaller percentage of the same stock. *(See also: REVERSE SPLIT)*

Split offering: A new offering of a bond issue that consists of serial and term maturity bonds.

Split order: A large order that, if executed all at once, would upset an otherwise orderly market and so is split up into several smaller orders to be executed over a period of time.

Split rating: A situation that exists when two or more rating services give the same security different ratings.

Split up: The separating of a parent company from its subsidiaries. (Example: The split up of AT&T into seven individual regional telephone companies providing local service and the parent company continuing to provide long distance telephone service.)

Sponsor: The underwriter or promoter of a security or investment.

Spot commodity: The actual physical commodity as distinguished from the futures. *(See also: CASH COMMODITY)*

Spot delivery month: The nearest delivery month of a traded commodity contract.

Spot market: The market in which commodities are sold for cash and delivered immediately.

Spot month: The nearest trading month of a commodity futures contract.

Spot price: The price at which a spot or cash commodity is quoted.

Spot secondary distribution: This is a block-trading procedure in which a secondary distribution is not registered and is announced suddenly. Also known as "unregistered secondary distribution."

Spousal IRA: An IRA account owned by the nonworking spouse of a working person.

Spread: 1) The difference between the bid and asked prices. 2) An option and commodity trading technique in which there is a simultaneous purchase and sale of similar but different contracts. *(See also: STRADDLE)*

Spreading: The investment technique of buying and selling options of the same class on the same underlying security to take advantage of the profit potential of price movement.

Spread load: The sales charge of a contractual-type mutual fund that is paid over a four year period of time.

Spread option: The simultaneous purchase and sale of put or call options against the same security but with different exercise prices or expiration months.

Spread order: A simultaneous order to buy and sell put or call options specifying an exact difference in the premium paid for the buy side and the premium received on the sell side, noted as a net debit or credit.

Spread position: The status of an account in which a spread has been executed.

Spreadsheet: The accounting reports of a company, whether entered by hand or by computer.

Squeeze: Any situation which forces action by others, such as price movements that touch off stop orders.

SRO: Self-regulatory organization.

ss: Indicates on a ticker tape a transaction in actual number of shares rather than round lots. (Example: T Pr 27ss98 indicates 27 shares of AT&T Preferred stock was traded at 98.)

ST: Indicates on a ticker tape a transaction had been "stopped" and guaranteed a minimum price by the specialist.

Stabilizing: A manuever of a managing underwriter to prevent a sudden drop in price of a new issue due to low volume by buying the security at or slightly below the offering price.

Stag: Term used to describe a speculator who is a short-term or day trader.

Stagflation: Stagnation in the economy accompanied by a rise in prices.

Staggered board of directors: Board of directors members who are elected on a staggered basis of a few each year in order to help thwart unfriendly takeover attempts.

Staggering maturities: A debt security trading strategy in which an investor purchases various bonds with staggered maturity dates.

Stagnation: 1) An economic period of no, slow or negative growth. 2) An investment period of low volume and inactive trading.

Standard deduction: The income tax deduction allowed to individual taxpayers who elect not to itemize.

Standard deviation: A statistical measure of the probability of the degree of change of an individual item as compared to the degree of change of a group of items as a whole, commonly used in portfolio theory to calculate probable future performance of a portfolio.

Standard Industrial Classification System (SIC): A standardized numbering system for companies used for quick identification of the type of business, size, and other pertinent data.

Standard and Poor's Corporation: A subsidiary of McGraw-Hill involved in providing a widely diverse range of services to the financial community.

Standard and Poor's 100 and 500 Indices: Broad based weighted indices based on the average performance of 100 & 500 common stocks respectively.

Standard and Poor's Rating Service: One of several rating services that ranks stocks and bonds according to financial risk.

Standby commitment underwriting: A brokerage firm agreement to purchase any part of an issue that had not been subscribed in a rights offering.

STANY: Popular acronym for the Security Traders' Association of New York.

Stapled stock: Common stock of two companies under the same parent company or manager that are sold as one unit. Usually one certificate is issued with the information on one company printed on the front and the other company printed on the back.

STARS: An acronym for Short-Term Auction-Rate Stock.

Start-up money: The first funds used to start up a business. Also known as "venture capital" and "seed money."

State bank: A bank that has its charter granted by a state regulatory authority and generally has all the rights and privileges available to nationally chartered banks.

Stated value: The amount per share that is credited on the books of a company to the capital stock account. Has no relation to the price per share at which the stock trades.

Statement: A summary of activities that have occurred since the last accounting period, usually monthly, quarterly and/or annually.

Statement of condition: A statement of the financial condition of an individual or company including all assets, liabilities and equities.

Statement of income/operations: A summary of the income and operating expenses of a company during an accounting period, usually quarterly or annually.

Statutory book income: Income before federal and foreign taxes, used in the computation of corporate alternative minimum tax.

Statutory investment: A permitted investment specifically authorized by state law for trusts within that state's jurisdiction.

Statutory underwriter: An individual, group or other entity who purchases unregistered securities, files an effective registration statement with the Securities and Exchange Commission (SEC) then offers the securities for sale to the public. Also known as "voluntary underwriter."

Statutory voting right: A voting procedure that permits a shareholder to cast one vote per share owned for each director. *(See also: CUMULATIVE VOTING)*

Staying power: The financial and mental ability of an investor to continue holding a losing position.

Steenth: An abbreviation of a sixteenth, used in giving quotes in fractional figures.

Sticky deal: A new securities issue that is felt will be difficult to sell.

Stock: A proportionate share of ownership in a company. The total number of shares is set by the company's charter.

Stock ahead: A phrase used to describe the situation in which an order to buy or sell a security cannot be filled because of other orders at the same price that were previously entered.

Stock certificate: Written evidence of ownership in a corporation.

Stock dividend: A dividend declared by the board of directors of a corporation that is paid in stock rather than cash.

Stock exchange: A place of business organized for the purpose of providing an orderly and efficient marketplace for the trading of stock and related securities.

Stockholder: The owner of one or more shares of stock in a corporation. Also known as a "shareholder."

Stockholder of record: A stockholder whose name is registered on the books of the issuing corporation.

Stockholders' equity: The residual claims that stockholders have against a company's assets, calculated by subtracting the total liabilities from the total assets. Also known as "net worth."

Stock index future: A futures contract based on the performance of a stock index such as the New York Stock Exchange or Standard and Poor's 100 Indices.

Stock list: A department within a stock exchange involved in the investigation of requirements for the listing of companies to be traded on that exchange.

Stock market: An all inclusive term referring to the trading of stocks and related securities on all exchanges including the over the counter market.

Stock option: 1) The right to purchase (call) or sell (put) shares of stock at a specified price at any time prior to the expiration date. 2) An employee incentive and compensation plan by which an employee is allowed to purchase shares of the company at a certain price during a specified period of time.

Stock power: A standardized form that matches the information contained on the back of a security certificate used for endorsement purposes if the registered owner of the security does not have the certificate available for endorsement.

Stock purchase plan: An employee incentive and compensation plan by which an employee is allowed to purchase shares of the company at a certain price during a specified period of time.

Stock record: The record of securities received by a brokerage firm.

Stock split: The division of the outstanding shares of stock of a corporation into a larger number of shares. (Example: The board of directors of a corporation with 500,000 shares of outstanding stock declares a two-for-one stock split. The price of the shares just preceeding the split closed at $68.00 per share. Following the split, there are now one million shares outstanding valued at $34.00 per share. A stock split is a technique used to make outstanding stock seem more affordable and attractive to the buying public.)

Stock symbol/stock ticker symbol: Unique identification system given to securities to facilitate trading and ticker reporting. Some of the better known symbols are "T" for AT&T, "GM" for General Motors, "P" for Phillips Petroleum, "S" for Sears and "OEX" for Standard and Poor's 100 Index.

Stock watcher: The computerized system on the New York Stock Exchange that monitors all trading activities and stock movements in order to help identify trading patterns that may indicate manipulation or other illegal activities.

Stop-limit order: An order to buy or sell a security that is to be executed at the indicated limit price only after the limit price is touched. There is no guarantee of execution.

Stop-loss order: An order which is to be executed at market only when and if the price indicated on the order is touched.

Stop-out price: The lowest dollar price at which a U.S. Treasury bill was sold during a particular auction. Used to average with the beginning auction price to ascertain the price at which smaller investors may purchase.

Stopped-out: Said of a position in which a stop-loss order had been activated following the stop price being touched.

Stopped-out price: The price at which a stop order was executed. (Example: A stop-loss order was placed for $19.00, when the price reaches $19.00, the order becomes a market order, the next trade was at $18½ which is the stopped-out price.)

Stopping order: A guarantee by a specialist to execute an order at a specific price or better for a public order submitted by a floor broker.

Story: The "story" told to influence an investment decision to buy the security.

Straddle: An option and commodity trading technique in which there is a simultaneous purchase and sale of similar but different contracts. Also known as "spread."

Straight bond: A bond that is not convertible to any other type of security.

Straight-line depreciation: The simple accounting method of depreciating the value of an asset the same amount each year.

Strap: A triple option contract that includes one put and two call options, all with the same underlying security, exercise price and maturity. Sold at a lower premium than the total of the three individual options. Also known as "strip."

Strategy: A specific plan by which investment decisions are based.

Street: Short for Wall Street, even though the actual Wall Street is an area in the middle of the New York City financial district where many securities firms and exchanges started in business. The term now is synonymous with the entire stock market and includes stock activities anywhere in the U.S.

Street name: Securities registered in the name of a brokerage firm but credited to the account of a client. Street name securities are used in margin accounts and accounts in which the client wishes the brokerage firm to hold the securities.

Strike price interval: The amount of dollars per share between the strike price intervals in a series of options (Example: Options are often available in $5 intervals.)

Strike/striking price: The price at which the underlying security of an option may be exercised. Also known as "exercise price."

Strip: 1) The practice of separating a debt security principal from its coupons and selling them as separate entities. *(See also: ZERO COUPON BOND)* 2) The purchase of a stock in order to receive a declared dividend. 3) A triple options contract that includes one put and two call options, all with the same underlying security, exercise price and maturity, sold at a lower premium than the total of the three individual options. Also known as "strap."

Student Loan Marketing Association (SLMA):   A publicly traded corporation established by federal decree in 1972 which guarantees student loans. Also known as "Sallie Mae."

Subchapter M: An Internal Revenue Service regulation that allows qualifying investment companies and real estate investment trusts to pass interest, dividend income and capital gains directly through to the shareholders. Also known as the "conduit theory."

Subchapter S Corporation: A corporate structure that is allowed to be taxed as a partnership rather than a corporation. Must meet very specific guidelines in order to qualify as a Subchapter S Corporation.

Subject: An indication that a bid or offer quote is subject to be negotiated.

Subject market: A bid or offer on an over-the-counter security that cannot be accepted prior to approval by the client.

Subject quote: A quote that represents only an indication of the market, not a firm bid or offer.

Subordinated: A class of security that is junior to other securities of the same type as to claims on assets in the case of liquidation or bankruptcy.

Subordinated debenture: A type of bond that has unsecured junior claims to interest and principal subordinated to ordinary debentures or other debt obligations of the issuing corporation.

Subscription: An agreement to buy a newly issued security.

Subscription privilege: A privilege given to current shareholders and/or convertible security holders to buy a proportionate amount of shares of a new issue in the same company. Also known as "preemptive right."

Subscription right: A paper given to current shareholders of a company offering them the opportunity to retain percentage ownership during a new offering through the purchase of additional shares.

Subscription warrant: A certificate, sometimes offered with a newly offered security as an inducement to buy giving the holder the right to purchase additional securities at a specific price within a certain period of time (could be perpetually).

Subsidiary: A company in which more than 50 percent of the voting shares of stock are owned by another company (called the parent company). *(See also: HOLDING COMPANY)*

Substantive: A legal term meaning substantial or important.

Substitution: The replacement of one security with another of the same type. (Example: The selling of a seven percent bond and the purchase of a ten percent bond would be a substitution.)

Suitability: The aptness of an investment according to the needs and investment experience of a client.

Suiter: The entity engaged in the process of taking over another company.

Summary complaint proceedings: The procedure used by a respondent to plead guilty to a minor infraction of the National Association of Securities Dealers Rules of Fair Practice.

Sunrise industries: A term used to describe industries that are emerging and expected to grow and be a major factor in the future economy replacing declining sunset industries.

Sunset provision: A provision in a law that sets its own expiration date unless specifically reinstated by Congress.

Sunshine laws: State or federal laws that require most regulatory meetings be held in public view—"out in the sunshine"—with disclosure of most of the decisions and records.

Super-sinker bond: A bond with a long-term maturity date and interest comparable to other long-term bonds but because of the type of project being funded, usually housing, it is expected to be called within the next three to five years.

Supervisory analyst: A research analyst deemed qualified (subsequent to passing a NYSE exam) to approve publicly distributed research reports.

FIGURE 25:   Support

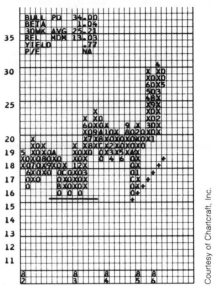

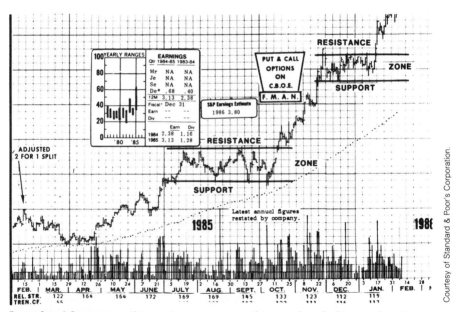

Supply-side economics: An economic theory that believes drastic tax
reductions stimulate investments by corporations and individuals,
which helps all in the economy.

Support: A technical term used to describe the bottom of a stock's
trading range. Figure 25.

Supranationals: Special agencies formed by groups of countries to support their economies and trade relationships and sometimes to finance economic development with supranational bond issues. (Examples: the International Monetary Fund, World Bank and Asian Development Bank.)

Surtax: A special tax occasionally imposed by Congress on individuals and corporations above certain income levels.

Surveillance department of exchanges: The department within an exchange that watches for unusual trading patterns that might indicate illegal maneuvers.

Suspended trading: A temporary halt in the trading of a security, usually as the result of impending news causing an imbalance of orders.

Suspense account: An account initiated by a broker-dealer to hold money or securities until such time as they are reconciled and deposited into the owner's account.

Suspension: The halting of trading privileges of a client due to infractions of settlement or margin rules by the client.

Swapping: The selling of one security and the purchase of another either similar to or the same as the one as being sold. Usually accomplished for tax purposes or to increase yields.

Sweetener: A feature added to a new issue to make the issue more attractive to the buying public, such as a right or warrant. *(See also: KICKER)*

SWIFT: The acronym for the Society for Worldwide Interbank Finance Telecommunications, an automated network for the facilitation of transfer of currency and financial information.

Switching: 1) The simultaneous closing of an open commodity position and the opening of another in the same commodity but in a later month. 2) The simultaneous closing of an open position in a security and the opening of another different security. (Example: A client switches by selling an open long position of 1,000 shares of the XYZ Company at $30 per share and buying 3,000 shares of the ABC Company at $10 per share.)

Symbol: A unique identification system given to securities to facilitate trading and ticker reporting. Some of the better known symbols are: T (AT&T), GM (General Motors), P (Phillips Petroleum), S (Sears), and OEX (Standard and Poor's 100 Index Options).

Syndicate: A group of investment bankers formed to underwrite and distribute a new or secondary issue of securities.

Syndicated offering: The offering of a new or secondary offering by a syndicate.

Syndicate manager: The leading underwriter of a new or secondary offering by a syndicate.

Synergy: An ideal merger situation in which the combined performance of the companies merged exceeds the total performance of the separate companies.

Systematic risk: The measure of a stock's volatility relative to the rest of the market.

TAB: An acronym for tax anticipation bill.

Tag ends: Slang for the remainder of a new debt offering in which the majority of the issue has already been sold.

Tailgating: An unethical practice of entering orders for a broker's personal account after those of a client who has either consistently made profitable trades or is in a position to have knowledgeable information.

Take: 1) Realized gains. 2) Lottery or gambling gains. 3) Open to bribery. 4) Seizure of a debtor's property. 5) The acceptance of an offering price of a security by the broker-dealer.

Take a bath: To incur a substantial realized loss in a transaction.

Take a flier: To invest in a highly speculative and risky security.

Take a position: To buy long or sell short a security as an opening transaction.

Takedown: 1) The amount of shares accepted by each participating investment banker in a new or secondary offering. 2) The price at which a new or secondary offering is allocated to the members of the underwriting group.

Take-or-pay contract: A contract in which the buyer is obligated to pay for the goods or services being provided whether or not taken.

Take-out: The amount of cash withdrawn from a margin account due to a credit balance, usually the result of the liquidation of a position.

Take-over: To assume ownership of a company by the purchase of more than the majority of outstanding shares accomplished by friendly or unfriendly merger or acquisition.

Take-over arbitrage: The simultaneous purchase of stock in a company being bought out and the selling short of stock of the proposed acquirer.

Taking delivery: The acceptance of goods, a security or commodity as the result of contract terms or purchase.

TAN: An acronym for tax anticipation note.

Tandem spread: An investment strategy similar to but not actually a spread whereby one security is bought long and another historically price-related security is sold short, with a resulting gain realized should the difference in prices widen, and a loss resulting should the prices narrow.

Tangible asset: An asset that is physical in nature. *(See also: INTANGIBLE ASSET)*

Tangible cost: The costs in oil and/or gas drilling associated with items that can be used over a period of time such as machinery and equipment.

Tape: The telegraphic system that prints or displays the stock symbol, volume and last sale price, usually within one minute of the transaction.

Tape delay: A delay in the reporting of transactions on the broad tape usually due to very heavy volume.

Tape racing: An unethical ploy by a broker in which personal orders are placed before a very large order by a client in order to take advantage of the expected price movement generated by the client's order.

Target company: A business that is being sought by a potential acquirer.

Target price: The price: 1) An investor hopes a security will reach. 2) An acquirer desires to purchase a takeover target. or 3) The underlying security reaches in order for an option trade to become profitable.

Tariff: A government imposed duty on export or import articles.

Taxable income: Net income subject to income tax after all deductions have been taken.

Tax-advantaged investment: An investment intended to reduce or eliminate the tax liability of an individual.

Tax anticipation bill (TAB):   A short term U.S. treasury debt obligation bought at a discount to face value, used by corporations as a credit at full face value against federal income tax liabilities.

Tax anticipation note (TAN):   A short term municipal debt obligation used to finance current expenditures pending receipt of expected tax revenue.

Tax basis: The actual cost of an asset or security adjusted for any commissions or other charges to be added or subtracted.

Tax bracket: The percentage rate of taxable income of an individual or joint income tax filing that is to be paid to the federal government as income tax.

Tax credit: A direct, dollar for dollar credit against taxes owed by an individual or joint income tax filing.

Tax deferred: Tax liability on an investment that has been deferred to a later period of time.

Tax district bond: A municipal bond issued by a specific tax district and in which the payment of interest and principal is made from taxes within the district.

Tax exempt/tax free security: A security in which the interest is exempt from taxation by federal, state and/or local authorities.

Tax free rollover: The transfer of assets from one custodian of a retirement plan to another custodian with the provision all rollover conditions have been met.

Tax loss carryforward: Capital gains or losses retain their short or long term status, are in excess of the annual deduction permitted on a tax form and are allowed by law to be taken in subsequent tax years. (Caution: Tax laws change constantly. Check with a tax attorney, accountant or other qualified financial adviser as to the current limits and allowances.)

Tax managed utility mutual fund: A mutual fund that invests in utility stocks and reinvests the dividends into additional shares of the utility. Mutual fund shareholders receive no distributions but realize profits due to increased net asset value upon selling the shares of the mutual fund.

Tax preference item: Any item specified by the IRS to be used in the calculation of the alternative minimum tax liability.

Tax Reform Acts of 1969, 1976, 1978, 1984 and 1986:   The years in which legislation was enacted providing major revisions in previous tax laws.

Tax selling: The selling of a security in order to realize a capital gain or loss in a particular accounting year.

Tax shelter: An investment intended to reduce or eliminate the tax liability of an individual.

Tax umbrella: Tax loss carryforwards that are used to shield current and future profits from taxes.

Tax year: The 12 month period of time a business chooses for tax liability and accounting purposes.

TBA: Acronym for to be announced, usually referring to the price that will be decided at a future date of a new issue.

Tear sheet: Rating and research companies, such as Moody's and Standard & Poor's, providing subscription services of loose-leaf books comprised of "sheets" upon which reports on publicly-traded companies are printed. Often these sheets are "torn out" and sent to clients in order to provide information on the essential background and financial history of a company.

Technical analysis: An analysis of the market as a whole and/or individual securities based on supply and demand. Items taken into consideration include price movements, volume trends and chart patterns. *(See also: FUNDAMENTAL RESEARCH)*

Technical indicator: An indication made by technical analysis that certain events are probable based upon that analysis.

Technical rally: A short-term rise in a market, security or commodity during a general bearish trend.

Technical research: An analysis of the market as a whole and/or individual securities based on supply and demand. Items taken into consideration include price movements, volume, trends and chart patterns. *(See also: FUNDAMENTAL RESEARCH)*

Technical sign: An easily recognizable signal by technical analysts that should be significant in the projected price movement of a security or commodity.

Technician: Someone who analyzes securities based on technical data rather than fundamental data.

Teeny: Wall Street slang for $\frac{1}{16}$.

Telephone booths: The communications facilities used by floor brokers and others to receive orders to buy and sell securities and to report the details of executed orders.

Telephone privilege switching: The ability to transfer shares by telephone from one mutual fund to another managed by the same family of funds.

Tenant: Part owner of an asset, security or account.

Tenants by the entireties: A state designation of "joint tenants with rights of survivorship" in which the surviving owner(s) receive the(ir) proportionate share of the ownership should one of the principals become deceased.

Tenants in common (ten in com; TIC):   A legal form of joint ownership that, upon the death of one of the owners, the proportionate ownership share of the assets held are passed on to the estate of the deceased.

Tender: 1) Commodity—The issuance of transferable notices that announce the intention of delivery of an actual commodity. 2) Stock—The delivery of one stock in exchange for cash and/or stock in another company due to a buyout or merger.

Tender offer: An offer to exchange securities for cash and/or other securities.

Ten in com: Tenants in common.

10-K report: The Securities and Exchange Commission (SEC) required annual report of every issuer of a registered security that includes information on total sales, revenue, pretax operating income, sales by product, source and application of funds and other pertinent information.

Tennessee Valley Authority (TVA): A federal agency established in 1933 to develop power and nonpower projects in and around the Tennessee Valley. Financed through the sale of bonds and notes.

Ten percent guideline: The guideline of municipal bond analysts in which funded debt over ten percent of taxable property assessed value is excessive.

Ten-year forward averaging: A special income tax advantage available only on lump-sum distributions from a qualified employee retirement plan allowing the recipient to elect ten-year forward tax averaging rather than rolling over the assets into an Individual Retirement Account.

Term: 1) The period of time in which a contract is in force. 2) The provision(s) specifying the nature of a contract or agreement. 3) The period of time an elected official holds office.

Term bond: A bond issue in which all bonds mature on the same date.

Term certificate: A long term certificate of deposit (CD).

Term life insurance: A life insurance contract that builds up no cash value and in which the premium goes up or the coverage comes down every time the policy is renewed.

Term maturity: A bond issue in which all bonds mature on the same date.

Term repo: A repurchase agreement that is longer than the usual overnight agreement.

Test: 1) A measurement of knowledge, competence or qualifications. 2) The result of a financial ratio to determine information such as liquidity or others. 3) The price movement of a security up to and including but not past the current support or resistance levels.

Testamentary trust: A trust created by a will with the testamentary trustee authorized by the will of the decedent.

Theoretical value of a right or warrant: The market value of a right or warrant. Figured by subtracting the price of the right or warrant from the price of the stock and dividing the resulting figure by the number of rights or warrants needed to purchase one share of stock plus the share of stock being bought. (Example: A right is issued that allows the purchase of one share of stock at $20 and five rights. The stock is currently at $26.00. $26.00 − $20.00 = $6.00 divided by five plus one equals $1.00 value of each right.)

Thin market: The market condition in which the volume is low with few offers to buy or sell. May refer to an individual security or the market as a whole.

Third market: Over-the-counter trading of exchange listed securities by nonexchange members.

Third party account: An illegal type of brokerage account that is in the name of one person but is actually owned by another.

Third party release: A document signed by the owner(s) of an account that gives authority for the transfer of cash and/or securities to another. *(See also: AUTHORITY TO TRANSFER)*

30-day visible supply: The total dollar amount of new municipal bonds with maturities in excess of 13 months that will be brought to the market within 30 days.

30-day wash rule: An Internal Revenue Service (IRS) rule that states gains or losses may not be taken on the sale of a security if the security was purchased within 30 days before the sale or repurchased within 30 days after the sale.

3-5-10 rule: The Economic Recovery and Tax Act of 1981 Accelerated Cost Recovery System rule referring to the length of time for depreciation of vehicles (three years), equipment and machinery (five years) and leased buildings (ten years) for assets put into service after 1980.

Three-handed deal: A municipal bond issue consisting of serial maturities and two term maturities.

Thrifts: A descriptive term for savings banks, credit unions or savings and loan associations.

Through the roof: An investment in which the price has gone straight up.

Throwaway offer: An approximate bid or offer that is not firm and is for information purposes only.

Thundering herd: The nickname for Merrill Lynch, Pierce, Fenner & Smith used due to their advertising program and extremely large number of offices and personnel.

TIC: Tenants in common.

Tick: The price movement of a security from the last to the current trade, may be an up tick, down tick or zero tick.

Ticker: The telegraphic system that prints or displays the stock symbol, volume and last sale price, usually within one minute of the transaction.

Ticker symbol: The letters that identify a security on the ticker tape. Also known as "stock symbol."

Ticker tape: The telegraphic system that prints or displays the stock symbol, volume and last sale price, usually within one minute of the transaction.

Tier: The designation of a particular class or type of securities, generally the lower the tier the lower the claim on assets or the lower the status of a company.

Tiffany list: Slang for the list of issuers of the highest quality commercial paper.

TIGRs: An acronym for Treasury Investment Growth Receipts, a U.S. government-backed zero coupon bond, first introduced by Merrill Lynch, Pierce, Fenner and Smith.

Tight market: The market condition characterized by active trading with fairly high volume and narrow bid and asked range.

Tight money: An economic situation in which credit is tight due to action by the Federal Reserve to restrict the money supply.

Time deposit: A savings account or certificate of deposit (CD) held at a financial institution.

Time loan: A collateralized loan to a brokerage firm with a set rate of interest and specified maturity date. *(See also: BROKER'S LOANS)*

Time spread: An option or commodity trading technique in which simultaneous contracts are positioned on the same security but with different contract expiration months.

Time value: The value of an option contract over and above its intrinsic value. The closer the expiration date nears, the less time value remains in the value of the option.

Times fixed charge: Fixed-charge coverage.

Times interest earned ratio: A financial ratio used to determine the margin of safety with which the fixed interest charges are covered by earnings.

Tip: "Inside" or not publicly known information relating to a company that, once known, would affect the price of the stock.

Tippee: Slang for the one who receives insider information.

Toehold purchase: A shareholder position of just under five percent of the shares of a takeover candidate, five percent being the level at which the Securities and Exchange Commission (SEC), the exchange and the target company must be notified by the receipt of Schedule 13D explaining the acquisition.

Toll revenue bond: A municipal bond issue backed by revenues from a toll producing project.

Tombstone: A new issue advertisement that lists the name of the issuer, type of security, underwriter(s) and place where additional information is available.

Ton: Bond trader's jargon for $100 million.

Top-down approach to investing: The investment approach in which the general economic trend is studied and then companies are sought to hopefully benefit from the trend.

Top-heavy plan: A qualified employee retirement plan in which the present value of cumulative benefits for "key employees" exceeds 60 percent of the value for all employees.

Topping a bid: A bid higher than current which indicates a bullish move in the market.

Topping out: An individual company, industry or the market as a whole which is believed to have reached the maximum price and is expected to correct downward.

Total capitalization: The capital structure of a company including long-term debt and all equity.

Total cost: The principal amount paid for a security plus any fees, charges or commissions.

Total output: The total amount of goods and services available for purchase at a given period of time. Also known as "aggregate supply."

Total return: The total earnings of an investment including dividends, interest and/or gain realized on the liquidation of a position.

Total volume: The total number of trading units of all; a) Options traded on options exchanges, b) Stocks and bonds traded on national exchanges, c) Futures and options on futures traded around the world or d) Securities traded on the over-the-counter market.

To the buck: An expression used by U.S. government security traders indicating an offer is in even amounts and include no fractions. (Example: A Treasury bill offered at 99 is quoted as 99 to the buck.)

Tout: The aggressive promotion of a security designed to create buying interest in a security among investors.

Track record: The past performance record of a fund or portfolio manager.

Trade: 1) Another name for a business or company. 2) The exchange of goods and/or services for cash and/or other goods and/or services. 3) A completed transaction in a security or commodity.

Trade balance: The difference between the imports brought into a country and the exports shipped out to other countries.

Trade confirmation: A written notice to the buyer or seller of a security of the name, price, commission or fee and trade date of a transaction.

Trade date: The date on which a transaction occurred.

Trade deficit: More imports being brought into a nation than exports being sent out.

Trademark: A registered name, emblem, symbol or motto that identifies a product, service or company, protected with trademark laws against use by others.

Trader: An individual investor who buys and sells securities and/or commodities in the hopes of making profits.

Trade surplus: More exports going out of a nation than imports being brought in.

Trade through: An order executed on the floor of an exchange even though there is a more advantageous price available through the Intermarket Trading System. An unethical practice unless the order is of such size as to be difficult to execute at one price anyplace but on the floor.

Trading at a discount: A security that is trading below its face or stated value.

Trading at a premium: A security that is trading above its face or stated value.

Trading authorization: A power of attorney granted to someone other than the account owner, giving authority for trading privileges in the account. *(See also: LIMITED TRADING AUTHORITY, FULL TRADING AUTHORITY)*

Trading dividends: A corporate investment strategy of purchasing and selling stock in order to accumulate as many dividends as possible in order to benefit from Internal Revenue Service dividend exclusion laws. (Caution: Dividend exclusion amounts are subject to change. Check with a tax attorney, accountant or other qualified adviser for the current amounts.)

Trading floor: The trading area of an exchange.

Trading halt: A temporary halt in the trading of a security, usually as the result of impending news causing an imbalance of orders.

Trading limit: The maximum price movement a commodity may make, up or down, in any one trading day. *(See also: LIMIT UP, LIMIT DOWN)*

Trading on equity: A debt issued by a corporation in which the debt service may be lower than the expected return of invested capital.

Trading pattern: The long-term price range of a security or commodity as plotted on a chart with a line drawn connecting the lowest prices and a line drawn connecting the highest prices at which the security has traded within a specified period of time. The upward or downward slant of the two lines indicate whether the long term trend is up or down. Figure 26.

Trading post: The area in an exchange where specialists and floor brokers trade specific securities.

Trading range: The range between the high and low prices of a security over a specified period of time.

Trading ring: The designated area on the New York Stock Exchange floor where listed bond trading activity occurs.

Trading through the fund: A debt security traded at such a price as to give a yield to maturity less than that of the federal fund rate, usually an indication of an expected lowering of the federal fund rate.

Trading unit: The normally accepted number of shares of stock (round lot of 100) or dollar amount of bonds ($5,000) or multiples thereof, which are usually traded.

Trading variation: The common minimum fractional point fluctuation of a security including: a) Stocks, corporate and municipal bonds, and options more than $3–⅛th; b) Options less than $3–¹⁄₁₆th

FIGURE 26:   Trading Pattern

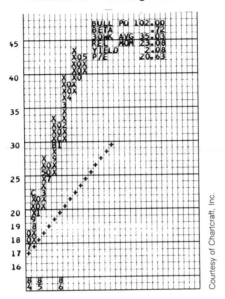

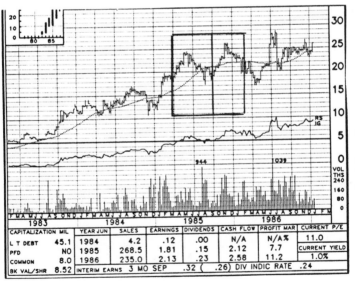

Courtesy of Chartcraft, Inc.

Courtesy of Standard & Poor's Corporation.

c) Medium and long-term U.S. Government notes and bonds—1/32nd; and d) Short term U.S. Government bills–1/64th. Futures commodity contracts fluctuate in cents and fractions of cents with the exchanges setting the trading variations on each type of commodity.

Trading volume: The number of shares of stock or commodity contracts that changed hands during a trading day.

Transaction: Instructions to buy, sell or transfer a security, commodity futures contract or cash which have been completed.

Transfer: The change of ownership of a security from the seller to the buyer.

Transferable notice: Notice given by the seller of a futures commodity contract for the preparation of actual delivery.

Transfer agent: The entity responsible for recording the name, address, social security number and number of shares owned by the company, delivering and receiving the certificates as required and making any changes as needed in the ownership records.

Transfer and hold: Instructions by a buyer of a security to transfer the stock into the name of the account and hold in local safe keeping (the brokerage firm's vault).

Transfer and ship: Instructions by the buyer of a security to transfer the stock into the designated name and deliver the certificates to the new owner.

Transfer tax: A tax imposed by certain states for the transfer of securities regardless of the residence of the buyer or seller.

Transmittal letter: A letter accompanying the delivery of a certificate that describes the security and the reason for delivery.

Treasuries: An all inclusive name for negotiable debt securities issued by the U.S. government.

Treasury bill: A U.S. government debt security with a maturity date of 90 days to one year bought at a discount to face value. Pays no interest payment and matures at full face value.

Treasury bill auction: The weekly auction by the U.S. Treasury in which short term U.S. government debt obligations are bought at discount to face value.

Treasury bond: A U.S. government debt security with a maturity date of ten to 30 years with the yield based on the purchase price, pays interest semi-annually.

Treasury Investment Growth Receipts (TIGRs):   A U.S. Government-issued security that pays no current interest but is issued at a discount to face value with the yield figured by calculating the difference between the purchase and maturity prices as relates to the purchase price and length of maturity.

Treasury note: A U.S. government debt security with a maturity date of one to ten years with the yield based on the purchase price, pays interest semi-annually.

Treasury stock: Previously issued stock that has been repurchased by a company. May be held indefinitely, reissued or retired. Treasury stock is not entitled to dividends and has no voting rights.

Treasury zero certificate (TZ):   A U.S. Government-issued security that pays no current interest but is issued at a discount to face value with the yield figured by calculating the difference between the purchase and maturity prices as relates to the purchase price and length of maturity.

Trend: The general direction of price movement of the market as a whole or of individual securities or commodities.

Trendline: The straight line drawn on a chart connecting the lowest or highest points of price movements. Figure 27.

Triangle: A technical chart pattern where the price movements of a security or commodity are in a constant down or up trend so that when a line is drawn across the highest prices connecting to the sides of the chart, a triangle is formed. Figure 28.

Triple tax exempt: A municipal bond bought by a resident of the municipality of issue that exempts the interest from tax liability on the federal, state and local levels.

Triple witching hour: The concurrent date and time of expiration of: a) current month options, b) current month index options and c) index futures contracts.

Truncation: The elimination of paper, paperwork or processing.

Trust: 1) Faith and confidence in another. 2) A combination of business interest. 3) Property or money held for another by an entity having fiduciary responsibilities of the trust.

Trust company: A firm organized for the purpose of acting as trustee, fiduciary or agent in the administration of trust accounts and related services.

Trustee: An entity with fiduciary responsibility for the administration of an account held in trust for the benefit of another.

Trust indenture: The written agreement between a corporation and its creditors that details the terms of the debt issue including rate of interest, maturity date(s), call features, collateral and means of payment.

FIGURE 27:   Trend Line

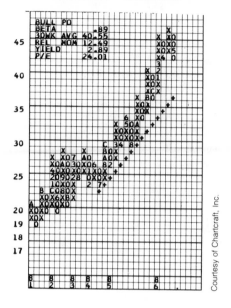

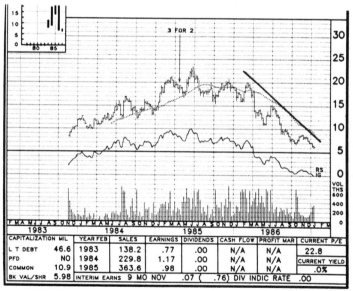

Trust Indenture Act of 1939:   The legislation that requires all corporate debt securities be registered under the Securities Act of 1933 and issued under a trust indenture.

FIGURE 28:   Triangle

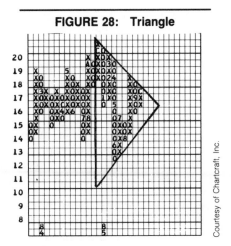

Trustee: The administrator of a trust.

Trustee of living trust: The administrator of a trust created by a living person with the authorization of the trustee created by the trust rather than by a will.

Trust in Securities Act: Another name for the Securities Act of 1933.

Truth in Lending Law: Federal legislation designed to protect the borrowing public by requiring lenders to fully disclose the true cost and the interest rate being applied in such a way as to be completely understood by the borrower.

Turkey: An investment that not only did not perform as expected but went down in price as well.

Turnaround: A marked improvement in the performance of a company as witnessed by increased earnings and price of the stock.

Turnover rate: 1) The total volume of traded shares on an exchange as a percentage of the total number of outstanding shares listed by the exchange. 2) The frequency a portfolio switches positions.

Type: The designation of an option as either a put or a call.

12b-1 mutual fund: A mutual fund, usually no-load, which assesses the shareholders for a portion of its advertising and promotion expenses.

20-Day period: The minimum time between the filing and the registration (effective date) of a new issue by the Securities and Exchange Commission (SEC). Also called the "cooling off period."

25 % rule: A guideline of the minimum amount of debt to annual budget used by an analyst of a municipal bond issue.

20 % cushion rule: A guideline used by an analyst of a municipal revenue bond issue in which revenues should exceed debt service by 20 percent.

Twisting: The unethical practice of switching a client from one investment or insurance policy to another in order to generate additional commissions for the broker. Also called "churning" or "churn and burn."

Two-dollar broker: The designation of a member of an exchange who freelances by executing trades for various member firms when their own floor brokers are especially busy. Originally, the fee charged was $2 per round lot, hence the name two dollar broker.

Twofer: A slang term used for the investment strategy of the purchase of one call and the sale of two calls with the calls sold having a higher exercise price than the one bought but with all calls having the same expiration date.

200-day moving average: A technical indicator that averages the price movements of an individual security or a market index or average for current day plus the previous 199 days, used to indicate the long range trend.

Two-sided market: The market condition in which both the bid and asked sides of a security are firm and both buyers and sellers may expect transactions to be completed at the quoted prices. Also known as a "two-way market."

Type of option: The designation of an option as either a put or a call.

TZ: Short for Treasury zero certificates.

U: An indication in a newspaper report that signifies a new annual high for a security.

U-4: The uniform application in the securities industry used to register security agents, representatives and principals.

U-5: The uniform document of the securities industry used to notify all entities with whom a representative is registered of any changes in the employment of the individual.

UBI: Unit of beneficial interest.

Ultra vires activities: Activities of a company that are not authorized by its charter and are, therefore, subject to suit.

Unable: A response from a trading floor when asked about the status of an order meaning there has been no execution due to price or unavailability of the security or commodity.

Uncovered call writer: The seller of a call option as an opening transaction in which the underlying security is not owned by the seller.

Uncovered option: An opening transaction sale of an option in which the underlying security is not owned by the seller.

Underbanked: Said of an issue being underwritten in which the investment banker has difficulty putting an underwriting group or syndicate together.

Underbooked: Said of an issue being underwritten in which there are few indications of interest from the buying public.

Undercapitalization: The situation by a company in which there is not enough capital (cash) to carry on business.

Underlying: The security or commodity against which one has the right to buy or sell, according to the terms of an option contract.

Underlying debt: The municipal bond situation in which an entity higher than the issuing authority is partly responsible for the debt service of the bond issue.

Underlying security: The security or commodity against which one has the right to buy or sell according to the terms of an option contract.

Undervalued: A security that is trading at less than the book value or less than comparable companies.

Underwrite: The system whereby an investment banker or syndicate buys a new issue of securities from the issuer and then sells the issue to the buying public.

Underwriter: A financial organization that acts as an investment banker or agent serving as intermediary between the issuer of a security and the buying public.

Underwriting: The procedure used by investment bankers to channel investment capital from investors to the issuers of new or secondary securities.

Underwriting agreement: The agreement between the issuer of a security and the managing underwriter as agent for the underwriting group that spells out the terms of the responsibilities of all parties involved in bringing the issue to the buying public.

Underwriting group: A group of underwriters formed for the express purpose of bringing an individual new issue to the buying public.

Underwriting manager: Managing underwriter.

Underwriting spread: The difference between the public offering price of a new or secondary issue and the amount paid to the issuer.

Underwriting syndicate: The group of brokerage firms that agree to become joint underwriters of a particular offering of securities.

Undigested securities: Any newly issued securities that remain unsold to the buying public due to lack of demand (buyers).

Undistributed earnings/net income/profits: The amount of net income remaining after all dividends have been paid to common and preferred shareholders.

Unearned income: Income derived from sources other than wages, tips or salaries earned for personal services. Unearned income includes such items as rental income, dividends and interest.

Unencumbered: An asset that has no lien against it, such as a clear mortgage or securities held in a cash account.

Uniform Gifts to Minors Act (UGMA):   The authorization by the state of residence that allows gifts to minors and allows an adult to act as custodian for the minor.

Uniform Practice Code (UPC):   The National Association of Securities Dealers (NASD) code that governs the uniform dealings among brokerage firms.

Uniform Securities Agent State Law Exam: The series No. 63 National Association of Securities Dealers (NASD) exam, required by many states for registered representatives or principals who wish to conduct business in those states.

Unissued stock: Shares of stock or a mutual fund that have been authorized but not issued.

Unit: One trading interest. May be a share, bond or contract.

United States Government Securities: Any debt security issued by and a direct obligation of the U.S. government.

Unit investment trust: An investment company security sold in units, consisting of a portfolio of securities, usually bonds. A fixed trust returns the principal of retired issues to the investor on a pro rata basis and is, therefore, a self-liquidating trust. A nonfixed trust reinvests principal into other securities.

Unit of beneficial interest (UBI):   A share in the ownership of an investment trust created by a corporation in order to attract capital. The trust includes certain income producing assets of the company in which the income and any gains realized on the sale of the assets are returned to the unit owners. Also known as "shares of beneficial interest" (SBI).

Unit of trading: The normally accepted number of shares of stock (round lot of 100) or dollar amount of bonds ($5,000) or multiples thereof that are usually traded.

Universal life insurance: A type of insurance product that combines a term insurance policy with a savings portion.

Unleveraged program: A limited partnership in which the money borrowed to finance the assets is less than 50 percent of the value of the assets.

Unlimited tax bond: A municipal bond that is backed by a pledge of the municipality to levy additional taxes if needed for the payment of interest or repayment of principal.

Unlisted security: A stock or bond not listed on any exchange that is traded on the over-the-counter network.

Unloading: The liquidating of positions during adverse price movements to preclude further loss.

Unpaid dividend: A dividend declared by the board of directors of a company but which has not yet reached its payment date.

Unrealized profit or (loss):   Profit or (loss) that has not been actually taken as the security position has not yet been liquidated.

Unregistered security: A security that is not registered with the Securities and Exchange Commission (SEC) and is sold with the use of an investment letter between the issuer and the buyer stating the securities are for investment only and not for resale.

Unsecured debt: A debt obligation not secured by the pledge of assets or collateral, an unsecured bond is called a debenture.

Unwind a trade: 1) The liquidation of a securities position by an offsetting transaction. 2) The correction of a trade made in error.

Up-and-out option: An over-the-counter call option with a provision that if the price of the underlying shares go "up" over a specific price, the option is cancelled "and-out".

Upset price: The minimum price which will be accepted at an auction.

Upside potential: The amount of possible upward movement of the price of an investment.

Upstairs market: A transaction completed within a brokerage firm rather than through the floor of an exchange or on the over the counter market.

Uptick: The term used to describe a transaction in which the price was higher than the previous trade. *(See also: DOWN TICK, PLUS TICK, ZERO TICK)*

Up trend: The value of a security or the market as a whole that is tending to go up more than it goes down.

UR: An acronym for under review. Used as an indication on a corporate and municipal calendar on bond issues that are still being reviewed by the rating company and have yet to be assigned a rating.

U.S. savings bond: A U.S. government bond that is issued either at a discount to face value (pays no current interest) or at discount or premium to face value (pays a periodic interest). There are no local or state taxes due and no federal taxes due until the bonds are redeemed. Bondholders of Series EE bonds may defer payment of taxes by exchanging the bonds for Series HH bonds.

Utility revenue bond: A municipal bond issue used to finance a public utility with the revenues from the utility used to pay the interest and repay the principal.

Utility stock: Stock issued by a public service utility company such as telephone, gas or electricity.

Value broker: A discount broker who charges commissions based on the dollar value of the transaction rather than the number and price of shares or contracts traded.

Value change: The change in the price of a stock adjusted for the number of shares outstanding. Used in the computation of a weighted index.

Value date: Synonymous with settlement date.

Value Line Report: An advisory service report issued by Value Line that gives fundamental information on individual companies as well as timeliness, safety, beta coefficient and many other pertinent facts.

VA mortgage (VA): Home mortgage loans granted to veterans by a lending institution and guaranteed by the Veterans Administration.

Variable annuity: An annuity (insurance product) in which the premium is turned into accumulation units of a security portfolio. The accumulation units fluctuate in value according to the prices of the securities in the portfolio. Payout (annuitization) is based upon the value of the accumulation units.

Variable cost: Production costs that change directly with the amount of production needed to complete a product.

Variable hedging: An option position in which an investor writes (sells) more call options than are covered by the investor's long position in the underlying security. Also known as "variable ratio writing."

Variable rate debt instrument: A debt such as a loan, mortgage or bond which has an interest rate tied to an index of some type (such as the Consumer Price Index, Prime Rate or Government Bond Index) which changes up or down as the index changes. *(See also: FIXED RATE SECURITY)*

FIGURE 29:   Vertical Line Chart

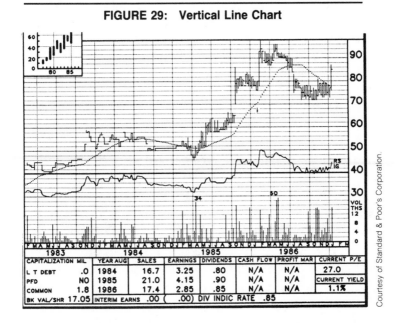

CAPITALIZATION MIL		YEAR AUG	SALES	EARNINGS	DIVIDENDS	CASH FLOW	PROFIT MAR	CURRENT P/E
L T DEBT	.0	1984	16.7	3.25	.80	N/A	N/A	27.0
PFD	NO	1985	21.0	4.15	.90	N/A	N/A	CURRENT YIELD
COMMON	1.8	1986	17.4	2.85	.85	N/A	N/A	1.1%
BK VAL/SHR 17.05		INTERIM EARNS	.00	(	.00)	DIV INDIC RATE	.85	

Courtesy of Standard & Poor's Corporation.

Variable ratio writing: An option in which an investor writes (sells) more call options than are covered by the investor's long position in the underlying security.

Vault cash: The money kept in the vault of a bank as a reserve against client deposits.

Velocity: The number of times the same dollar is spent in a given period of time.

Venture capital: The financing required for the start-up of a new company or venture. Also known as "seed money."

Venture capital limited partnership: A limited partnership that is formed to raise money for the start-up or purchase of a new or newly formed company.

Vertical line chart: A technical chart for a security, index or average in which a line is drawn on the vertical bar representing the range between the high and low prices and a short horizontal mark is placed on that line at the closing price. Shows the daily as well as the longer term price volatility. Figure 29.

Vertical spread: An option strategy involving the purchase of one option and the simultaneous sell of another option with the same expiration date but with a different strike price with both the buy and the sell sides either put or call options.

Vesting: The gradual participation by the employees of ownership of an employer-qualified plan based on factors such as length of time with the company (tenure), age and whether or not a full time employee. (Caution: Each company sets its own vesting schedule within the limits set by law. Check with the personnel department regarding vesting rights.)

Veterans Administration mortgage (VA):   Home mortgage loans granted to veterans by a lending institution and guaranteed by the Veterans Administration.

V formation: A technical chart pattern that forms a V, supposedly indicates a security has bottomed out. An inverted V indicates a security has topped out. Figure 30 on page 249.

vi: A newspaper symbol used to designate a corporation is in the process of reorganization under the U.S. bankruptcy laws.

Visible supply: The supplies of a commodity in distribution centers, afloat and all other supplies "in sight."

Voidable: A transaction that may be cancelled at some date in the future because the transaction was illegal in the first place. (Example: An order to buy a security was placed by someone for another without trading authority for that account.)

Volatile: The rapid and extreme price change of a security or the market as a whole.

Volatility: The degree to which a security is subject to sudden and unexpected price changes.

Volume: The number of units (shares or contracts) traded in a security or the entire market during a given period of time.

Volume deleted: An indication of the broad tape meaning only the symbol and price will appear on transactions under 5,000 shares, usually necessary when the tape is running behind two or more minutes.

Volume of trade theory: A technical theory that attempts to verify market strength or weakness by the measurement of trading volume.

Voluntary accumulation plan: Mutual fund investments in which any investments are voluntary and do not require the investor to make additional deposits.

Voluntary association: An unincorporated business organization structured much like a partnership with all members having unlimited financial responsibility. (Example: The New York Stock Exchange was a voluntary association until it became a not-for-profit corporation in 1971.)

FIGURE 30:   V Formation

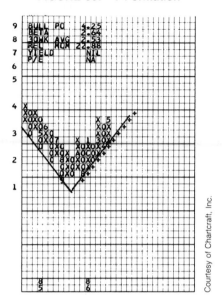

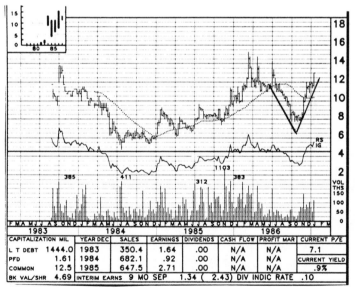

Voluntary bankruptcy: A legal action taken in response to the filing under Chapter 11 of the Bankruptcy Code by an insolvent business or individual.

Voluntary underwriter: An individual, group or other type of entity who purchases unregistered securities, files an effective registration statement with the Securities and Exchange Commission (SEC) then offers the securities for sale to the public. Also known as "statutory underwriter."

Voting right: The common shareholder's right to vote on the affairs of the company. May be delegated by the stockholder to another person (proxy). *(See also: CUMULATIVE VOTING)*

Voting trust certificate: The transfer of common stock voting power (proxy) to a group of trustees, usually to facilitate the reorganization of a company under Chapter 11 of the bankruptcy code.

Waiting period: The twenty day minimum required by the Securities and Exchange Commission between the filing and the registration of a new security.

Wallflower: A security that is no longer attractive to investors.

Wall Street: Synonymous with: 1) the New York financial district located at the lower end of Manhattan Island, 2) the New York Stock Exchange, and 3) the entire investment community.

Wanted for cash: An indication on the ticker tape announcing a bidder will pay cash the same day for a security rather than the usual settlement period of five business days.

War babies: Slang for stocks and bonds issued by companies engaged in the business of defense.

Warehouse receipt: A negotiable receipt that lists goods or commodities kept in a warehouse. Can be used to transfer ownership.

Warrant (WT):   A certificate (sometimes offered with a newly offered security as an inducement to buy) giving the holder the right to purchase securities at a specific price within a certain period of time (could be perpetually).

Wash sale: Disallowance of capital loss by the Internal Revenue Service (IRS) when a purchase of the same security within 30 days of the sale date of the same security that established a capital loss.

Wasting asset: An asset (other than land) that has a limited use or life, including such items as oil and gas reserves, business machines and option contracts.

Watch list: A list of securities that are being watched for unusual trading activity. Usually takeover candidates or others with unusually heavy volume.

Watered stock: Stock in an overvalued company.

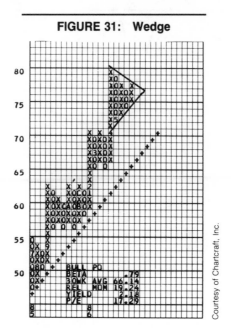

FIGURE 31: Wedge

Courtesy of Chartcraft, Inc.

Weak market: The market as a whole with more sellers than buyers, relatively small volume and generally declining prices.

Wedge: A technical chart pattern that indicates the high and low price range of a security, index or average is narrowing. Figure 31.

We offer retail (WOR): An expression used to indicate certain securities are offered at a net price to the buyer as all transaction costs are paid by the seller.

Western account: An underwriting agreement in which each participant is only responsible for selling the individually underwritten specific quantity of shares or bonds. *(See also: EASTERN ACCOUNT)*

W formation: A technical pattern indicating a double bottom (two periods of low prices) formation. A reverse W indicates a double top (two periods of high prices). Figure 32.

When distributed (WD): Terminology used to describe a newly issued security that has not yet been distributed. Often trades on a WD basis. (Example: The XYZ Company went public and sold 1,000,000 shares in the offering. The day after new issue, the stock was trading on a WD basis.)

When issued: The shortened version of "when, as and if issued." Used to indicate a provisional purchase of a newly authorized debt or equity security that has not yet been issued.

FIGURE 32:   W Formation
Straight Formation

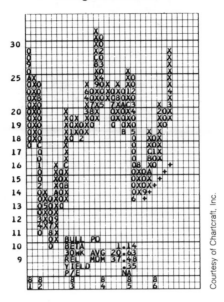

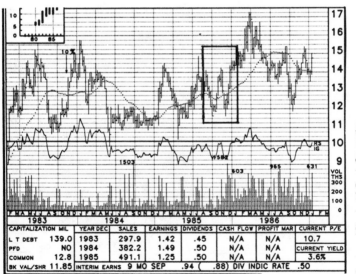

Courtesy of Chartcraft, Inc.

Courtesy of Standard & Poor's Corporation.

Whipsawed: Said of an investor who has continually been on the wrong side of the transactions during an extremely volatile market.

Inverted Formation

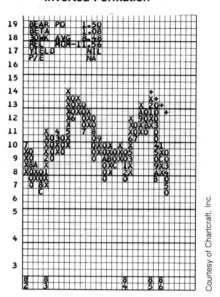

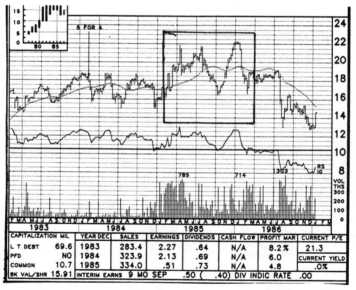

Courtesy of Chartcraft, Inc.

Courtesy of Standard & Poor's Corporation.

White knight: A strategy in response to an unfriendly takeover attempt in which the takeover target searches for rescue by a friendly acquirer.

White's Rating: A service by White's Tax Exempt Bond Rating Service providing classification of municipal securities based on market factors rather than creditworthiness.

Whole life insurance: An insurance policy that combines the coverage of a term policy with the benefit of building cash values.

Wholesale Price Index: The former name of the Producer Price Index. A monthly report issued by the U.S. Department of Labor Statistics that measures the change in wholesale prices.

Wholesaler: 1) A representative of an investment company such as a mutual fund or public limited partnership whose responsibilities include informing registered representatives and current or possible clients about the benefits of ownership in the security represented. 2) An investment banker acting as underwriter in a new or secondary offering.

Wholesale transaction: The purchase of an over-the-counter security from one broker-dealer to another.

Whoops: The popular name given to the $7 billion bond issue of the Washington Public Power Supply System as several of the bonds went into default and litigation—the largest dollar value of municipal bond default in history.

Wide open: Said of an issue being underwritten in which the investment banker has difficulty putting an underwriting group or syndicate together.

Wide opening: An unusually wide spread between the bid and asked prices of a security.

Widget: A catch-all phrase used to mean any type of hypothetical manufactured product.

Widow and orphan stock: A relatively safe and high dividend paying stock which would be suitable for even "widows and orphans" to own.

Wildcat drilling: The exploration for gas and oil in unproven fields.

Will: A legal document that spells out the wishes of an individual as to the disposal of the individual's estate after death.

Windfall profit: Profit from the sale of goods or products attributed to demand or shortages driving the price up rather than lower production costs. (Example: The cost of copper went very high due to increased demand and shortages while the cost of mining copper stayed relatively stable.)

Windfall profit tax: A special federal tax occasionally levied against companies with windfall profits.

Window: 1) The discount window of a Federal Reserve Bank. 2) The cage, or cashiering, department of a brokerage firm. 3) The limited time during which an investment opportunity is available.

Window dressing: The selling of losing or unpopular positions by the manager of a portfolio (usually just before an accounting period), in order to present to the shareholders only profitable and popular positions.

Wire: The communications system used by broker-dealers to communicate directly with exchanges and among branch and home offices.

Wire house: A firm operating a private communications system "wire" to the exchanges, its own branch offices or other firms. Used collectively to mean all brokerage firms.

Wire room: The brokerage firm department responsible for the transmittal of an order to the proper exchange or destination.

Wire transfer: Ownership transfer of cash or securities accomplished through the use of electronic rather than physical means.

Withdrawal plan: A program available to most investors of open-end mutual fund that allows a fixed-payment withdrawal when the account exceeds the minimum requirement as specified in the prospectus. Payment may usually be made on a monthly, quarterly, semi-annual or annual basis.

Withholding: 1) Taxes deducted as credit against tax liability. 2) The holding of shares of a hot issue for the account of the broker or family member rather than offering the shares to the public. A violation of the rules of fair practice of the National Association of Securities Dealers.

With or without: A term used in the placement of an odd-lot limit order meaning the order is to be executed at the limit price only, not at the last price, which would be a market order, including an ⅛th point differential. *(See also: ODD-LOT DIFFERENTIAL)*

Without an offer: A response to a request for a quote meaning the dealer is willing to buy the security at the bid price but is unwilling to sell due to lack of shares or not wishing to sell short.

With rights of survivorship: A legal term that refers to assets owned by two or more persons. Should one of the owners die, the assets pass to the remaining owners rather than the heirs of the deceased.

W-9:   The Internal Revenue Service form required to be signed by clients of financial institutions stating certain information about the client's social security or tax identification number as well as whether or not the client is subject to "back-up withholding."

Wooden ticket: The slang expression used for a nonviable confirmation of trade (highly illegal). *(See also: BUCKET SHOP)*

WOR: We offer retail.

Working capital: A measure of the liquidity of a company calculated by subtracting current liabilities from current assets.

Working control: Ownership by an individual or group of enough voting stock of a company necessary to exercise control. May or may not require 51 percent or more.

Workout quotation: An estimate of a quotation on a security subject to the brokerage firm finding the stock to buy or sell. *(See also: SUBJECT QUOTE)*

World Bank: The common name for the International Bank for Reconstruction and Development, which was organized in 1944 to help finance the reconstruction of Europe and Asia after World War II. Now used to finance a nation's infrastructure under the condition of the loans. Must be backed by the borrowing country's government. May not compete with local banks, but may be a participating consortium member.

Wraparound annuity: An annuity (insurance product) contract that allows the owner to switch from one type of investment to another within the limits outlined in the annuity contract.

Wraparound mortgage: A mortgage which increases the indebtedness of the owner while still leaving the original mortgage intact. Payments are usually made to the wraparound mortgagee who in turn makes the scheduled payments to the original lienholder.

Wrinkle: A new and unusual feature or security which makes an investment more attractive to a potential buyer. (Example: Options on foreign currencies were a new wrinkle when added to the growing list of options on commodity futures.)

Write: When referring to options, write means "to sell."

Write off: An accounting term used when referring to the amount charged off to the depreciation or amortization of an asset.

Writer: A person who sells a put or call option contract and assumes the obligation to sell (call) or buy (put) the underlying security at the option's exercise price.

Writing naked: The writing (selling) of a call option by someone who doesn't own the underlying security.

Writing puts to acquire stock: An investment strategy using the income derived from the sale of a put option exercisable at a price the writer (seller) would purchase the underlying security. If the security goes up in price, the put expires, allowing the writer to keep the premium received. If the security goes down in price, the put is exercised and the writer is able to use the premium received as part of the purchase price of the security. (Example: A put option is sold at $6.00 per share for 100 shares of XYZ Company [currently trading at $45.00] with a strike price of $40.00 due to expire in two months. The put option [if previously not bought back by the seller] will expire or be exercised. Scenario 1) The stock goes to $50, the option expires and the writer keeps the premium. Scenario 2) The stock goes to $38, the option is exercised at $40, the writer uses the premium received from the put option giving the buyer a cost basis of $34 per share.)

WT: Warrant.

X or XD: A newspaper indication that a stock is trading ex-dividend (without dividend) or a bond is trading flat (without accrued interest).

XCH: Means ex-clearing, an indication that a trade was completed outside regular clearing facilities.

X-dividend date: The last day that a stock trades with the latest declared dividend, usually four business days prior to record date. After x-dividend date, the purchaser of the stock is not entitled to the dividend. Also known as "ex-date" and "ex-dividend date."

XR: A newspaper indication that a stock is trading ex-rights (without rights attached).

XW: A newspaper indication a stock is trading ex-warrants (without warrants attached).

Yankee bond market: Bonds issued by a foreign bank or corporation and sold in the U.S. market using dollar denominations.

Yankee certificates of deposit: A certificate of deposit issued by a foreign bank and sold in the U.S. market with dollar denominations.

Yellow sheets: Wholesale corporate bond quotations among dealers, published daily by the National Quotation Bureau.

Yen bond: A bond issued in Japanese yen currency.

Yield: The return on investment, whether in the form of dividends or interest, based on the price paid for the security.

Yield advantage: The advantage received in the form of additional earnings when a convertible security is purchased rather than the common stock. (Example: A convertible preferred stock yields a seven percent dividend, while the common stock pays three percent so the yield advantage would be four percent.)

Yield curve: A chart analysis of bond interest plotted from the shortest to the longest maturity dates. Used to graphically show the relationship of short to long term interest rates. A positive yield curve shows long term rates higher than short term. A negative yield curve shows short term rates higher than long term. Figure 33.

Yield equivalence: The yield of a corporate bond compared to a municipal bond after an individual's tax bracket has been taken into consideration.

Yield spread: The difference in yields between similar or dissimilar securities. (Example: An investor may compare the yield spread between a long term bond and a preferred stock.)

Yield to average life: The yield of a debt security calculated on the average length of time the debt security is expected to be retired. Used for mortgage bonds and bonds with sinking funds.

FIGURE 33:   Yield Curve

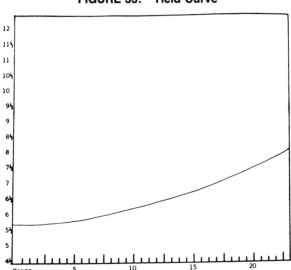

Yield to call (YTC):   The yield to maturity calculated at the earliest call date of a debt security rather than the maturity date.

Yield to maturity (YTM):   The yield of a debt security taking the price paid for the bond into account. The yield will be higher when the bond has been bought at a discount, lower when bought at a premium and when bought at par the yield to maturity is the same interest rate as stated on the bond.

Yoyo stock or market: An individual security or the market as a whole that rapidly goes up, down, up, down, etc., just like a yoyo.

YTC: Yield to call.

YTM: Yield to maturity.

Z

Z: 1) Used by newspapers to indicate volume is being reported in actual shares, not round lots. 2) Used in newspapers to indicate a mutual fund closing price was not received by press time.

Zero coupon bond: A bond that pays no interest but is priced at a discount to face value at maturity. The interest rate is stated as yield to maturity, compounded rather than simple interest. (Caution: Many different types of zero coupon bonds are available, both taxable and nontaxable. When taxable, income tax is due on the difference between the purchase price and the face value on a pro-rated basis.) *(See also: PHANTOM INCOME)*

Zero-minus tick: A sale of a security that was made at the same price as the previous price but lower than the last different price.

Zero-plus tick: A sale of a security that was made at a price that was the same as the previous price but higher than the last different price.

Zero tax bracket: The maximum amount of earned income not subject to federal income tax. (Caution: The zero tax bracket changes occur often. Check with a tax attorney, accountant or other qualified adviser about individual tax liabilities.)

Zero tick: A sale of a security that was made at a price that was the same as the previous price.

Ziatech: A Japanese word for fast-track trading techniques in financial markets, often computer assisted, that the U.S. has pioneered and that are increasingly popular in Japan.

COMMON ABBREVIATIONS

ACRS: accelerated cost recovery system
A-D: advance-decline
ADB: adjusted debit balance
ADR: American depository receipt
AGI: adjusted gross income
AMEX: American Stock Exchange
AMPS: Auction Market Preferred Stock
AMT: alternative minimum tax
AON: all-or-none
APR: annual percentage rate
BOD: board of directors
BOT: bought
BSE: Boston Stock Exchange
BW: bid wanted
CAPM: Capital Asset Pricing Model
CARDs: Certificates for Amortizing Revolving Debts
CARs: Certificates for Automotive Receivables
CATS: Certificate of Accrual on Treasury Securities
CBOE: Chicago Board Options Exchange
CBOT: Chicago Board of Trade
CD: certificate of deposit
CEO: chief executive officer
C&F: cash and freight
CFO: chief financial officer
CFP: certified financial planner
CFTC: Commodity Futures Trading Commission
CME: Chicago Mercantile Exchange
CMV: current market value
C.O.D.: cash on delivery
COLTS: Continuously Offered Long-Term Securities
COMEX: Commodity Exchange of New York
COO: chief operating officer
CPA: certified public accountant
CPI: Consumer Price Index
CR: credit; credit balance
CSE: Cincinnati Stock Exchange
CTS: Consolidated Tape System

CUSIP: Committee on Uniform Securities Identification Procedures
CV: convertible security
DARTS: Dutch Auction-Rate Transferable Securities
DEFRA: Deficit Reduction Act of 1984
DI: disposable income
DJIA: Dow Jones Industrial Average
DK: don't know
DNR: do not reduce
DR: debt recorded
DTC: Depository Trust Company
DVP: delivery versus payment
ECU: European Currency Unit
EPS: earnings per share
ERISA: Employee Retirement Income Security Act
ERTA: Economic Recovery Tax Act of 1981
ESOP: Employee Stock Ownership Plan
F: foreign market
Fannie Mae: Federal National Mortgage Association
FAO: for the account of
FAQ: fair average quality
FASB: Financial Accounting Standards Board
FASTBACs: First Automotive Short-Term Bonds and Certificates
FBO: for the benefit of
FDIC: Federal Deposit Insurance Corporation
FED: Federal Reserve System
FHA: Federal Housing Administration
FHLMC: Federal Home Loan Mortgage Corporation
FICB: Federal Intermediate Credit Bank
FIFO: first in, first out
FIRSTS: Floating-Interest Rate Short-Term Securities
FLB: Federal Land Bank
FMAN: February, May, August and November
FMV: fair market value
FNMA: Federal National Mortgage Association
FOB: free on board
FOCUS Report: Financial and Operational Combined Uniform
    Single Report
FOK: fill or kill
FOMC: Federal Open Market Committee
Freddie Mac: Federal Home Loan Mortgage Corporation
FRN: floating rate note
FSLIC: Federal Savings and Loan Insurance Corporation
FTC: Federal Trade Commission
FVO: for valuation only
FYI: for your information
GAAP: generally accepted accounting principles
Ginnie Mae: Government National Mortgage Association
GNMA: Government National Mortgage Association
GNP: Gross National Product

GO: general obligation
GTC: good til cancelled
GTM: good this month
GTW: good this week
HOMES: Homeowner Mortgage Eurosecurities
House: London Stock Exchange
HUD: U.S. Department of Housing and Urban Development
IBRD: International Bank for Reconstruction and Development
ICC: Interstate Commerce Commission
IMF: International Monetary Fund
IMM: International Monetary Market
IOC: immediate-or-cancel
IPO: initial public offering
IRA: individual retirement account
IRR: internal rate of return
IRS: Internal Revenue Service
ITC: investment tax credit
ITS: inter-market trading system
JAJO: January, April, July, October
JTWROS: joint tenancy with right of survivorship
KCBT: Kansas City Board of Trade
LIBOR: London Interbank Offered Rate
LIFO: last in, first out
LMV: long market value
LOC: letter of credit
LOI: letter of intent
LPOA: limited power of attorney
LSK: local safekeeping
LTD: limited company
LYONs: Liquid Yield Option Notes
M: 1,000; U.S. money supply
M1: money supply that includes money in circulation
MAPS: Market Auction Preferred Stock
MIG: Moody's investment grade
MITs: market if touched orders
MJSD: March, June, September, December
MM: million
MSE: Midwest Stock Exchange
MSRB: Municipal Securities Rulemaking Board
N: New York Stock Exchange trading; newly listed; note
NASD: National Association of Securities Dealers
NASDAQ: National Association of Securities Dealers
    Automated Quotations
NAV: net asset value
NC: noncallable
NH: not held
NMAB: National Market Advisory Board
NMS: National Market System
NOL: net operating loss

NOW account: Negotiable Order of Withdrawal account
NR: not rated
NSCC: National Securities Clearing Corporation
NYFE: New York Futures Exchange
NYMEX: New York Mercantile Exchange
NYSE: New York Stock Exchange
O: over-the-counter
OAR: original accretion rate
OB: or better
OBO: order book official
OCC: Options Clearing Corporation
OID: original issue discount
OMB: Office of Management and Budget
OPM: other people's money
OPOSSMS: Options to Purchase Or Sell Specific Mortgage-backed
    Securities
OPRA: Options Price Reporting Authority
OTC: over-the-counter
OW: offer wanted
p: put options
PBGC: Pension Benefit Guaranty Corporation
PHLX: Philadelphia Stock Exchange
PN: project note
PPI: Producer Price Index
PSA: Public Securities Association
PSE: Pacific Stock Exchange
P/E: price-to-earnings ratio
P&L: profit and loss
POA: power of attorney
P&S: purchase and sales department
PV: par value
PVD: payment versus delivery
PX: price
Q: company to be bankrupted or liquidated
QT: questioned trade; fiscal quarter
RAN: revenue anticipation note
R&D: research and development
REIT: real estate investment trust
REMIC: real estate mortgage investment conduit
REORG: reorganization department
REPO: repurchase agreement
ROI: return on investment
ROP: registered options principal
RP: repurchase agreement
RR: registered representative
RTD: rated; returned
S: round lot; stock split or dividend
Sallie Mae: Student Loan Marketing Association
SBA: Small Business Administration

SBI: shares of beneficial interest
SDRs: special drawing rights
SEC: Securities and Exchange Commission
SECO: Securities and Exchange Commission Organization
SEP: simplified employee pension
SIA: Securities Industry Association
SIAC: Securities Industry Automation Corporation
SIC: Standard Industrial Classification
SIPC: Securities Investors Protection Corporation
SLMA: Student Loan Marketing Association
SMA: special miscellaneous account
SPA: single premium annuity
SRO: self-regulatory organization
SRP: salary reduction plan
ss: actual number of shares
ST: stopped
STANY: Security Traders' Association of New York
STARS: Short-Term Auction-Rate Stock
Steenth: one sixteenth
Street: Wall Street
SWIFT: Society for Worldwide Interbank Finance Telecommunications
TAB: tax anticipation bill
TAN: tax anticipation note
TBA: to be announced
Ten in com: tenants in common
TIC: tenants in common
TIGRs: Treasury Investment Growth Receipts
Ton: $100 million
TVA: Tennessee Valley Authority
TZ: Treasury zero certificates
U: annual high
UBI: unit of beneficial interest
UGMA: Uniform Gifts to Minors Act
UPC: Uniform Practice Code
UR: under review
VA: Veterans Administration
vi: corporation reorganizing under bankruptcy laws
WD: when distributed
WOR: we offer retail
WT: warrant
X: ex-dividend
XCH: ex-change
XD: ex-dividend
XR: ex-rights
XW: ex-warrants
YTC: yield to call
YTM: yield to maturity
Z: actual shares

REFERENCE LIST

Accounting year *(See: Fiscal year)*
ACRS *(See: Accelerated cost recovery system)*
ADR *(See: American depository receipt)*
Advance-Decline Line *(See: Breadth of market theory)*
Aftermath *(See: Secondary market)*
AMT *(See: Alternative minimum tax)*
Analyst *(See: Financial analyst)*
Annuitant *(See: Annuity)*
AON *(See: All-or-none order)*
Arbitration *(See: Board of arbitration)*
Asked price *(See: Asked)*
Auditor's report *(See: Accountant's opinion)*
Averaging *(See: Constant dollar plan)*
Bed-bug letter *(See: Deficiency Letter)*
BETA *(See: BETA coefficient)*
Burn *(See: Churn and burn)*
Buy limit order *(See: Limit order)*
Cage *(See: Cashiering department)*
Call loan rate *(See: Broker's loan rate)*
Call premium *(See: Premium)*
Call provision *(See: Call feature)*
Capital appreciation *(See: Appreciation)*
Capital investment *(See: Capital expenditure)*
Cash order *(See: Cash sale)*
Cash transaction *(See: Cash sale)*
CATS *(See: Certificates of Accrual on Treasury Securities)*
CBOE *(See: Chicago Board Options Exchange)*
CBOT *(See: Chicago Board of Trade)*
CD *(See: Certificate of deposit)*
CEO *(See: Chief executive officer)*
Certificateless municipals *(See: Book entry)*
C & F *(See: Cash and freight)*
CFP *(See: Certified financial planner)*

CFTC *(See: Commodities Futures Trading Commission)*
Class A/Class B stock *(See: Classified stock)*
Close a position *(See: Closing transaction)*
Closed-end management company *(See: Closed-end investment company)*
Closing price *(See: Close)*
Closing purchase *(See: Closing transaction)*
Closing sale *(See: Closing transaction)*
CMV *(See: Current market value)*
COMEX *(See: Commodity Exchange of New York)*
Computerized buy program *(See: Buy program)*
Computerized sell program *(See: Sell program)*
Confidence theory *(See: Barron's Confidence Index)*
Confirmation *(See: Trade confirmation)*
Consolidated balance sheet *(See: Balance sheet)*
Consolidated tape *(See: Ticker tape)*
Corporate calendar *(See: Calendar)*
Cost basis *(See: Basis)*
Cost of carrying *(See: Carrying charge)*
Cost-of-Living Index *(See: Consumer Price Index)*
Cost of Sale *(See: Basis)*
Coupon bond *(See: Bearer bond)*
Covenant of equal coverage *(See: Negative pledge clause)*
CPI *(See: Consumer Price Index)*
Credit agreement *(See: Hypothecation agreement)*
Crush *(See: Putting on the crush; Reverse a crush)*
CSE *(See: Cincinnati Stock Exchange)*
Curb *(See: American Stock Exchange)*
Current maturity *(See: Original maturity)*
Current return *(See: Current return yield)*
CUSIP *(See: Committee on Uniform Securities Identification Procedures)*
Customer's loan consent *(See: Consent to loan agreement)*
Customer statement *(See: Accountant's opinion)*
CV *(See: Convertible security)*
Deed of trust *(See: Trust indenture)*
Deferral of taxes *(See: Tax deferred)*
Deferred interest bond *(See: Zero coupon bond)*
Delayed delivery *(See: Seller's option)*
Delivery against cost *(See: Delivery versus payment)*
Delivery against sale *(See: Delivery versus payment)*
Delivery grades *(See: Contract grade)*
Delphi Forecast *(See: Jury of executive opinion)*
Depletion *(See: Depletion accounting)*
Depository receipt *(See: American depository receipt)*
DI *(See: Disposable income)*
Direct placement *(See: Private placement)*
Discount bond *(See: Discount)*

Distributing syndicate *(See: Syndicate)*
DJIA *(See: Dow Jones Industrial Average)*
DK *(See: Don't know)*
DNR *(See: Do not reduce)*
Dual security *(See: Guaranteed bond or stock)*
DVP *(See: Delivery versus payment)*
Earned surplus *(See: Retained earnings)*
Economic expansion *(See: Economic growth rate)*
Either or order *(See: Alternative order)*
End load *(See: Back-end load)*
EPS *(See: Earnings per share)*
Equipment Bond *(See: Equipment bond/trust certificate)*
Equity REIT *(See: Real estate investment trust)*
Equity Turnover *(See: Capital turnover)*
ERISA *(See: Employee Retirement Income Security Act)*
ESOP *(See: Employee Stock Ownership Plan)*
Excess margin *(See: Excess equity/margin)*
Exchange acquisition *(See: Exchange trade)*
Exchange distribution *(See: Exchange trade)*
Ex-dividend date *(See: Ex-date)*
Fannie Mae *(See: Federal National Mortgage Association)*
FAO *(See: For the account of)*
FAQ *(See: Fair average quality)*
Favorite Fifty *(See: Nifty Fifty)*
FBO *(See: For the benefit of)*
FDIC *(See: Federal Deposit Insurance Corporation)*
Fed, The *(See: Federal Reserve System)*
Federal Farm Credit Bank *(See: Federal Farm Credit System)*
Federal Reserve Open Market Committee *(See: Federal Open Market Committee)*
Fed funds *(See: Federal funds)*
FHA *(See: Federal Housing Administration)*
FHLMC *(See: Federal Home Loan Mortgage Corporation)*
Fidelity bond *(See: Blanket fidelity bond)*
FIFO *(See: First in, first out)*
Financial position *(See: Financial condition)*
Financial pyramid *(See: Pyramid)*
Financial risk *(See: Downside risk)*
Fixed trust *(See: Unit investment trust)*
Flexible exchange rate *(See: Floating exchange rate)*
Floating an issue *(See: New issue)*
Floating rate note *(See: Floater)*
Floating supply *(See: Float)*
Fluctuation limits *(See: Daily trading limit)*
FNMA *(See: Federal National Mortgage Association)*
FOB *(See: Free on board)*

FOK *(See: Fill-or-kill order)*
FOMC *(See: Federal Open Market Committee)*
Foreign corporation *(See: Alien corporation)*
For valuation only *(See: For your information)*
Freddie Mac *(See: Federal Home Loan Mortgage Corporation)*
Free box *(See: Box)*
Free crowd *(See: Active bond crowd)*
FTC *(See: Federal Trade Commission)*
Full disclosure act *(See: Securities Act of 1933)*
Fundamental analysis *(See: Fundamental research analysis)*
Fund manager *(See: Manager)*
Futures contracts *(See: Futures)*
FYI *(See: For your information)*
General loan and collateral agreement *(See: Broker's loans)*
Ginnie Mae *(See: Government National Mortgage Association)*
GNMA *(See: Government National Mortgage Association)*
GNP *(See: Gross National Product)*
Gold fix *(See: Fix)*
Good money *(See: Federal funds)*
Government bond calendar *(See: Calendar)*
GTC *(See: Good til cancelled order)*
GTM *(See: Good this month order)*
GTW *(See: Good this week order)*
Hard currency *(See: Hard money)*
House maintenance call *(See: Maintenance call)*
HUD *(See: Housing and Urban Development)*
ICC *(See: Interstate Commerce Commission)*
IMF *(See: International Monetary Fund)*
IMM *(See: International Monetary Market)*
Immediate payment annuity *(See: Immediate annuity)*
Import duty *(See: Immediate annuity)*
Inactive bond *(See: Inactive stock)*
In and out trader *(See: Day trader)*
Income shares *(See: Dual purpose fund)*
Instinet *(See: Fourth market)*
Intermarket spread *(See: Interdelivery spread)*
Internal financing *(See: Internal expansion financing)*
Inter vivos trust *(See: Living trust)*
Investment credit *(See: Investment tax credit)*
Investment grade *(See: Bank quality)*
Investment trust *(See: Investment company)*
IPO *(See: Initial public offering)*
IRA *(See: Individual retirement account)*
IRS *(See: Internal Revenue Service)*
Joint bond *(See: Joint and several bond)*
JTWROS *(See: Joint tenancy with right of survivorship)*

Junior security *(See Junior issue)*
Justified price *(See: Fair market value)*
Lapsed option *(See: Expire worthless)*
Legal investments *(See: Legal investments list)*
Letter bond *(See: Investment letter)*
Letter of authorization *(See: Authority to transfer)*
Letter security *(See: Investment letter)*
Letter stock *(See: Investment letter)*
LIBOR *(See: London Interbank Offered Rate)*
LIFO *(See: Last-in, first-out)*
Limited trading authority *(See: Limited power of attorney)*
Lipper Gauge *(See: Lipper Mutual Fund Industry Average)*
LOC *(See: Letter of credit)*
LOI *(See: Letter of intent)*
LMV *(See: Long market value)*
Long bond *(See: Long bond coupon)*
Long-term gain or (loss) *(See: Long-term capital gain or [loss])*
LPOA *(See: Limited power of attorney)*
LSK *(See: Local safekeeping)*
Ltd *(See: Limited company)*
Maintenance requirement *(See: Minimum maintenance)*
Make a price *(See: Make a market/price)*
Margin agreement *(See: Hypothecation agreement)*
Marketability *(See: Liquidity)*
Market arbitrage *(See: Arbitrage)*
Market maker *(See: Make a market/price)*
Marketplace *(See: Market, The)*
Market research, *(See: Market analysis)*
MIG *(See: Moody's investment grade)*
Minus tick *(See: Down tick)*
MIT *(See: Market-if-touched order)*
Money Spread *(See: Vertical spread)*
Mortgage REIT *(See: Real estate investment trust)*
MSRB *(See: Municipal Securities Rulemaking Board)*
Multiple *(See: Price to earnings ratio)*
Municipal bond calendar *(See: Calendar)*
Mutual improvement certificate *(See: Municipal improvement certificate)*
NASD *(See: National Association of Securities Dealers)*
NASDAQ *(See: National Association of Securities Dealers Automated Quotations)*
NAV *(See: Net asset value)*
NC *(See: Noncallable)*
Negative yield curve *(See: Inverted yield curve)*
Negotiable certificate of deposit *(See: Certificate of deposit)*
Net earnings *(See: Net income/earnings)*
Net estate *(See: Gross estate)*
Net profit *(See: Net income/earnings)*

Net quick assets *(See: Acid test ratio)*
Net worth *(See: Stockholders' Equity)*
New York Curb Exchange *(See: American Stock Exchange)*
Nominal interest rate *(See: Nominal yield)*
Nominal quotation *(See: For your information)*
Nonpublic information *(See: Insider information)*
NR *(See: Not rated)*
NSCC *(See: National Securities Clearing Corporation)*
NYFE *(See: New York Futures Exchange)*
NYSE *(See: New York Stock Exchange)*
NYSE Rule 396 *(See: Nine bond rule)*
OAR *(See: Original accretion rate)*
OB *(See: Limit or better order)*
OBO *(See: Order Book Official)*
OCC *(See: Options Clearing Corporation)*
Offering *(See: Primary offering; Secondary offering)*
Offering circular *(See: Prospectus)*
OID *(See: Original issue discount)*
OMB *(See: Office of Management and Budget)*
On a scale *(See: Scale order)*
One cancels the other *(See: Alternative order)*
On margin *(See: Margin)*
Open Order *(See: Good til cancelled order)*
Operating leverage *(See: Leverage)*
OPM, *(See: Other people's money)*
OPRA *(See: Options Price Reporting Authority)*
Or better *(See: Limit or better order)*
OTC *(See: Over-the-counter)*
OTC margin stock *(See: Margin security)*
Oversubscribed *(See: Over booked)*
OW *(See: Offer wanted)*
Paid in surplus *(See: Paid in capital/surplus)*
Parent company *(See: Holding company)*
Paris club *(See: Group of ten)*
Par value *(See: Par)*
P/E *(See: Price-to-earnings ratio)*
Pegging *(See: Fixing)*
Pipeline *(See: In the pipeline)*
P&L *(See: Profit and loss statement)*
POA *(See: Power of attorney)*
Pooling of interest *(See: Pool)*
Preference item *(See: Tax preference item)*
Preference shares *(See: Prior preferred stock)*
Pretax profits *(See: Pretax earnings/profits)*
Price gap *(See: Gap)*
Price limit *(See: Limit price)*

Profit margin *(See: Margin of profit)*
Promissory note *(See: Note)*
Pro rata basis *(See: Pro rata/pro rata basis)*
Protective covenant *(See: Protective convenant)*
P&S *(See: Purchase and sales department)*
Public offering *(See: Primary offering)*
Purchase group *(See: Syndicate)*
PV *(See: Par value)*
PVD *(See: Payment versus delivery)*
Qualified plan *(See: Qualified retirement plan)*
RAN *(See: Revenue anticipation note)*
Rate of exchange *(See: Exchange rate)*
Rate of inflation *(See: Consumer Price Index; Inflation rate)*
R&D *(See: Research and development)*
Real rate of return *(See: Aftertax real rate of return)*
Receivables *(See: Accounts receivable)*
Receive versus payment *(See: Delivery versus payment)*
Reciprocal immunity *(See: Mutual exclusion doctrine)*
Redeemable bond *(See: Callable)*
Red herring *(See: Preliminary prospectus)*
Refinancing *(See: Refunding)*
Regional Fund *(See: Specialized mutual fund)*
Registered competitive trader *(See: Floor trader)*
Registered coupon bond *(See: Registered bond)*
Registered investment company *(See: Investment company)*
REIT *(See: Real estate investment trust)*
Repo *(See: Repurchase agreement)*
Restrictive convenant *(See: Restrictive convenant)*
Retirement account *(See: Qualified retirement plan)*
Return on investment *(See: Return on capital/principal)*
Rigged market *(See: Manipulation)*
Rights of survivorship *(See: Joint tenancy with right of survivorship)*
Risk *(See: Downside risk)*
ROI *(See: Return on investment)*
ROP *(See: Registered options principal)*
RP *(See: Repurchase agreement)*
RR *(See: Registered representative)*
Safekeeping *(See: Local safekeeping)*
Sales load *(See: Sales charge)*
Sallie Mae *(See: Student Loan Marketing Association)*
SBA *(See: Small Business Administration)*
SBI *(See: Shares of beneficial interest)*
SDRs *(See: Special drawing rights)*
SEC *(See: Securities and Exchange Commission)*
SECO *(See: Securities and Exchange Commission Organization)*
Secondary offering *(See: Secondary distribution)*

Securities analyst *(See: Financial analyst)*
Selling short *(See: Short sale)*
Selling short against the box *(See: Short against the box)*
Sell-stop order *(See: Stop-loss order)*
SEP *(See: Simplified employee pension [SEP])*
Series of option *(See: Option series)*
Shares authorized *(See: Authorized stock)*
Shares of beneficial interest *(See: Unit of beneficial interest)*
Shares outstanding *(See: Issued and outstanding)*
Shelter *(See: Tax shelter)*
Short sale against the box *(See: Short against the box)*
Short-term gain or [loss] *(See: Short-term capital gain or [loss])*
SIA *(See: Securities Industry Association)*
Siamese stock *(See: Paired stock)*
SIC *(See: Standard Industrial Classification System)*
SIPC *(See: Securities Investors Protection Corporation)*
SLMA *(See: Student Loan Marketing Association)*
SMA *(See: Special miscellaneous account)*
Social and economic risk *(See: Economic and social risk)*
SPA *(See: Single premium annuity)*
Special bid *(See: Special offering)*
Special block sale *(See: Specialist block purchase or sale)*
Special district bond *(See: Special assessment bond)*
Split *(See: Stock split)*
Split down *(See: Reverse split)*
SRO *(See: Self-regulatory organization)*
Standby commitment *(See: Standby commitment underwriting)*
Stapled stock *(See: Paired stock)*
Start-up money *(See: Seed money)*
Statement of income *(See: Profit and loss statement)*
Statement of operations *(See: Profit and loss statement)*
Statutory underwriter *(See: Voluntary underwriter)*
Stock purchase plan *(See: Stock option)*
Stock symbol *(See: Symbol)*
Stock ticker symbol *(See: Symbol)*
Straddle *(See: Spread)*
Strike price *(See: Exercise price)*
Striking price *(See: Exercise price)*
Subscription right *(See: Right)*
Subscription warrant *(See: Warrant)*
Systematic risk *(See: BETA coefficient)*
Takeover arbitrage *(See: Risk arbitrage)*
Tape *(See: Broad tape; Ticker tape)*
Tax free *(See: Tax exempt/tax free security)*
Technical analysis *(See: Technical research)*
Telephone privilege *(See: Telephone privilege switching)*

Ten in com *(See: Tenants in common)*
Term bond *(See: Term maturity)*
3-5-10 Rule *(See: Accelerated cost recovery system)*
TIC *(See: Tenants in common)*
Ticker *(See: Ticker tape)*
Times fixed charge *(See: Fixed-charge coverage)*
Total output *(See: Aggregate supply)*
Trade balance *(See: Balance of trade)*
Trading authorization *(See: Full trading authorization; Limited trading authorization)*
Trading floor *(See: Floor)*
Trading halt *(See: Suspended trading)*
Trading limit *(See: Daily trading limit; Limit up; Limit down)*
Trading post *(See: Post)*
Type of option *(See: Class)*
Underlying security *(See: Underlying)*
Underwriter *(See: Investment banker)*
Underwriting manager *(See: Managing underwriter)*
Undistributed profits, earnings or net income *(See: Retained earning)*
Unit of trading *(See: Trading unit)*
Unregistered security *(See: Investment letter)*
VA mortgage *(See: Veterans Administration Mortgage)*
Variable ratio writing *(See: Variable hedging)*
Wholesale Price Index *(See: Producer Price Index)*
Wide open *(See: Underbanked)*
Wire room *(See: Order department)*
With rights of survivorship *(See: Joint tenancy with right of survivorship)*
WOR *(See: We offer retail)*
World Bank *(See: International Bank for Reconstruction and Development)*
Writing naked *(See: Naked option)*
XD *(See: Ex-dividend)*
X-Dividend Date *(See: Ex-dividend date)*
Yield equivalent *(See: Equivalent taxable yield)*
YTC *(See: Yield to call)*
YTM *(See: Yield to maturity)*

HOW TO INTERPRET THE WALL STREET
JOURNAL REPORTS

An essential element of investing is the ability to monitor the value of securities. Newspapers and reporting services around the world provide the latest information to their subscribers. Because of the large numbers of securities being reported, abbreviations are used to conserve page space. When the abbreviations and terminology are understood, interpreting the information being reported becomes quite simple.

The following section has been included to provide a detailed explanation of various headings and abbreviations used in reporting. Most newspapers use fairly standard methods of reporting security prices. Check the legends printed in the newspaper you use for any differences. (Caution: Some newspapers print their legends on a space available basis, so the legend may not appear every day.)

Explanatory Notes

EXPLANATORY NOTES
(For New York and American Exchange listed issues)

Sales figures are unofficial.

PE ratios are based on primary per share earnings as reported by the companies for the most recent four quarters. Extraordinary items generally are excluded.

The 52-Week High and Low columns show the highest and the lowest price of the stock in consolidated trading during the preceding 52 weeks plus the current week, but not the current trading day. The 52-week high and low columns are adjusted to reflect stock payouts of 10 percent or more.

u – Indicates a new 52-week high. d – Indicates a new 52-week low.

g – Dividend or earnings in Canadian money. Stock trades in U.S. dollars. No yield or PE shown unless stated in U.S. money. n – New issue in the past 52 weeks. The high-low range begins with the start of trading and does not cover the entire 52 week period. pp – Two installments. s – Split or stock dividend of 25 per cent or more in the past 52 weeks. The high-low range is adjusted from the old stock. Dividend begins with the date of split or stock dividend. v – Trading halted on primary market.

Unless otherwise noted, rates of dividends in the foregoing table are annual disbursements based on the last quarterly or semi-annual declaration. Special or extra dividends or payments not designated as regular are identified in the following footnotes.

a – Also extra or extras. b – Annual rate plus stock dividend. c – Liquidating dividend. e – Declared or paid in preceding 12 months. i – Declared or paid after stock dividend or split up. j – Paid this year, dividend omitted, deferred or no action taken at last dividend meeting. k – Declared or paid this year, an accumulative issue with dividends in arrears. r – Declared or paid in preceding 12 months plus stock dividend. t – Paid in stock in preceding 12 months, estimated cash value on ex-dividend or ex-distribution date.

x – Ex-dividend or ex-rights. y – Ex-dividend and sales in full. z – Sales in full.

pf – Preferred. rt – Rights. un – Units. wd – When distributed. wi – When issued. wt – Warrants. ww – With warrants.

vi – In bankruptcy or receivership or being reorganized under the Bankruptcy Act, or securities assumed by such companies.

Courtesy of Dow Jones & Company, Inc.

a	Also extra dividend or dividends.
b	Annual dividend rate plus stock dividend.
c	Liquidating dividend.
d	Indicates a new 52 week low.
e	Dividend declared or paid in preceding 12 months.
g	Dividend or earnings in Canadian money.
i	Dividend declared or paid after stock dividend or split.
j	Dividend paid this year, dividend omitted, deferred or no action taken at last dividend meeting.
k	Dividend declared or paid this year, an accumulative issue with dividend in arrears.
n	New issue in the past 52 weeks. The high low range begins with the start of trading and does not cover the entire 52 weeks period.
pf	Preferred (followed by letter indicating series if applicable).
pp	Dividend paid in two installments.
r	Dividend declared or paid in preceding 12 months; plus stock dividend.
rt	Rights.
s	Split or stock dividend of 25 percent or more in the past 52 weeks. The high-low range is adjusted from the old stock. Dividend begins with the date of split or stock dividend.
t	Dividend paid in stock in preceding 12 months; estimated cash value on ex-dividend or ex-distribution date.
u	Indicates a new 52 week high.
un	Units.

v	Trading halted on primary market.
vi	In bankruptcy or receivership or being reorganized under the Bankruptcy Act, or securities assumed by such companies.
wd	When distributed.
wi	When issued.
wt	Warrants.
ww	With warrants.
x	Ex-dividend or ex-rights.
xw	Without warrants.
y	Ex-dividend and sales in full.
z	Sales in full.

AMERICAN, NEW YORK COMPOSITE TRANSACTIONS AND NASDAQ (OTC) MARKETS

Column headings and meanings:

52 Weeks   (365 Days)

High: The highest price at which the stock has traded in the preceding 52 weeks. Annual high.

Low: The lowest price at which the stock has traded in the preceding 52 weeks. Annual low.

Stock: The abbreviated name of the company, not usually the ticker symbol.

Div: Dividend. The annualized dividend based on the last quarterly or semi-annual declaration. (Example: A company declares a quarterly dividend of $0.25 per share. The annual dividend shown assumes the dividend will stay constant for the next three declarations for an annual dividend of $1.00 per share.)

YLD %:   The dividend yield of the stock based on the closing price.

P-E Ratio: The price-to-earnings ratio. (Example: The price of XYZ stock closed at $45 per share, annual earnings per share is $2.50. The P-E is 18.)

Sales 100s: The number of round lots (unofficial) of 100 each that traded hands during the sessions being reported (i.e., A figure reported of 627 means 62,700 shares, not including odd lots, were traded.)

High: The highest price at which the shares were traded during the trading session.

Low: The lowest price at which the shares were traded during the trading session.

Close: The last price at which the shares were traded during the trading session.

FIGURE 2

TUESDAY, FEBRUARY 24, 1987

NEW YORK STOCK EXCHANGE COMPOSITE TRANSACTIONS

Monday, February 23, 1987

Quotations include trades on the Midwest, Pacific, Philadelphia, Boston and Cincinnati stock exchanges and reported by the National Association of Securities Dealers and Instinet

Courtesy of Dow Jones & Company, Inc.

Net Chg: Net Change. The net difference in the closing price of the shares of the trading session being reported from the last previous trading session, could be higher (+), lower (–) or unchanged (. . .). The net change subtracted from the current closing price results in the closing price of the previous trading session. (Example: A close of 20½ (–¾) equals the closing price of 21¼ the previous trading session.)

MUTUAL FUND QUOTATIONS

Column 1 Most names of the funds are abbreviated.

Bold face type The name of the "family" or management company.

Indented under bold faced type The names of the individual funds being managed within a family.

Not bold face type, not indented The name of an individual fund (not part of a family of funds).

Column 2 Fund type. Composition of portfolio. (NOTE: Fund type may not always be indicated.)
  Apr Appreciation (growth).
  Bal Balanced (equity and debt securities).
  B or BD or Bnd Bond.
  Conv Convertible securities.
  Egy Energy stocks.
  Eur European stocks.
  Ex Tax exempt.
  Fin Financial securities.
  Gld Gold mining stocks.
  Gov or Govt Government securities.
  Gr or Grw Growth.
  HiY or HY High yield bonds.
  I or Inc Income.
  Ins Insured tax-free bonds.
  Intl International.
  Mbnd Municipal bond.
  Mtge Mortgage securities.
  Pfd Preferred stock.
  Shrt Short term bond.
  Stk Stock.
  Tech Technical (equity securities).
    -Legends (also listed in column 2).
  d Ex-dividend.
  f Previous day quotation.

FIGURE 3

MUTUAL FUND QUOTATIONS

Monday, February 23, 1987

Price ranges for investment companies, as quoted by the National Association of Securities Dealers. NAV stands for net asset value per share; the offering includes net asset value plus maximum sales charge, if any.

	NAV	Offer Price	NAV Chg.
GNMA	9.25	9.71	...
US Govt	9.16	9.62	...
TxFr Pa	8.19	8.60	...
TFr USA	11.96	12.56	
TF USAI	11.07	11.62	...
Delw Fd	21.70	23.72	-.20
Delta Td	8.80	9.62	-.07
Destiny I	14.82	(z)	-.11
Destiny II	19.20	(z)	-.03
D.I.T.			
Cap Gr	15.52	N.L.	-.19
Cur In	10.51	N.L.	...
Gov Sec	10.29	N.L.	+.01
OTC Gr	28.64	N.L.	-.13
DFA FxIn	101.80	N.L.	+.05
DFA Small	10.16	N.L.	-.05
D G DvSrs	27.40	N.L.	-.25
DodgC Bal	x36.21	N.L.	-.61
DodgC Stk	x37.02	N.L.	-.61
Double Ex	11.97	12.47	...
Drexel Burnham:			
DB Fund	23.43	24.28	-.15
DSTGv r	10.71	N.L.	+.02
DSTOp r	10.75	N.L.	-.07
DST Cv r	10.61	N.L.	-.05
DSTBd r	11.85	N.L.	-.01
DST Gr r	13.60	N.L.	-.12
DST E r	15.21	N.L.	+.02
FenInt r	12.87	N.L.	-.04
TxFr Ltd	10.89	11.06	-.01
TF Long	10.65	N.L.	...
Dreyfus Group:			
A Bonds	15.23	N.L.	+.01
CalT Ex	15.80	N.L.	...
Cap Val	21.70	N.L.	-.10
Cnv Sec	9.36	N.L.	+.02
Dreyf Fd	12.92	14.12	-.08
Dreyf Lv	17.93	19.60	-.12
GNMA	(z)	(z)	...
Growth	11.83	N.L.	-.04
Insr TE	18.75	N.L.	-.01
Intrmd	14.37	N.L.	...
Mass Tx	16.98	N.L.	...
New Ldr	23.91	N.L.	-.21
NYT Ex	16.17	N.L.	...
Str Inc	13.76	14.19	+.01
Str Inv	15.19	15.66	-.10
Tax ExB	13.19	N.L.	-.01
Third Cn	7.37	N.L.	-.03
Eagle Gth	8.04	8.79	-.11
Eaton Vance Funds:			
Cal Mn r	10.81	N.L.	...
EH Stk	14.83	15.99	-.13
Gov Obli	12.28	12.89	...
Growth	8.24	8.65	-.09
Hi Inc r	10.30	N.L.	...
Hi Mun r	10.58	N.L.	-.01
High Yld	5.40	5.67	+.01
Inc Bost	10.78	11.32	-.01
Invests	8.24	8.65	-.05
Muni Bd	9.42	9.89	+.01
Naut Fd	14.54	15.27	-.11
Spc Eqty	19.36	20.87	-.19
Tot Ret	10.77	11.31	-.10
VS Specl	12.52	13.14	-.13
Empir Bld	17.98	18.88	+.02
Equitec Siebel:			
AggrGr r	14.34	N.L.	-.02
HiYld r	9.89	N.L.	+.01
TotlRet r	14.78	N.L.	-.12
USGvt r	9.91	N.L.	+.01
Eq Strat	16.52	N.L.	-.01
Evergrn	14.15	N.L.	-.06
Evrgrn TR	20.35	N.L.	-.10
Fairmnt	58.25	N.L.	-.59
Farm B Gr	16.09	N.L.	-.03
Federated Group:			
Fed Flt	10.13	N.L.	...
Fed StkB	16.32	N.L.	-.08
Cash Tr	10.94	N.L.	...
Exch Fd	56.45	N.L.	-.45
FIMT	10.61	N.L.	...
FT Intl	22.10	N.L.	-.04
GNMA	11.50	N.L.	...
Grow Tr	17.97	N.L.	-.12
Hi Yld	11.21	N.L.	...
Incm Tr	10.76	N.L.	-.03
Intrmd	10.14	N.L.	...
SIGT	10.42	N.L.	...
SIMT	10.36	N.L.	...
Stock Tr	25.09	N.L.	-.28
US Govt	10.03	N.L.	...
Fidelity Investments:			

	NAV	Offer Price	NAV Chg.
HY Inv	10.70	11.15	.
Incom f	10.88	N.L.	+.02
GabelliA	12.72	N.L.	-.06
Gatewy Gr	11.29	N.L.	-.07
Gatewy Op	14.78	N.L.	-.10
Geico ARP	25.69	N.L.	-.02
GenAgg G	22.85	N.L.	-.22
Genl Elec Invest:			
Elf TxE	11.56	N.L.	...
Elfn Inc	11.55	N.L.	-.01
Elfn Tr	30.79	N.L.	-.29
S&S LT	11.97	N.L.	-.01
S&S Pro	39.05	N.L.	-.33
GenlSec r	12.33	N.L.	-.04
Genl TxEx	15.08	N.L.	...
Gintel Group:			
Cap App	12.85	N.L.	-.12
Erisa	43.39	N.L.	.43
Gintl Fd	76.19	N.L.	.89
Grad EstG	17.32	N.L.	.18
Grad Opp	13.55	N.L.	.08
GIT Investment:			
Eq Spec	17.99	N.L.	.11
Income	9.61	N.L.	...
TxFr HY	11.61	N.L.	..
Granit Gr	17.09	N.L.	-.11
Grth IndSh	10.56	N.L.	-.03
GrF Wash	12.60	13.26	-.03
GT Global:			
Europe	(z)	(z)	...
Intl	(z)	(z)	...
Japan	(z)	(z)	...
Pacific	(z)	(z)	...
Guardian Funds:			
Bond	12.36	N.L.	+.02
Park Av	24.57	26.85	-.09
Stock	20.16	N.L.	-.06
Hamltn Fd	7.69	8.40	-.05
Harbor G	12.34	N.L.	.09
Hartwll Gt	14.62	N.L.	15
Hartwll Lv	21.34	N.L.	.1)
Heartlnd	16.28	17.05	-.07
Hrtg Cap	12.57	12.96	.07
Hrtg Conv	10.04	10.57	.03
HorcM Gr	25.57	N.L.	-.24
Hutton EF Group:			
Bond r	12.26	N.L.	...
Growth r	15.24	N.L.	-.18
OptnIn r	9.56	N.L.	-.10
GovSec r	10.40	N.L.	-.01
BasVal r	13.63	N.L.	-.10
Cal Muni	11.23	11.70	-.01
Nat Mun	12.20	12.71	..
NY Muni	11.48	11.96	+.02
PrecMt r	14.44	N.L.	+.10
SplEq r	15.30	N.L.	-.13
IDEX	14.68	16.04	.15
IDEX II	12.20	13.33	.11
IndsFd Am	3.52	N.L.	.06
Industrial Group:			
Ind Am	10.71	11.70	.11
Ind Govt	9.26	9.93	+.01
Ind Opt	9.23	10.09	.07
Integrated Resources:			
CapAp r	14.62	N.L.	-.17
HmInv r	10.74	N.L.	-.01
Tax Free	12.59	13.22	+.01
Int CapG	7.22	7.41	-.06
Investment Portfolios			
GovtPl r	8.48	N.L.	...
HiYield r	10.19	N.L.	+.01
Option r	7.96	N.L.	-.06
Equity r	12.73	N.L.	-.10
TotalRt r	9.89	N.L.	-.05
ITB Group:			
InvT Bos	13.87	14.91	-.17
InvT Hip	14.58	15.64	.
InT MTF	17.20	17.96	+.01
IDS Mutual Fund Grp:			
IDS Bnd	5.40	5/60	-.01
IDS Disc	8.89	9.36	.10
IDS Eqty	11.25	11.84	.09
IDS Extl	5.31	5.59	...
IDS Fed	5.28	5.56	...
IDS Gth	25.14	26.47	-.29

	NAV	Offer Price	NAV Chg.
Intl Hldg	15.59	16.67	-.07
Inter TP	11.92	12.16	...
Muni Ins	8.36	8.71	..
Mun HY	10.90	11.35	..
NY Mn r	11.45	N.L.	...
Ltd Mat	9.91	10.01	...
MuniI r	10.13	N.L.	+.01
NatRes r	14.50	N.L.	-.07
Pacific	34.73	37.14	-.23
Phoenx	13.63	14.58	-.06
Retire r	11.93	N.L.	-.05
RetInc r	10.07	N.L.	-.01
RetGIB r	10.54	N.L.	...
Sci Tech	13.44	14.37	-.05
Sp'l Valu	16.25	17.38	-.02
MetL EqIc	10.23	10.71	.04
MetL HI	7.67	8.03	.
Mid Amer	6.82	7.45	.04
MidA HGr	5.25	5.74	.01
Midas Gld	9.50	10.11	+.05
Monitrd	20.07	20.80	.09
MSB Fund	24.76	N.L.	.22
Mutl Beac	21.37	N.L.	.02
Muti BnFd	15.11	16.51	.17
Mutual of Omaha Funds:			
Amer	10.80	N.L.	..
Growth	8.34	9.07	.12
Incom	9.48	10.30	.04
Tax Free	12.03	13.08	+.01
MutlQI Fd	22.46	N.L.	-.04
Mutl Shars	67.51	N.L.	-.13
NtlAvia Tc	12.84	14.03	-.09
Natl Ind	13.69	N.L.	-.08
National Securities Funds:			
Balanc	15.13	16.31	-.09
Bond	3.25	3.50	+.01
Cal TEx	13.48	14.23	+.01
Fed Sec	11.23	12.04	...
Preferd	8.81	9.50	
Income	8.47	9.13	.05
Real Est	10.67	11.57	.02
Stock	10.20	11.00	.08
Tax ExB	10.49	11.07	..
Totl Ret	8.07	8.70	.05
Grwth	12.62	13.61	.08
Fairfld	(z)	(z)	...
Natl Telcm	16.30	17.81	-.18
Nationwide Funds:			
Fund	15.58	16.84	-.13
Growth	9.91	10.71	-.14
Bond	10.19	11.02	...
Tax Free	10.10	N.L.	-.01
New England Funds:			
Equity	22.58	24.15	-.19
Grwth	34.07	36.44	.07
Income	(z)	(z)	..
Gvt Sec	(z)	(z)	..
Ret Eqty	26.08	27.89	.33
Tax Ex	(z)	(z)	
Neuberger Berman Mngt:			
Energy	21.23	N.L.	.22
Guardn	44.62	N.L.	.31
Liberty	4.79	N.L.	+.01
Ltd Mat	10.16	N.L.	...
Manhtn	10.34	N.L.	-.10
Partner	19.75	N.L.	-.18
Newton Gr	24.79	N.L.	-.26
Newtn Inc	8.39	N.L.	+.01
NY Muni	1.24	N.L.	...
Nicholas Group:			
Nichls r	38.80	N.L.	-.22
NichII r	19.03	N.L.	-.06
Nich Inc	4.05	N.L.	+.01
NodCal Inc	12.11	N.L.	-.04
NomuraP f	22.41	N.L.	-.14
Noeast Gr	21.60	N.L.	-.19
Noeast Tr	14.14	N.L.	+.01
North Star Funds:			
Apollo	12.14	N.L.	-.11
Bond	(z)	(z)	
Region	21.11	N.L.	.15
Reserv	(z)	(z)	..
Stock	16.80	N.L.	-.09
Nova Fund	18.64	N.L.	+.01
Nuveen BF	9.09	9.47	...

	NAV	Offer Price	NAV Chg.
High Yld	9.78	N.L.	...
Value	9.46	N.L.	-.04
Safeco Group:			
Cal TxFr	12.26	N.L.	...
Equity	11.30	N.L.	.09
Growth	16.57	N.L.	.10
Income	16.86	N.L.	-11
Muni	14.29	N.L.	.01
US Gov	(z)	(z)	..
Salem Gro	14.27	N.L.	.10
SBSF Fd	13.86	N.L.	-.09
Scudder Funds:			
Cal TxFr	11.28	N.L.	+.01
Cptl Gro	18.18	N.L.	-.10
Devl Fd	25.18	N.L.	-.08
Gen 90	(z)	(z)	...
Global	13.97	N.L.	-.08
Gvt Mtg	(z)	(z)	...
Gro Inc	(z)	(z)	...
Income	13.47	N.L.	-.01
Intl Fnd	42.15	N.L.	-.14
Muni Bd	d9.10	N.L.	-.05
NY TxFr	11.50	N.L.	+.01
TxFr 90	d10.45	N.L.	-.06
TxFr 87	d10.01	N.L.	-.03
TxFr 93	d11.12	N.L.	15
Security Funds:			
Action	11.05	(z)	06
Bond Fd	8.30	8.71	+.01
Equity	6.14	6.71	.06
Invest	9.96	10.89	.05
Omni	3.32	3.63	.01
Ultra Fd	7.74	8.46	-.06
Selected Funds:			
Selct Am	14.15	N.L.	-.10
Selct Spl	21.11	N.L.	-.12
Seligman Group:			
Captl Fd	14.81	16.19	-.08
Colo Tx	7.29	7.65	...
Com Stk	15.13	16.31	-.14
Com Info	14.03	15.33	-.10
Growth	6.25	6.74	-.06
Income	13.94	14.64	-.02
La TxEx	8.22	8.63	+.01
Mass Tx	8.20	8.61	+.01
MD Tx	7.84	8.23	.01
Mi TxEx	8.57	9.00	+.01
Minn Tx	8.05	8.45	.01
Mo Tx	7.57	7.95	.01
Ntl TxEx	8.54	8.97	.
NY TxE	8.36	8.78	...
Ohio Tax	8.34	8.76	...
Pa TxQ	7.82	8.21	...
Cal THY	6.67	6.98	...
Cal TxQ	6.89	7.21	-.01
Govt Gtd	8.09	8.49	+.02
Secu Mtg	7.34	7.71	...
High Yld	7.87	8.26	+.01
Sentinel Group Funds:			
Bal Fund	13.48	14.73	-.09
Bond Fd	6.65	7.27	...
Com Stk	27.23	29.76	.37
Growth	16.98	16.56	.19
Sentry Fd	14.77	16.05	.09
Sequoia	42.17	N.L.	-.09
SFT EQTY	12.59	13.76	-.12
Shearson Funds:			
Aggr Gr	18.88	19.87	.28
ATTGr r	83.68	N.L.	-.70
ATTInc r	102.11	N.L.	-.55
Apprec	29.86	31.43	-.27
Fund Val	7.45	7.84	-.09
Glob Opp	32.82	34.55	-.05
High Yld	x19.32	20.34	-.16
Cal Muni	16.50	17.37	-.01
Mng Gvt	d13.39	14.09	-.04
Mg Muni	15.81	16.64	-.01
NY Muni	17.00	17.89	-.01
Spl Conv	x13.73	N.L.	-.11
Spl GlBd	16.22	N.L.	+.07
SplGro r	15.32	N.L.	-.09
Spl Hln	x14.59	N.L.	-.11
Spl Intl r	21.45	N.L.	-.08
Spl Mtgs	12.10	N.L.	-.01
Spl TE r	17.50	N.L.	...
Spl Ing r	d11.74	N.L.	-.01
SplLtg r	d9.28	N.L.	-.01
Spl Opt r	x14.39	N.L.	-.06
SplPlus r	16.50	N.L.	-.14
Shrm Dean	5.76	N.L.	+.05
Sierra Gro	14.02	N.L.	-.15
Sigma Funds:			

nl No initial load.
r Redemption charge may apply.
s Stock split dividend.
z Quote not available.

Column 3 NAV Net Asset Value. The total value of all securities plus cash divided by the number of issued shares; the price at which shares are sold on the day reported.

Column 4 Offer Price—The price at which shares may be purchased (the total of the net asset value plus any sales charge), if N.L. appears, the shares are bought at the net asset value as there is no initial sales charge. (Does not indicate whether or not there is a sales charge when principal is withdrawn.)

Column 5 NAV Chg.—Net Asset Value Change. The net change in the net asset value of the current price of the shares from the net asset value of the previous trading session, reported in dollars and cents, could be higher (+), lower (–) or unchanged (. . .), the net asset value change subtracted from the current closing price results in the closing price of the previous trading session (i.e., a net asset value of $13.12 (–.03) equals a net asset value of $13.15 for the previous trading session.)

STOCK MARKET DATA BANK

Major Indexes:

Column 1 High.—The highest point the index reached in the previous 12 months.

Column 2 Low.—The lowest point the index reached in the previous 12 months.

Column 3 The name of the index or average and the number (if appropriate) of issues comprising the index/average.

Column 4 Close.—The final point the index/average reached at the end of the trading session.

Column 5 NET CH.—The difference in the index of the current closing value of the previous trading session. The change subtracted from the current closing value results in the closing value of the previous trading session. (i.e., A current value of 2104.47 (–1.97) equals the close at the previous trading session of 2106.44.)

Column 6 % CHANGE.—The percentage change of the closing value on the day being reported from the close of the previous trading session.

Column 7 12 MO CH.—Twelve Month Change. The point difference between the closing value of the day being reported and the closing value of 12 months ago.

Column 8 %.—The percentage change between the current value and the closing value of 12 months ago.

Column 9 From 12/31.—The point difference between the current value and the closing value on the last trading day of the previous year.

Column 10 %.—The percentage change between the current value and the closing value on the last trading day of the previous year.

FIGURE 4

STOCK MARKET DATA BANK — Feb. 23, 1987

Major Indexes

HIGH	LOW	(12 MOS)	CLOSE	NET CH	% CH	12 MO CH	%	FROM 12/31	%
DOW JONES AVERAGES									
2244.09	1686.42	30 Industrials	x2216.54	– 18.70	– 0.84	+ 518.26	+30.52	+ 320.59	+16.91
953.00	709.13	20 Transportation	938.95	– 12.60	– 1.32	+ 145.98	+18.41	+ 131.78	+16.33
227.83	179.63	15 Utilities	x220.41	– 1.61	– 0.73	+ 35.76	+19.37	+ 14.40	+ 6.99
859.22	670.98	65 Composite	x849.19	– 8.23	– 0.96	+ 172.57	+25.50	+ 112.36	+15.25
NEW YORK STOCK EXCHANGE									
162.82	128.93	Composite	161.12	– 1.70	– 1.04	+ 31.92	+24.71	+ 22.54	+16.26
192.76	147.11	Industrials	190.57	– 1.89	– 0.98	+ 43.32	+29.42	+ 30.46	+19.02
80.85	66.29	Utilities	77.63	– 0.66	– 0.84	+ 11.01	+16.68	+ 3.86	+ 5.23
138.47	105.58	Transportation	136.15	– 2.05	– 1.48	+ 9.55	+ 7.54	+ 18.50	+15.72
162.77	138.01	Finance	159.99	– 2.70	– 1.66	+ 14.83	+10.22	+ 19.94	+14.24
STANDARD & POOR'S INDEXES									
285.57	223.79	500 Index	282.38	– 3.10	– 1.09	+ 58.04	+25.87	+ 40.21	+16.60
324.72	246.98	400 Industrials	320.15	– 3.26	– 1.01	+ 72.69	+29.37	+ 50.22	+18.60
230.40	176.16	20 Transportation	226.02	– 4.12	– 1.79	+ 14.95	+31.55	+ 28.75	+14.57
124.04	99.02	40 Utilities	119.23	– 0.93	– 0.77	+ 19.57	+19.64	+ 6.94	+ 6.18
31.35	26.16	40 Financials	30.50	– 0.71	– 2.27	+ 2.16	+ 7.62	+ 3.58	+13.30
NASDAQ									
418.18	343.67	OTC Composite	415.22	– 2.02	– 0.48	+ 59.73	+16.80	+ 66.39	+19.03
439.35	339.13	Industrials	432.08	– 2.24	– 0.52	+ 77.11	+21.72	+ 82.75	+23.69
469.73	399.10	Insurance	466.31	– 3.42	– 0.73	+ 30.64	+ 7.03	+ 62.18	+15.39
499.42	387.95	Banks	498.22	– 1.20	– 0.24	+ 110.27	+28.42	+ 85.69	+20.77
179.20	146.10	Nat. Mkt. Comp.	177.82	– 0.87	-0.49	+ 26.69	+17.66	+ 28.78	+19.31
167.88	127.41	Nat. Mkt. Indus.	164.83	– 0.86	– 0.52	+ 31.77	+23.88	+ 32.26	+24.33
OTHERS									
319.25	249.73	AMEX	316.33	– 1.57	– 0.49	+ 66.60	+26.67	+ 53.06	+20.15
1567.0	1212.6	Fin. Times Indus.	1556.9	– 10.1	– 0.64	+ 281.7	+22.09	+ 243.0	+18.49
20228.09	13503.49	Nikkei Stock Avg.	19940.50	–139.89	– 0.70	+6437.01	+47.67	+1239.20	+ 6.63
263.74	218.79	Value-Line	261.56	– 2.18	– 0.83	+ 35.35	+15.63	+ 35.94	+15.93
2871.33	2303.76	Wilshire 5000	2842.15	– 29.17	– 1.02	+ 534.66	+23.17	+ 407.20	+16.72

Most Active Issues

NYSE	VOLUME	CLOSE	CH
Amer T&T	3,387,200	23	– ⅜
GTE Corp	3,223,400	41¼	– ¼
IBM	2,897,700	143⅜	+ 3¾
Navistar	2,579,200	7⅝	– ⅛
SearsRoeb	2,214,900	51¾	– 1¼
ArchDnM	1,841,000	18⅞	– ⅜
Citicorp	1,738,500	54½	– 3¾
MorganJP	1,650,000	45¾	– 1½
Pan Am	1,588,600	4¾	– ⅝
KanPwLt	1,442,600	56	– ½
Exxon	1,400,700	80	– 1⅜
HewlettPk	1,361,600	52⅜	+ ⅝
EstKodak	1,360,600	79	– 1
GenElec	1,265,900	100⅜	– ⅝
BankTr NY	1,196,700	46¼	– 1¾

NASDAQ			
Seagate Tch	3,513,400	35⅞	+ 1¼
MCI Comm	2,165,100	5⅜	– ¼
Apple Cptr	1,574,100	63⅛	+ 1⅞
Intel Cp	1,459,100	34⅞	– ⅜
Ashton	1,423,900	25¾	....
Glaxo Hold	1,339,600	23⅛	– ⅜
Lotus Devel	1,018,100	69½	+ 2¼

AMEX			
Wickes	1,141,400	4	....
Amdahl	436,600	36¾	+ ⅜
NY Times	356,100	46¼	+ ¼
WangLabB	343,500	15	– ⅛
HomeShop	312,800	28⅛	....
TexasAirCp	311,500	48	– ⅞
TaiwanFd	282,400	34¾	– 4½

Diaries

NYSE	MON	FRI	WK AGO
Issues traded	1,977	2,004	Closed
Advances	439	829	Closed
Declines	1,166	787	Closed
Unchanged	372	388	Closed
New highs	68	116	Closed
New lows	5	5	Closed
Adv Vol (000)	31,231	85,238	Closed
Decl Vol (000)	126,204	77,235	Closed
Total Vol (000)	170,450	175,750	Closed
Block trades	2,931	3,137	Closed
NASDAQ			
Issues traded	4,548	4,546	Closed
Advances	930	1,220	Closed
Declines	1,359	1,059	Closed
Unchanged	2,259	2,267	Closed
New highs	124	161	Closed
New lows	27	16	Closed
Adv Vol (000)	38,845	63,077	Closed
Decl Vol (000)	59,394	50,998	Closed
Total Vol (000)	140,128	155,712	Closed
Block trades	1,926	2,312	Closed
AMEX			
Issues traded	823	832	Closed
Advances	253	312	Closed
Declines	368	291	Closed
Unchanged	202	229	Closed
New highs	23	31	Closed
New lows	4	2	Closed
Adv Vol (000)	3,820	5,670	Closed
Decl Vol (000)	5,311	5,065	Closed
Total Vol (000)	11,730	12,790	Closed
CompVol (000)	12,623	11,488	Closed
Block trades	163	163	Closed

FIGURE 4: ***(Concluded)***

Percentage Gainers . . . and Losers

NYSE	CLOSE	CH	% CH		CLOSE	CH	% CH
vjManville	3	+ ⅜	+ 14.3	Copwld	5⅜	– 3¼	– 37.7
Plessey	37½	+ 4¼	+ 12.8	Pan Am	4¾	– ⅝	– 11.6
Am Motors	3½	+ ⅜	+ 12.0	KoreaFd	52½	– 5⅞	– 10.1
GalvstHou	2⅝	+ ¼	+ 10.5	KaufBd pfB	113	– 12	– 9.6
Carling	13¼	+ 1¼	+ 10.4	RepGyps	9	– ⅞	– 8.9
Wurlitzer	2¾	+ ¼	+ 10.0	KaufBroad	20¾	– 1⅞	– 8.3
Cenergy	7⅛	+ ⅝	+ 9.6	PioneerEl	30¼	– 2⅝	– 8.0
ICN Pharm	18½	+ 1½	+ 8.8	ThompMed	14⅝	– 1⅛	– 7.1
NewmontGold	21¾	+ 1½	+ 7.4	UnStkyds	8⅛	– ⅝	– 7.1
Am Motr pf	29⅛	+ 1⅞	+ 6.9	Datapoint	5	– ⅜	– 7.0
vjAmfesco	2	+ ⅛	+ 6.7	Tidewatr	5	– ⅜	– 7.0
Elscint	2	+ ⅛	+ 6.7	FloatPnt	15⅝	– 1⅛	– 6.7
HomestdFn	12¼	+ ¾	+ 6.5	Citicorp	54½	– 3¾	– 6.4
Lennar	28⅞	+ 1¾	+ 6.5	ContlIll	5½	– ⅜	– 6.4
Ipco Corp	13½	+ ¾	+ 5.9	BkBoston	31⅜	– 2⅛	– 6.3
GIANT Group	30⅜	+ 1⅝	+ 5.7	Wstn Union	3¾	– ¼	– 6.3
TelecomCp	2⅜	+ ⅛	+ 5.6	AMCA Int	7⅞	– ½	– 6.0
OTC							
Progrmng&Sys	12	+ 3	+ 33.3	UtdNewMex	11	– 3½	– 24.1
Plymerc	5⅜	+ 1 5/16	+ 32.3	Benihan	4	– 1⅛	– 22.0
Detec Elct	4½	+ 1	+ 28.6	Daxor	17¾	– 4½	– 20.2
Levon Rsc	2 13/16	+ 9/16	+ 25.0	CamilStMortz	2	– ½	– 20.0
Kevlin	3¼	+ ⅝	+ 23.8	Alaska Ntl	2½	– ½	– 16.7
Telcrft	7½	+ 1⅜	+ 22.4	Zymos	3¼	– ⅝	– 16.1
Intervoice	2¾	+ ½	+ 22.2	Totl Aset	2⅝	– ½	– 16.0
Medicl St	8⅛	+ 1⅜	+ 20.4	VLI Cp	4¾	– ⅞	– 15.6
Mich Anthny	14	+ 2¼	+ 19.1	Sutron	2¾	– ½	– 15.4
Stuarts DS	8⅝	+ 1⅜	+ 19.0	Seeq Tch	6⅜	– 1⅛	– 15.0
Xytronyx	14¼	+ 2¼	+ 18.8	Endtronic	10	– 1¾	– 14.9
HomeIntensive	5	+ ¾	+ 17.6	Homac Inc	3	– ½	– 14.3
AMEX							
Sorg Inc	23	+ 4¼	+ 22.7	Horn Har wt	2¼	– ⅜	– 14.3
Punta Gorda	3⅝	+ ⅝	+ 20.8	Penril Cp	4¾	– ⅝	– 11.6
La Jolla Bcp	8⅛	+ 1⅛	+ 16.1	Taiwan Fd	34¾	– 4½	– 11.5
Dyneer Cp	2	+ ¼	+ 14.3	Rockaway	13¼	– 1⅝	– 10.9
Ookiep	8½	+ 1	+ 13.3	May Engy	2¼	– ¼	– 10.0
Ntl Hlth Cp	16¼	+ 1⅞	+ 13.0	Acton Cp	2⅝	– ¼	– 8.7
Versar	12	+ 1⅜	+ 12.9	Kapok Cp	2⅞	– ¼	– 8.0
Pico Prod	3⅝	+ ⅜	+ 11.5	A Att 2 Sc	4¾	– ⅜	– 7.3
Calprop	9⅞	+ 1	+ 11.3	ETZ Lavud	11¼	– ¾	– 6.3
Whrhse Entr	13¼	+ 1¼	+ 10.4	Manufact Hme	11⅛	– ¾	– 6.3
Graham Cp	8⅛	+ ¾	+ 10.2	Selas Corp	5⅝	-- ⅜	– 6.3
Bank Bldg	12¼	+ 1⅛	+ 10.1	Atari Cp	23⅞	– 1½	– 5.9

Breakdown of Trading in NYSE Stocks

BY MARKET	Mon	Fri	WK AGO
New York	170,450,000	175,750,000	Closed
Midwest	10,908,000	12,078,900	"
Pacific	6,907,800	6,936,300	"
NASD	3,679,460	6,011,320	"
Phila	3,033,200	2,979,400	"
Boston	2,773,000	2,743,200	"
Cincinnati	905,500	522,100	"
Instinet	112,900	572,100	"
Composite	198,769,860	207,593,320	"

x-Ex-dividends of Minnesota Mng & Mfg 93 cents and Sears Roebuck & Co. 50 cents lowered the Industrial average by 1.69. Philadelphia Elec. 55 cents lowered the Utility average by 0.29. These lowered the Composite average by 0.53.

½-HOURLY	Mon	Fri	WK AGO
9:30-10	20,660,000	28,860,000	Closed
10-10:30	19,350,000	17,720,000	"
10:30-11	20,940,000	13,570,000	"
11-11:30	18,610,000	14,120,000	"
11:30-12	10,640,000	11,690,000	"
12-12:30	8,210,000	9,980,000	"
12:30-1	8,130,000	8,460,000	"
1-1:30	7,910,000	7,740,000	"
1:30-2	7,630,000	7,490,000	"
2-2:30	10,060,000	9,020,000	"
2:30-3	16,240,000	8,780,000	"
3-3:30	10,090,000	10,140,000	"
3:30-4	11,980,000	28,180,000	"

Most Active Issues:

Column 1 Bold print—The exchange.
Not bold print—The abbreviated name of the stock.

Column 2 VOLUME—The actual number of shares traded of the stock.

Column 3 CLOSE—The last price at which the stock traded on the day being reported.

Column 4 CH—The net amount of change between the closing price of the security from the day being reported to the closing price on the previous trading session.

Diaries:

Column 1 Bold print—The name of the exchange.
Not bold print—The name of the market statistic being reviewed.

Column 2 The statistic on the day being reviewed.

Column 3 The statistic on the previous day.

Column 4 The statistic on the previous week.

Percentage Gainers . . . And Losers:

Column 1 The abbreviated name of the company.

Column 2 Close—The last price at which the stock traded.

Column 3 CH—The dollar difference between the closing price of the trading session being reported and the closing price of the previous trading session.

Column 4 % CH—The percentage change between the closing price of the trading session being reported and the closing price of the previous trading session.

Breakdown of Trading in NYSE Stocks:

Column 1 Indicates the exchange on which the NYSE stocks were traded

Column 2 The total volume of shares traded on the day being reported.

Column 3 The total volume of shares traded on the previous trading session.

Column 4 The total volume of shares traded on the day one week previous.

For both Breakdown of Trading in NYSE Stocks & ½ HOURLY:

Column 1 Indicates the ½ hour period being reported.

Column 2 The total volume of shares traded on the day being reported.

Column 3 The total volume of shares traded on the previous trading session.

Column 4 The total volume of shares traded on the day one week previous.

FUTURES PRICES

FIGURE 5

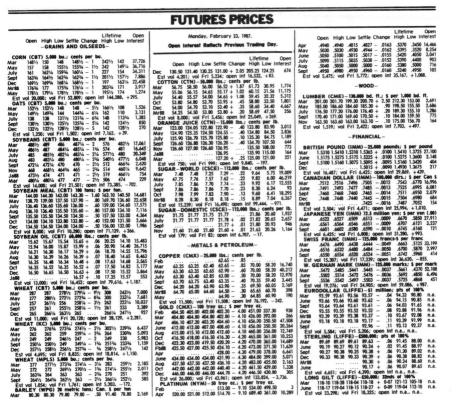

Courtesy of Dow Jones & Company, Inc.

Column 1 Indicates the month of the futures contract being reported.

Column 2 Open—The first price at which the futures contract traded on the day being reported.

FIGURE 5: *(Concluded)*

Column 3 High—The highest price at which the futures contract traded during the trading session.

Column 4 Low—The lowest price at which the futures contract traded during the trading session.

Column 5 Settle—The adjusted closing price of the futures contract on the day being reported.

Column 6 Change—The difference between the settlement prices of the futures contract on the day being reported and the previous trading session.

Column 7 Lifetime High—The highest price the futures contract traded since becoming available.

Column 8 Lifetime Low—The lowest price the futures contract traded since becoming available.

Column 9 Open Interest—The number of futures contracts outstanding as of the previous trading session.

OPTIONS — (LISTED STOCK) INDEX & FUTURES

FIGURE 6

LISTED OPTIONS QUOTATIONS

Monday, February 23, 1987

Closing prices of all options. Sales unit usually is 100 shares. Stock close is New York or American exchange final price.

Option & NY Close	Strike Price	Calls—Last Feb	Calls—Last Mar	Calls—Last Apr	Puts—Last Feb	Puts—Last Mar	Puts—Last Apr
99 1/2	85	s	r	r	s	r	3/4
99 1/2	90	10 1/2	11	12 7/8	3/16	7/16	r
99 1/2	95	6 3/8	7 3/8	9 3/8	3/4	1 5/8	r
99 1/2	100	2 15/16	4 1/8	6 5/8	2 3/4	3 3/8	5 3/8
99 1/2	105	1 3/16	2 1/4	4 1/8	6 1/8	6 1/2	r
99 1/2	110	9/16	1 1/8	2 7/8	r	r	r
99 1/2	115	r	1/2	r	r	r	r
GerbPd	40	r	4 1/4	5 3/4	r	1/2	r
43 7/8	45	1	1 1/2	2 5/8	1 1/4	2 3/4	r
43 7/8	50	3/16	3/8	1 1/4	r	r	r
43 7/8	55	s	1/8	s	s	r	s
Glenfd	25	r	r	r	r	7/16	r
30 1/2	30	2 1/16	2 7/16	r	1 1/16	r	2 5/8
30 1/2	35	r	1/2	1 9/16	r	r	r
Goodyr	35	s	19	r	s	r	r
54 3/4	40	r	14 3/4	15	r	1/16	r
54 3/4	45	9 3/4	9 5/8	r	r	r	r
54 3/4	50	5	5 5/8	7 1/2	r	3/4	r
54 3/4	55	1 3/4	2 3/4	4	1 7/8	2 7/8	3 1/2
54 3/4	60	r	15/16	2 1/4	r	r	r
Gould	15	s	4 3/4	r	s	r	r
19 1/2	17 1/2	2 1/8	2 3/4	r	r	r	r
19 1/2	20	3/4	1 5/16	2	15/16	1 1/2	r
19 1/2	22 1/2	1/4	9/16	1 5/16	r	r	r
Greyhd	30	r	r	r	r	3/16	r
36	35	1 1/4	1 3/4	r	15/16	1 1/8	1 3/4
36	40	r	3/8	7/8	r	r	r
Houshl	50	r	r	6 1/8	r	3/8	3/4
55 3/8	55	1 3/4	2	r	r	1 1/2	r
Hutton	35	4 3/4	5	r	3/16	1/2	1 1/8
39 1/2	40	1 1/4	2 1/16	3 5/8	1 5/8	2 1/8	3 1/2
39 1/2	45	5/16	13/16	2 1/4	r	6	r
39 1/2	50	s	5/16	1	s	r	r
39 1/2	55	s	3/16	s	s	r	s
Inco	10	r	r	5 3/8	r	r	r
15 1/8	15	3/4	1 1/8	1 3/4	r	r	r
15 1/8	17 1/2	r	r	1/2	r	r	2 1/2
Intel	20	s	r	r	s	1/16	r
34 7/8	25	r	10	10 1/2	r	r	r
34 7/8	30	5 1/4	6 1/2	8	1/2	1	2 5/8
34 7/8	35	2 1/4	3 1/4	4 7/8	2 1/4	3	5 1/4
34 7/8	40	3/4	1 3/8	3 1/4	6 1/8	6 1/4	r
Intgph	15	s	r	9 1/4	s	1/8	r
24	17 1/2	s	6 1/2	r	s	r	r
24	20	r	4 1/2	r	1/8	r	r
24	22 1/2	r	2 7/8	r	5/8	1 1/4	2 3/8
24	25	1 1/4	2	3	1 7/8	2 1/4	r
24	30	1/4	11/16	1 5/8	r	6 1/4	r
Iomega	5	r	1 9/16	r	r	r	r
6 1/4	7 1/2	r	1/2	5/8	r	r	r
6 1/4	10	r	1/8	r	r	3 7/8	3 3/4
KimbCl	100	r	r	r	3/16	r	r
109 7/8	105	5 1/2	r	r	r	1 1/8	2 7/8
109 7/8	110	2 1/8	3 1/4	r	r	3	r
109 7/8	115	7/8	1 5/8	r	r	7 3/8	r

Option & NY Close	Strike Price	Calls—Last Mar	Calls—Last Jun	Calls—Last Sep	Puts—Last Mar	Puts—Last Jun	Puts—Last Sep
46 1/2	55	1/16	s	s	r	s	s
Chevrn	40	8	r	r	r	5/16	r
47 7/8	45	3 5/8	5	5 1/8	1/4	1 3/16	2
47 7/8	50	11/16	2	2 7/8	2 3/8	3 1/2	4 1/2
47 7/8	55	1/8	3/4	1 1/8	r	r	r
Circus	17 1/2	r	3 5/8	r	r	r	r
20 1/2	20	1 1/4	2 3/8	r	r	r	r
20 1/2	22 1/2	3/8	1 1/4	r	r	r	r
Coastl	35	12	r	r	r	r	r
47	40	r	8 1/2	r	r	r	r
47	45	2 7/8	5	r	r	2	r
47	50	r	2 5/8	3 5/8	r	r	r
Deere	22 1/2	6 3/4	r	r	r	r	r
29 5/8	25	4 1/4	r	r	3/16	r	r
29 5/8	30	15/16	2 1/8	3 1/4	1 1/2	r	r
29 5/8	35	r	11/16	1 3/16	r	r	r
EmrsEl	85	r	r	r	r	3/8	r
103 3/4	90	r	r	r	1/8	r	1
103 3/4	95	r	11 1/2	r	3/16	1 1/2	r
103 3/4	100	5 1/8	r	10	3/4	r	4
103 3/4	105	2 1/4	5	7	2 1/2	4 3/4	r
103 3/4	110	7/8	3 1/4	4 1/4	r	r	r
103 3/4	115	r	r	2 7/8	r	r	r
G T E	40	1 3/4	2 3/4	3 1/4	5/8	1 1/8	r
41 1/4	45	1/4	5/8	1 1/4	r	r	r
GTE o	36 5/8	4 7/8	5 3/8	5 3/4	r	r	r
41 1/4	40	1 1/2	r	r	3/8	r	r
41 1/4	43 3/8	5/16	1 1/4	1 5/8	2 3/8	2 5/8	3 1/4
GenRe	50	r	14 1/4	r	r	r	r
64 1/4	55	9	10 3/4	11 1/2	3/16	r	r
64 1/4	60	5 1/8	r	r	5/8	r	r
64 1/4	65	1 13/16	3 3/4	r	r	r	4 1/2
Gillet	45	15	r	r	1/16	5/16	r
59 3/4	50	10 1/2	12 1/4	12 3/4	3/16	13/16	r
59 3/4	55	6	7 3/4	9 1/4	13/16	2	2 5/8
59 3/4	60	2 3/4	5	6 1/2	2 5/8	4 3/8	5
59 3/4	65	1 3/16	3 3/8	4 3/4	6 1/2	r	r
59 3/4	70	1/2	1 3/4	s	r	r	s
Hecla	7 1/2	r	r	r	r	1/16	r
13	10	3	3 1/4	3 1/2	1/16	r	r
13	12 1/2	1	1 1/2	r	5/16	r	7/8
13	15	1/8	1/2	7/8	1 7/8	r	2 7/16
Hercul	50	12 5/8	r	r	1/16	r	r
62 5/8	55	7 3/4	9 1/4	9 1/2	r	13/16	r
62 5/8	60	3 1/8	5 1/4	r	3/4	2	r
62 5/8	65	1 1/16	3	r	r	r	r
Kellog	50	10 1/2	r	r	r	3/4	1 1/4
60 1/8	55	6	7 3/8	8 1/2	1/4	1 3/8	2 1/2
60 1/8	60	2	4 3/8	5 3/4	2	r	4 3/8
60 1/8	65	3/4	2 1/8	4 1/2	r	r	r
NiagMP	15	r	r	2 5/8	r	r	r
17 3/8	17 1/2	3/16	1/2	3/4	3/8	1 1/8	1 1/4
17 3/8	20	r	r	1/8	r	r	r
PacGE	25	2	r	r	r	11/16	1 1/8
26 5/8	30	r	r	1/4	r	r	r

Courtesy of Dow Jones & Company, Inc.

FIGURE 6: *(Concluded)*

Kraft	50	r	6½	r	¾	⅜	r
56⅛	55	2¼	3	4¾	r	1½	r
56⅛	60	⅝	1	2⅜	r	r	r
Kroger	30	2⅝	r	r	r	r	r
32⅜	35	r	9/16	1½	r	2¾	r
Lilly	70	s	r	20⅝	s	r	¼
89⅞	75	r	15	r	r	r	r
89⅞	80	r	11¼	12¼	⅜	1	r
89⅞	85	6	7½	9½	1⅛	2⅜	4
89⅞	90	2⅞	4⅝	7	2⅝	4½	6
89⅞	95	1⅜	2¾	5	6¼	r	r
LinB	45	s	20¼	s	s	r	s
65½	60	s	8¼	s	s	⅞	s
Lotus	50	s	r	r	s	½	3
69½	55	10½	2¼	r	⅝	1½	r
69½	60	r	12	16	1⅜	2⅝	7
69½	65	8	9⅞	r	2⅜	4½	r
69½	70	5⅜	7½	11¾	5¼	9	12¼
69½	75	3½	5½	11	8¼	r	r
69½	80	2	3⅞	r	r	r	r
Lypho	20	r	r	5⅜	3/16	½	r
24⅜	22½	r	r	4¼	r	r	r
24⅜	25	1½	1 13/16	3⅛	r	r	r
24⅜	30	r	9/16	r	r	r	r
ManHan	40	s	6½	6¾	s	⅜	¾
46⅝	45	2⅛	2¼	2 13/16	¾	1⅜	2¼
46⅝	50	5/16	½	1⅛	3¼	4½	5¼
Masco	30	r	5½	6¼	r	r	¾
35⅜	35	r	1¾	r	r	1⅝	2⅜
35⅜	40	r	⅜	r	r	r	r
Mattel	10	1¾	2	2⅝	3/16	r	¾
11⅝	12½	7/16	¾	1½	1 3/16	1⅜	r
11⅝	15	⅛	5/16	r	3½	r	r
Merril	30	s	14¼	s	s	r	s
43⅜	35	9¼	9¾	10¼	1/16	1/16	r
43⅜	40	3¾	4½	5⅝	¼	⅝	1⅜
43⅜	45	15/16	1 13/16	3⅛	2¼	2¾	3¾
43⅜	50	3/16	⅝	1 9/16	r	7⅛	r
MesaLP	15	r	1⅝	r	r	⅛	r
16¾	17½	r	¼	⅜	r	r	1¾
Motrla	35	s	r	r	s	1/16	r
47	40	6¾	8	8½	r	½	1 1/16
47	45	3¼	4¼	6	1⅛	1⅞	3
47	50	1⅛	2⅛	3⅝	4	4⅝	r
47	55	r	⅞	2	r	r	r
Mylan	12½	2⅜	2 15/16	3⅜	r	3/16	½
15	15	15/16	1 9/16	2⅛	13/16	1⅛	1½
15	17½	⅜	13/16	1¼	r	3	r
NetwSy	17½	1	1⅝	r	⅞	r	r
17½	20	r	⅝	r	r	r	r
Nordst	40	r	r	r	r	1/16	r
53	45	r	r	10	r	r	1⅛
53	50	3⅝	4½	6¼	r	1⅜	r
53	55	r	2¼	3⅞	r	r	5⅛
Phelps	17½	s	r	r	s	r	1/16
29⅞	20	s	9⅝	r	s	r	r
29⅞	22½	r	7	r	r	⅛	r
29⅞	25	r	5¼	5	r	⅜	r
29⅞	30	1	1½	2⅝	1⅞	r	r
29⅞	35	r	½	r	r	r	r
Pitnev	40	2⅝	2 15/16	r	⅞	1¼	r
Pfizer	55	17	r	r	r	3/16	r
71⅞	60	r	13½	r	1/16	½	r
71⅞	65	8	9¾	11	⅛	1⅜	1⅞
71⅞	70	3⅝	6½	8¼	1¼	3	4
71⅞	75	1 5/16	4¼	5¾	3½	5¼	6
71⅞	80	½	2⅜	r	r	8½	r
Ph Mor	60	24⅞	r	s	r	r	s
84⅛	70	14½	r	r	r	½	r
84⅛	75	10	11⅝	13¼	r	1⅝	r
84⅛	80	4⅞	8⅛	9⅛	1 1/16	3	4¼
84⅛	85	2 5/16	5¾	7½	3¼	5½	6⅝
84⅛	90	13/16	3½	5⅛	6⅝	8⅝	9½
84⅛	95	¼	1⅞	3¾	r	12	r
84⅛	100	1/16	1⅛	2⅜	r	r	r
PrimeC	20	2⅛	3⅜	3½	7/16	1	r
21⅝	22½	¾	2	2⅝	1¾	r	r
21⅝	25	5/16	1⅛	1 13/16	r	r	r
Revlon	12½	2½	r	r	¼	r	1
14½	15	⅞	1¾	2¾	r	2	r
14½	17½	5/16	⅞	1½	r	r	3⅞
SFeSP	30	4	4¾	r	r	r	1⅛
33⅜	35	⅝	1¾	2⅝	2	2⅝	r
33⅜	40	r	⅝	1¼	r	r	r
Seagte	12½	24	r	s	r	r	s
35⅞	17½	19⅛	17⅝	r	r	r	r
35⅞	20	14¾	r	r	r	r	r
35⅞	22½	12¾	14½	r	r	½	r
35⅞	25	8¾	11½	11½	3/16	9/16	r
35⅞	30	7	9	10⅝	11/16	1⅞	2¾
35⅞	35	3⅝	6	8⅛	2⅛	3⅞	5
35⅞	40	1 13/16	4¼	6	5¼	r	r
35⅞	45	¾	2¾	4½	r	r	r
StdOil	45	r	11½	r	r	r	r
55½	50	r	6⅞	r	¼	13/16	r
55½	55	2	3⅜	4½	1⅛	2⅝	3½
55½	60	7/16	1⅝	r	4⅝	r	r
55½	65	⅛	r	r	r	r	r
Telex	55	36⅝	r	s	r	r	s
95⅜	60	35	33¼	s	r	⅛	s
95⅜	65	r	r	r	r	r	½
95⅜	70	24¾	r	25¼	r	r	¾
95⅜	75	20½	18	r	1/16	1	r
95⅜	80	15	17	r	r	1½	2⅛
95⅜	85	10¾	14	16¾	⅜	3⅜	4
95⅜	90	6¾	8½	12½	1¼	5¼	6
95⅜	95	3½	7¼	8⅛	3¼	r	r
Valero	7½	1¾	2¼	r	⅛	r	r
9⅜	10	5/16	¾	1 3/16	1	1⅜	1⅝
9⅜	12½	1/16	¼	7/16	r	r	r
Whitkr	25	r	r	9½	r	r	r
33⅝	30	3¾	r	r	3/16	r	r
		May	**Aug**	**Nov**	**May**	**Aug**	**Nov**
A M R	50	9½	r	s	7/16	1 1/16	s
58¼	55	5⅜	r	r	1½	2¼	3
58¼	60	2⅝	4⅜	r	4	5	r
58¼	65	1¼	r	r	r	r	9
A S A	30	r	11½	s	3/16	½	s
40⅞	35	6½	7⅜	8	½	1¼	r
40⅞	40	3	3⅞	5	2	2⅞	r
40⅞	45	1	2¼	3	5¼	6	r
AmCan	80	r	r	s	r	7/16	s

Column 1 Strike Price—The price at which the underlying security may be exercised.

Columns 2, 3, & 4 The closing or settlement premium of the closest three contract months in which call options are available to be traded.

FIGURE 7

INDEX OPTIONS

Monday, February 23, 1987

Chicago Board

S&P 100 INDEX

Strike	Calls—Last			Puts—Last		
Price	Mar	Apr	May	Mar	Apr	May
220	53	....	....	1/16	....	....
225	48	49	....	1/16	3/16	....
230	44	45	....	1/16	¼	....
235	39¼	37½	....	1/16	⅜	11/16
240	35	35	....	⅛	9/16	1
245	28½	31½	31½	3/16	⅞	1⅝
250	24	27	24½	7/16	1 7/16	2⅜
255	19	20⅜	23	¾	2⅛	3⅜
260	14¾	17	18½	1⅝	3⅜	4¾
265	10⅞	14⅛	15½	2⅞	4⅞	6⅝
270	7⅜	10½	12⅞	4⅞	7¼	8¾
275	5	7⅞	10¼	7⅜	9⅜	10⅝
280	3⅛	5¾	7¾	10½	12⅛	12⅞
285	1 13/16	4¼	6¼	14	17½	....
290	15/16	2¾	4½	18	19½	....

Total call volume 224,986 Total call open int. 474,173
Total put volume 212,461 Total put open int. 1,320,314
The index: High 275.11; Low 268.97; Close 272.21, −2.85

S&P 500 INDEX

Strike	Calls—Last			Puts—Last		
Price	Mar	Apr	Jun	Mar	Apr	Jun
225	....	....	....	....	....	⅛
230	....	....	....	....	....	⅜
235	....	....	....	....	....	13/16
240	....	....	....	....	....	1 1/6
245	....	....	....	⅛	....	1⅝
250	....	....	....	⅛	....	....
255	....	....	....	¼	....	2⅞
260	....	....	....	⅜	....	3⅝
265	17	....	....	¾	....	5⅜
270	14⅝	....	....	1⅝	....	6⅛
275	12¾	13⅝	....	2⅜	5¾	....
280	7⅞	10⅜	....	4¾	6⅜	11½
285	5	7½	11¾	7¼	9	13¾
290	3⅛	6⅝	9½	9⅝	12	....
295	2¼	....	8⅛	11⅝	....	....
300	1 1/16	....	7	19	....	....

Total call volume 13,379 Total call open int. 125,035
Total put volume 15,921 Total put open int. 153,399
The index: High 285.50; Low 279.37; Close 282.38, −3.10.

American Exchange

MAJOR MARKET INDEX

Strike	Calls—Last			Puts—Last		
Price	Mar	Apr	May	Mar	Apr	May
400	33	30½	....	1 5/16	3½	....
405	23	25	....	2¼	4¾	....
410	23½	25	....	3½	5⅞	....
415	17	22	....	4⅝	7	....
420	13½	20	....	6½	9⅜	11¾
425	10¾	14¾	....	9	12¾	14½
430	8⅜	12	....	11⅜	14¼	18½
435	6½	10⅞	13⅝	13¼	16¼	....

Total call volume 31,088 Total call open int. 90,947
Total put volume 23,011 Total put open int. 179,925
The index: High 430.49; Low 420.58; Close 425.37, −3.84

COMPUTER TECHNOLOGY INDEX

Strike	Calls—Last			Puts—Last		
Price	Mar	Apr	May	Mar	Apr	May
115	....	....	....	....	⅜	....
125	7¼	....	....	1½	2¼	....
130	2½	4⅛	....	2½	....	....
135	1½	....	....	....	....	....

Total call volume 25 Total call open int. 1,027
Total put volume 74 Total put open int. 408
The index: High 132.41; Low 128.02; Close 131.41, +1.16

OIL INDEX

Strike	Calls—Last			Puts—Last		
Price	Mar	Apr	May	Mar	Apr	May
155	....	....	....	¾	....	....
160	....	....	....	2 5/16	3¼	....
165	3¼	5¼	....	5⅜	5¾	6¾
170	1½	....	....	7¾	....	....

Total call volume 66 Total call open int. 1,498

Strike	Calls—Last			Puts Last		
Price	Feb	Mar	Apr	Feb	Mar	Apr
142½	....	....	....	1/16	....	....
145	16¾	....	....	¼	½	....
147½	....	....	....	¼	....	....
150	12	....	....	⅜	1	....
152½	....	....	....	¾	....	....
155	7⅜	9⅜	....	1 3/16	2⅜	....
157½	5½	....	....	1 13/16	....	....
160	4⅛	6 5/16	....	2 13/16	4 3/16	....
162½	3	4½	....	1¼	....	....
165	1⅞	3⅝	....	6½	7½	....
170	⅞	2⅜	3	10¾	....	10⅞
175	¼	....	....	....	....	....

Total call volume 4,341. Total call open int. 16,177.
Total put volume 4,313. Total put open int. 17,173.
The index: High 162.73; Low 159.63; Close 161.12, −1.70

NYSE BETA INDEX

Strike	Calls—Last			Puts—Last		
Price	Mar	Apr	May	Mar	Apr	May
350	....	....	....	1¾	....	....
355	....	....	....	3½	....	....
360	....	....	....	4⅛	8⅛	....
370	7½	....	....	8	....	....
380	3⅞	....	....	....	....	....
385	2¾	....	....	....	....	....

Total call volume 27. Total call open int. 93.
Total put volume 124. Total put open int. 515.
The index: High 373.63; Low 365.69; Close 369.92, −3.79

Philadelphia Exchange

GOLD/SILVER INDEX

Strike	Calls—Last			Puts—Last		
Price	Mar	Apr	May	Mar	Apr	May
70	....	....	....	1/16	....	....
80	....	....	....	⅝	1⅜	....
85	6¼	....	....	1 15/16	2¾	....
90	3¼	4⅝	....	4	4⅞	....
95	1 7/16	....	....	6⅞	....	....
100	⅞	1½	....	....	....	....

Total call volume 458 Total call open int. 1,217
Total put volume 298 Total put open int. 5,494
The index: High 90.23; Low 88.74; Close 89.63, −0.47

VALUE LINE INDEX OPTIONS

Strike	Calls—Last			Puts—Last		
Price	Mar	Apr	May	Mar	Apr	May
220	39⅝	....	....	....	....	....
235	....	....	....	¼	....	....
240	20	....	....	½	....	....
245	17	....	....	1	....	....
250	11¾	....	....	2	4⅞	....
255	8	....	....	3⅛	....	....
260	5⅜	....	....	5⅛	....	....
265	3⅛	6¾	6⅞	9⅜	....	....
270	1½	3½	....	13	....	....
275	¾	2 1/16	....	....	....	....

Total call volume 932 Total call open int. 6,034
Total put volume 402 Total put open int. 3,717
The index: High 263.79; Low 260.00; Close 261.56, −2.17

NATIONAL O-T-C INDEX

Strike	Calls—Last			Puts—Last		
Price	Mar	Apr	May	Mar	Apr	May
225	25½	....	....	....	....	....
235	....	....	....	1¼	....	....
245	9⅛	....	....	4	....	....
255	3⅜	....	....	....	....	....

Total call volume 14 Total call open int. 357
Total put volume 7 Total put open int. 1,555
The index: High 251.61; Low 247.73; Close 250.01, −1.36

Pacific Exchange

TECHNOLOGY INDEX

Strike	Calls—Last			Puts—Last		
Price	Mar	Apr	May	Mar	Apr	May
130	17⅜	....	....	....	....	....

FIGURE 7: *(Concluded)*

Total put volume 191 Total put open int. 2,315
The index: High 166.58; Low 163.38; Close 164.30, −2.16

INSTITUTIONAL INDEX

Strike Price	Calls–Last Mar	Calls–Last Apr	Calls–Last May	Puts–Last Mar	Puts–Last Apr	Puts–Last May
255	....	....	....	3/16	....	....
260	....	....	....	7/16	....	....
265	20¾	....	....	⅞	....	....
270	15½	....	....	1 3/16	....	....
275	11¼	....	....	2 9/16	....	....
280	9¼	....	....	3⅝	....	....
285	5⅞	....	....	....	....	....
290	3⅝	5¾	....	7⅝	10⅝	....

Total call volume 2,689 Total call open int. 26,160
Total put volume 1,655 Total put open int. 33,874
The index: High 286.82; Low 280.85; Close 283.73, −3.04

N.Y. Stock Exchange

NYSE INDEX OPTIONS

Strike Price	Calls–Last Mar	Calls–Last Apr	Calls–Last May	Puts–Last Mar	Puts–Last Apr	Puts–Last May
140	....	....	....	1/16	5/16	...
140	10¼	....	11½	1⅝	2½	4⅜
145	6	7	....	3¼	....	....
150	4⅞	5⅞	5¾	5¼	....	
155	2¾		4⅞	....	....	....

Total call volume 111 Total call open int. 748
Total put volume 57 Total put open int. 837
The index: High 148.99; Low 145.09; Close 147.99, −0.70

FINANCIAL NEWS COMPOSITE INDEX

Strike Price	Calls–Last Mar	Calls–Last Apr	Calls–Last May	Puts–Last Mar	Puts–Last Apr	Puts–Last May
180	21¼	....	....	3/16	....	....
185	17½	....	....	⅜	....	....
190	13½	....	....	¾	1⅞	....
192½	....	....	....	1 7/16	....	....
195	....	....	....	1⅞	....	....
197½	....	....	....	3⅛	....	....
200	5¼	....	....	3⅜	...	....
205	3⅛	....	....	6	....	....
210	1⅝	3⅜	....	....	....	....
220	5/16	....	....	....	....	....

Total call volume 1,255 Total call open int. 3,170
Total put volume 1,526 Total put open int. 12,548
The index: High 203.83; Low 199.08; Close 201.15, −2.57

Columns 5, 6, & 7 The closing or settlement premium of the closest three months in which put options are available to be traded.

Est or total volume Call and Put The estimated or actual total number of all call and put options of the underlying security.

Open Interest Calls and Puts The total number of outstanding call and put option contracts on the underlying security.

FIGURE 8

FUTURES OPTIONS

Monday, February 23, 1987.

-AGRICULTURAL-

CORN (CBT) 5,000 bu.; cents per bu.

Strike	Calls—Settle			Puts—Settle		
Price	May-c	Jly-c	Sep-c	May-p	Jly-p	Sep-p
130	....	....	....	....	....	....
140	17½	....	....	1⅛	1¾	....
150	9¼	14	....	3⅝	4¼	....
160	4⅜	8¼	13	8½	9	9
170	1¾	4¼	9	16	14½	15
180	⅝	2½	6	24⅞	22¼	21½

Est. vol. 2,000, Fri vol. 3,122 calls, 1,217 puts
Open interest Fri; 20,905 calls, 11,586 puts

SOYBEANS (CBT) 5,000 bu.; cents per bu.

Strike	Calls—Settle			Puts—Settle		
Price	May-c	Jly-c	Aug-c	May-p	Jly-p	Aug-p
450	....	....	....	½	1⅞	3½
475	12¾	14½	15	3¼	6½	9
500	2½	4¾	7¼	17¼	21	24
525	⅝	1⅞	3	....	42¾	....
550	¼	⅞	2	....	66¾	....
575	⅛	½	1½	....	....	....

Est. vol. 1,750, Fri vol. 1,593 calls, 599 puts
Open interest Fri; 30,871 calls, 10,474 puts

WHEAT (CBT) 5,000 bu.; cents per bu.

Strike	Calls—Settle			Puts—Settle		
Price	May-c	Jly-c	Sep-c	May-p	Jly-p	Sep-p
250	24	15½	18	1⅛	6¼	10
260	14¾	9½	11½	2¾	11	14
270	10½	6½	5	7½	....	....
280	5	3	4	13	....	....
290	2½	....	....	....	....	....
300	....	....	....	....	....	....

Est. vol. 650, Fri vol. 493 calls, 367 puts
Open interest Fri; 1,339 calls, 1,309 puts

COTTON (CTN) 50,000 lbs.; cents per lb.

Strike	Calls—Settle			Puts—Settle		
Price	May-c	Jly-c	Oc-c	May-p	Jly-p	Oct-p
53	3.20	3.80	4.20	1.10	2.25	3.30
54	2.60	3.30	3.70	1.48	2.75	3.85
55	2.25	2.80	3.30	1.95	3.25	4.40
56	1.70	2.40	2.90	2.50	3.70	5.00
57	1.36	2.00	....	3.10	4.30	....
58	1.06	1.70	2.25	3.80	4.90	6.20

Est. vol. 200; Fri vol. 48 calls; 55 puts
Open interest Fri; 1,218 calls; 2,926 puts

SUGAR—WORLD (CSCE) 112,000 lbs.; cents per lb.

Strike	Calls—Settle			Puts—Settle		
Price	May-c	Jly-c	Oc-c	May-p	Jly-p	Oct-p
6.00	1.67	1.89	2.18	0.05	0.15	0.28
7.00	0.90	1.19	1.49	0.26	0.45	0.59
8.00	0.44	0.76	1.02	0.80	1.02	1.12
9.00	0.21	0.47	0.69	1.59	1.73	1.79
10.00	0.12	0.30	0.52	2.50	2.56	2.62
11.00	0.07	....	....	....	....	....

Est. vol. 1,006; Fri vol. 631 calls; 153 puts
Open interest Fri; 18,208 calls; 5,177 puts

-OIL-

CRUDE OIL (NYM) 42,000 gal.; $ per bbl.

Strike	Calls—Settle			Puts—Settle		
Price	Apr-c	May-c	Ju-c	Apr-p	May-p	Jun-p
15	2.13	2.10	2.10	0.03	0.13	0.25
16	1.20	1.25	1.35	0.09	0.30	0.45

Strike	Calls—Settle			Puts—Settle		
Price	Apr-c	May-c	Ju-c	Apr-p	May-p	Jun-p
17	0.37	0.60	0.75	0.33	0.67	0.85
18	0.09	0.24	0.35	0.98	1.25	1.45
19	0.03	0.10	0.19	1.95	2.10	2.30
20	0.01	0.06	0.10	....	....	3.20

Est. vol. 3,583; Fri vol. 4,293 calls; 2,598 puts
Open interest Fri; 29,733 calls; 36,269 puts

CATTLE-LIVE (CME) 40,000 lbs.; cents per lb.

Strike	Calls—Settle			Puts—Settle		
Price	Apr-c	Jun-c	Aug-c	Apr-p	Jun-p	Aug-p
62	3.25	2.07	1.12'	0.25	1.92	4.17
64	1.75	1.25	0.65	0.75	3.10	....
66	0.72	0.70	0.37	1.72	4.52	....
68	0.25	0.35	....	3.25	....	....
70	0.07	....	....	....	....	....
72	....	....	....	....	....	....

Est. vol. 1,988, Fri vol. 1,916 calls, 1,474 puts
Open interest Fri; 3,811 calls, 3,090 puts

HOGS-LIVE (CME) 30,000 lbs.; cents per lb.

Strike	Calls—Settle			Puts—Settle		
Price	Apr-c	Jun-c	Jly-c	Apr-p	Jun-p	Jly-p
40	3.20	....	....	0.07	0.25	0.45
42	1.62	....	....	0.50	0.70	0.90
44	0.60	2.50	2.50	1.47	1.40	1.65
46	0.12	1.40	1.60	3.00	2.07	2.80
48	0.02	0.85	0.95	4.90	3.52	4.10
50	0.02	0.37	0.55	6.90	5.05	....

Est. vol. 286; Fri vol. 493 calls, 122 puts
Open interest Fri; 3,811 calls, 3,090 puts

-METALS-

COPPER (CMX) 25,000 lbs.; cents per lb.

Strike	Calls—Last			Puts—Last		
Price	May-c	Jly-c	Sep-c	May-p	Jly-p	Sep-p
58	4.95	5.20	5.65	0.05	0.25	0.45
60	3.20	3.70	4.15	0.30	0.75	0.95
62	1.60	2.20	2.85	0.70	1.25	1.65
64	0.90	1.50	2.05	2.00	2.60	2.75
66	0.40	0.90	1.40	3.50	3.95	4.15
68	0.25	0.65	1.20	5.35	5.60	5.65

Est. vol. 725, Fri vol. 679 calls, 57 puts
Open interest Fri; 23,955 calls, 3,822 puts

GOLD (CMX) 100 troy ounces; dollars per troy ounce

Strike	Calls—Last			Puts—Last		
Price	Apr-c	Jun-c	Aug-c	Apr-p	Jun-p	Aug-p
380	25.40	32.50	38.00	0.80	4.00	6.00
390	16.40	24.40	30.30	1.80	6.00	8.40
400	9.10	17.00	23.70	4.50	8.50	11.70
420	2.80	9.70	15.40	18.20	20.70	22.50
440	0.90	5.50	9.90	36.30	36.00	36.50
460	0.30	3.00	6.80	55.70	54.20	53.50

Est. vol. 5,500, Fri vol. 4,797 calls, 3,122 puts
Open interest Fri; 58,583 calls, 50,369 puts

SILVER (CMX) 5,000 troy ounces; cents per troy ounce

Strike	Calls—Last			Puts—Last		
Price	May-c	Jly-c	Sep-c	May-p	Jly-p	Sep-p
500	54.0	62.5	72.6	1.0	4.3	7.5
525	32.0	42.5	53.5	3.5	9.0	12.0
550	15.5	26.5	37.5	11.5	17.0	22.0
575	8.0	18.0	27.0	29.0	32.0	36.0
600	4.0	12.0	20.0	50.0	51.5	53.5
625	2.3	8.0	15.2	73.0	72.0	73.0

Est. vol. 1,650, Fri vol. 762 calls, 323 puts
Open interest Fri; 20,386 calls, 7,845 puts

FOREIGN CURRENCY OPTIONS
FIGURE 9

FOREIGN CURRENCY OPTIONS

Philadelphia Exchange

Monday, Feb. 23

Option & Underlying	Strike Price	Calls—Last			Puts—Last		
		Mar	Apr	Jun	Mar	Apr	Jun
50,000 Australian Dollars-cents per unit.							
ADollr	...66	r	r	r	0.39	r	r
66.77	...67	0.31	r	0.96	r	r	2.96
12,500 British Pounds-cents per unit.							
BPound	145	r	r	r	r	r	0.70
154.05	147½	r	r	r	r	r	1.40
154.05	.150	r	r	4.80	r	0.85	r
154.05	152½	r	r	3.25	0.60	1.80	3.40
154.05	.155	0.70	1.30	r	r	r	r
154.05	157½	r	r	1.40	r	r	r
154.05	.160	r	r	1.20	r	r	r
50,000 Canadian Dollars-cents per unit.							
CDollr	...71	r	r	r	r	r	0.03
75.10	...74	r	r	1.32	r	r	r
75.10	.74½	r	r	r	0.16	r	r
75.10	...75	0.38	0.55	r	r	r	r
75.10	.75½	0.21	0.40	0.68	r	r	r
75.10	...76	r	0.20	0.44	r	r	r
62,500 West German Marks-cents per unit.							
DMark	.. 46	8.68	s	r	r	s	r
54.38	...48	r	s	6.82	r	s	r
54.38	...49	5.65	r	r	0.01	r	r
54.38	...50	r	r	r	0.01	r	r
54.38	...51	3.40	r	r	r	0.10	0.27
54.38	...52	r	r	r	0.04	0.14	0.50
54.38	...53	r	r	2.61	0.14	0.36	0.70
54.38	...54	1.00	r	1.90	0.44	0.76	1.05
54.38	...55	0.36	0.80	1.50	0.78	1.16	1.44
54.38	...56	0.16	0.57	1.10	1.53	r	2.08
54.38	...57	0.08	0.33	0.66	r	r	r
54.38	...58	0.03	r	0.47	r	r	r
54.38	...59	r	r	0.39	r	r	r
54.38	...60	r	0.07	0.24	r	r	r
6,250,000 Japanese Yen-100ths of a cent per unit.							
JYen	... 61	r	r	r	0.02	r	r
65.05	...62	r	r	r	r	r	0.20
65.05	...63	r	r	r	r	r	0.35
65.05	...64	r	r	r	0.14	0.28	0.63
65.05	...65	r	r	r	0.43	0.63	0.94
65.05	...66	0.18	r	r	r	r	r
65.05	...67	0.08	r	r	r	r	r
62,500 Swiss Francs-cents per unit.							
SFranc	..62	r	r	r	0.11	r	r
64.34	...64	1.23	r	r	0.55	r	r
64.34	...65	0.54	1.16	1.82	0.92	r	1.82
64.34	...66	0.28	0.80	r	r	r	r
64.34	...67	0.14	r	r	r	r	r
64.34	..1.70	r	r	0.42	r	r	r

Total call vol. 21,153 Call open int. 463,358
Total put vol. 22,696 Put open int. 465,966
r—Not traded. s—No option offered.
Last is premium (purchase price).

Chicago Board Options Exchange

Monday, Feb. 23

Option & Underlying	Strike Price	Calls—Last			Puts—Last		
		Mar	Apr	Jun	Mar	Apr	Jun

Treasury Bonds $100,000 12s2013-points and 32nds.

		Mar	Apr	Jun	Mar	Apr	Jun
TBnd100x	142	1.01	s	s	r	s	s

50,000 Australian Dollars-cents per unit.

ADollr	...62	r	r	r	r	0.06	r

25,000 British Pounds-cents per unit.

BPound	145	r	r	r	r	r	0.85
154.13	.155	0.70	r	r	r	r	r
154.13	.160	r	r	1.00	r	r	r

100,000 Canadian Dollars-cents per unit.

CDollar	..74	r	r	r	0.05	r	r

125,000 West German Marks-cents per unit.

DMark	.. 51	r	r	r	r	r	0.27
54.41	...54	r	r	r	0.37	r	r
54.41	...55	0.53	r	r	r	r	r
54.41	...56	0.20	r	1.10	r	r	r
54.41	...57	0.08	r	r	r	r	r

12,500,000 Japanese Yen-100ths of a cent per unit.

JYen	... 60	5.14	s	r	r	s	r
65.06	...63	2.21	r	r	r	r	r
65.06	...65	r	r	r	r	0.61	r

125,000 Swiss Francs-cents per unit.

SFranc	..71	r	r	0.31	r	r	r

Total call volume 985 Total call open int. 24,384
Total put volume 654 Total put open int. 20,819
r—Not traded. s—No option offered.
Last is premium (purchase price).

Column 1 Indicates the option, underlying foreign currency and exchange rate.

Column 2 Strike Price—The price at which the underlying foreign currency option contract may be exercised.

Columns 3, 4 & 5 The last premium paid on each of the three closest contract months in which call options are available to be traded.

Columns 6, 7 & 8 The last premium paid on each of the three closest contract months in which put options are available to be traded.